Visible Borders, Invisible Economies

Latinx: The Future Is Now
A series edited by Lorgia García-Peña and Nicole Guidotti-Hernández

Books in the series

Marisel C. Moreno, *Crossing Waters: Undocumented Migration in Hispanophone Caribbean and Latinx Literature and Art*

Yajaira M. Padilla, *From Threatening Guerrillas to Forever Illegals: US Central Americans and the Politics of Non-Belonging*

Francisco J. Galarte, *Brown Trans Figurations: Rethinking Race, Gender, and Sexuality in Chicanx/Latinx Studies*

Visible Borders, Invisible Economies

Living Death in Latinx Narratives

KRISTY L. ULIBARRI

University of Texas Press ⋎ *Austin*

Requests for permission to reproduce material from this work should be sent to:
  Permissions
  University of Texas Press
  P.O. Box 7819
  Austin, TX 78713-7819
  utpress.utexas.edu/rp-form

∞ The paper used in this book meets the minimum requirements of ANSI/NISO Z39.48-1992 (R1997) (Permanence of Paper).

Cataloging-in-Publication data is available from the Library of Congress.

LCCN 2022007611
ISBN 978-1-4773-2601-5 (cloth)
ISBN 978-1-4773-2657-2 (pbk)
ISBN 978-1-4773-2602-2 (PDF)
ISBN 978-1-4773-2603-9 (ePub)

doi:10.7560/326015

For my family

Contents

Illustrations

Acknowledgments

This book has journeyed with me through three institutions, and because of that, many people have influenced and sat in company with this project. I must first thank my mentors and teachers. Many thanks go to Frances R. Aparicio. She took me under her wing many years ago and continuously inspires me in both academia and life, and much of this project comes from working with her during graduate school and on my dissertation. I have had the good fortune of having many teachers and mentors guide and inspire this book, namely Mark Canuel, Madhu Dubey, Marcus Embry, and Helen Jun. Thank you for reading and listening, for answering sudden emails full of anxiety, and for helping to cultivate my nascent ideas for this project. The time and support you all have given me is so appreciated. I would also like to thank my University of Texas Press editorial team: Nicole Guidotti-Hernández, Lorgia García-Peña, Kerry E. Webb, Andrew J. Hnatow, and Christina Vargas. You all have guided this project in significant ways. Thank you for taking such care with my manuscript and guiding me through my first book publication.

Meaningful institutional funding and support have helped this project along the way: the University of Illinois at Chicago's Lincoln Fellowship; grants from the College of Arts and Sciences and the Department of English at East Carolina University; grants and research funding from CAHSS, IRISE, the Latinx Center, and the Department of English and Literary Arts at the University of Denver; and the copyediting services of my colleague Brad Benz. This support has allowed this project to be fully realized.

The following have kindly given me permission to reproduce their artwork in this book: Michael Aushenker, Don Bartletti, Javier Hernandez, the *Los Angeles Times*, Dulce Pinzón, and David Taylor. The BBC graciously allowed a small textual reproduction of James Baldwin's debate at Cambridge with William F. Buckley, Jr. Last, Taylor and Francis granted permission to reproduce an extended version of my article "Documenting the U.S.-Mexico Border: Photography, Movement, and Paradox," originally published in *Art Journal* in 2019.

This book would not exist without the many critical engagements of my colleague-kin and research comrades. I have had the pleasure to cross many scholarly paths while working on this book, and my project has been strengthened by the numerous writing groups, reading groups, and conversations over the years. I would like to thank James Arnett, Jessi Bardill, Cynthia Barounis, Solveig Bosse, Craig Brown, Cynthia Cravens, Kim Chiew, Karen Christian, Smita Das, Lauren DeCarvalho, Caroline Gottschalk Druschke, Donna Beth Ellard, Angela Espinosa, Rafael A. Fajardo, Erin Frost, Anna Froula, Nick Garcia, Maia Gil-Adí, Daniel Goldberg, Myrriah Gómez, Lillian Gorman, Tayana Hardin, Sarah Hart Micke, Anita Huizar-Hernández, Mandy Jesser, Carlos Jimenez, Jr., Justin Joyce, Andrea Kitta, Chad Leahy, Surbhi Malik, Justin Mann, Gera Miles, Madeleine Monson-Rosen, Miguel Muñoz, Bill Orchard, Deb Ortega, R. D. Perry, Nadya Pittendrigh, Aleksandr Prigozhin, Stephanie Reich, Lina Reznicek-Parrado, John Ribó, Ixta Menchaca Rosa, Emilio Sauri, Orna Shaughnessy, Casey Stockstill, Rick Taylor, Lindsay Turner, Alberto Varon, John Waldron, and Snežana Žabić. You all have engaged with this project in some way, and I am so grateful for your various forms of support through the writing of this book. I deeply admire you all and am fortunate to be in your intellectual company.

On a more personal note, I thank my parents, Steve and Cheridee. Without your love and support, I would never have gotten to where I am. A shoutout to my brothers and their beautiful families—I am lucky to call you my friends, and the laughter we share is a constant light in my life. I also want to thank my love, Pete Franks. He has read countless drafts, argued over the minutiae ad nauseam, moved across the country twice, put up with my writing idiosyncrasies, fed me delicious food, and tramped through many woods by my side. Words cannot express how much impact you have had on this book and in my life. Thank you, mi familia, mo mhuintir.

Visible Borders, Invisible Economies

Introduction: Imagination in the Age of National Security and Market Neoliberalization

In her 2017 performance manifesto *Your Healing Is Killing Me*, Virginia Grise places pencil sketches of herself doing each exercise of Chairman Mao's 4-Minute Physical Fitness Plan alongside mixed-form writings that call out healing culture and its polluted politics of "self-care." While Grise explicitly states, "This is not a play," she describes the utilitarian exercises as being a "gestural vocabulary" that creates "collective movement" and requires us to "show up, be present in [our] own bodies, and stay connected to one another."[1] Readers are asked to not skip over them but to perform each exercise. Sketches of "Exercise 3: Presenting the Bow" bridge a memory of her childhood imaginary friend and a poem about matrilineal curandera rituals in the backyard. The book refuses clean distinctions between the three genres of the manifesto: performance, written text, and visual representation. Grise's approach assembles histories, experiences, and imaginaries. She recalls and interrogates trauma, eczema, black-market doctors, fear, heteronormative patriarchy, white supremacy, Ronald Reagan's death, settler colonialism, revolutionary impulse, and counting breaths. In the middle of the manifesto, she poetically lists all the things that are killing her: "Prescriptions that address the symptoms but not the cause are killing me" to "The lack of political imagination in this country is killing me" to "Pan-Latino(ism) is killing me, as Latino is not a politic nor an ideology and does nothing to prepare us to defend ourselves against what is actually killing us."[2]

In many ways, Grise's performance manifesto asks us to create new imaginaries for self-defense that counter the neoliberalized and individualized political economy of self-care. "Self-care" connotes what Wendy Brown describes as the economization of our everyday lives that demands us to practice self-investment.[3] Grise's narrative clearly draws on her own self, especially her

Chicanx, Chinese, and migrant histories, but these histories do not forward a self-centric or self-investing politics and do not homogenize the many different experiences embedded in these terms of identity, discourse, and practice. In one way, her use of "pan-Latino(ism)" describes what Suzanne Oboler historicizes through the ethnic label "Hispanic" (and now "Latino"), whereby migrants from Latin America discover upon arrival that their different national identities are inconsequential and swept under an umbrella term in the United States.[4] "Latino," of course, has historically worked both in and against pan-ethnicity. Oboler relates the tension experienced by people from Latin America who share many commonalities—a language, a history of Spanish colonialism, a common goal of Latino rights and social justice—but also have histories, racial backgrounds, social experiences, and cultural nuances very different from one another's.[5] For Oboler, these tensions within our communities around terms like "Latino" or "Hispanic" are productive, but more important, these terms ask us to recognize how these ethnic labels are state-sanctioned in the United States, where "the state's distributions and withdrawals of resources [have occurred] on the basis of those terms since the 1960s."[6] Significantly, Oboler closely aligns these labels and terms with "migrant." "Migrant" does certain work here in that it further delineates how these histories, experiences, and state-imposed statuses are shaped by the movement across figurative and literal borders: national territories, cultural practices, ideology and norm, forms of security, punishment, and criminalization.[7] Nevertheless, as Lorgia García-Peña argues, imaginations about Latinx borders also require disrupting the "locus of migration" by thinking about these spaces as embodied and by reading them through "contra*diction*."[8]

While these umbrella terms are problematic and politicized enough for Grise to wishfully reject them outright, they carry the baggage of this troubled and taut subject formation that is necessary for decoding narratives by and about peoples from Latin America in the United States. These terms must be utilized, then, as intersecting forms of collective being/becoming that undercut the self-centric and/or the homogenized singularity of Latino subjects, while also recognizing and calling out the political structures that shape us and, as Grise declares, kill us. These terms are not only steeped in political meaning, but they are increasingly and primarily economic as well, undergoing what Brown describes as the neoliberal movement from *homo politicus* to *homo oeconomicus*. The recent academic embrace of "Latinx" advances this recognition by asking us to confront the social, gender, and queer dimensions within these fraught differences and commonalities, and it starts to name the political and economic violences that erase and render invisible some of us more than others.[9] Thinking in the space of the collective, the relational, and the social opens up possibilities to imagine otherwise and to build coalition, and Grise is building communities in preparation.

Equally significant in Grise's performance manifesto is how she presents the cultural politics of healing as a part of a political economy that enacts various forms and structures of death. "Healing" alludes to medical, biological, and psychological endeavors that prolong or better one's life and livelihood, and as such, it is a term embedded with what we may call biopolitical codifications of "life." Nevertheless, Grise's performance manifesto pushes against the seeming centrality of life and livelihood in the term "healing." Death regularly undergirds the performance, written text, and visuals through the hauntings of the past, deaths from AIDS and cancer, imaginations and fear of violence, all the things that are "killing us." Death, however, describes here not a non-life state of a singular subject but a collective state that is woven into history, practice, and discourse in violent and systemic ways.

I begin my discussion with Grise's performance manifesto and its over-turning of terms and genre because her work lays out the many layers and crossings that trouble *Visible Borders, Invisible Economies.* Grise brings to-gether the three major narrative modes—prose texts, visual texts, and perfor-mance texts—that run through and overlap in the ensuing pages while also capturing a tension between biopolitics and necropolitics, the two theoretical lenses that shape my narrative engagements. And mostly, the manifesto calls for different forms of imagination while living and dying within the struc-tural violence of our contemporary political economy. In parallel, I bring together Latinx literature, photography, and film as overlapping forms of narrative-building that tell us something about the political economy. These visual and written narratives expose the violence and death operating behind common US discourses and practices of immigration, migrant labor, and ethno-racialized subjectivities. These narratives reveal the strategic interplay between a free-market economy and a hyperfortified nation-state that orders the social world and makes some populations more disposable than others.

This idea grows out of the history of free-trade economy, an enterprise that has become entrenched and normalized in our imaginations. This en-trenchment becomes ever-more specialized, especially in moments such as the initiation of the North American Free Trade Agreement (NAFTA) in 1993, further refined with the Dominican Republic–Central American Free Trade Agreement (CAFTA-DR) in 2004, two policies that allow capital to cross borders easily while people cannot. This phenomenon has ensured that the global economy's many forms of death and its ongoing (re)production of disposable populations and bodies go unquestioned, unrestricted, and unseen. Primarily concentrating on Latinx narratives published or released after the implementation of NAFTA, I argue that these narratives elucidate a cultural politics where national security is a contradictory but necessary performance, one that downplays and elides the various forms of social and political death and violence required for the neoliberalization of the market. By this, I mean that the national and political understandings of citizenship and immigration—especially regarding racialized migrant labor—allow for and conceal the exploitative, violent, and fatal practices of free-trade globalization. Latinx narratives particularly reveal this strategic interplay between political visibility and economic invisibility.

Seeing Shadows and Phantoms:
Theorizing Biopolitics and Necropolitics

By focusing on questions of visibility and invisibility, I am engaging with a historical and philosophical lineage about market economies in modern democracies. The critical stakes of my argument specifically arise from contemporary theories of neoliberal governmentality. Neoliberalism often defines a historical movement from Keynesianism, where democratic governments regulate the economy through policies such as the New Deal, to more free-market ideology and policy, where markets now control and supervise the nation-state.[10] Yet neoliberalism is predicated on a much longer history and critical tradition that reaches into colonialism and empire building and that becomes wrapped up in the ideas of biopolitics and necropolitics, where the relationship between national politics and global economies structures our very understandings and experiences of life, livelihood, and death. In particular, *Visible Borders, Invisible Economies* is interested in how Latinx and migrant narratives confront broader US political processes that center the nation's life or livelihood in discourses and practices that target and kill migrant and racialized populations. Simultaneously, these narratives reveal how economic processes and practices put into question this championing of the nation's so-called life, especially when market economies produce various forms of migrant and Latinx death. Initially, the distributions of death seem antithetical to national and political discourses and practices that uphold the life or livelihood of the nation, but these deaths often reinforce these political discourses and practices. For *Visible Borders, Invisible Economies*, market violence walks hand-in-hand with national security, nationalisms, and border fortification.

This logic first grows out of Foucauldian notions of biopolitics. In its broadest terms, biopolitics marks the shift from a sovereign figure who rules through the right to kill to a dispersed power that rises from new conceptions of population, the *dēmos*, and the rule of law. This shift arguably begins with classical liberalism and the beginnings of so-called modern democracy, where governance is by and for the people.[11] Defining modern democracy is contentious, but Wendy Brown argues that even within these critical tensions, there is still an insistence that it "stands opposed to tyranny and dictatorship, fascism and totalitarianism, aristocracy, plutocracy or corporatocracy." Under contemporary neoliberal forms, however, democracy transforms the populations and *dēmos* into economic subjects (*homines oeconomici*) who must self-invest.[12] Governance here is no longer about exercising rule through subjects but instead becomes an exercise in select administration and management by economic actors.[13]

The dispersed and democratic power that mark classical liberalism, then, eventually shift toward market forms of neoliberalism. Foucault argues that classical liberalism sets the stage by producing an "economy of power" that is internally sustained by the "interplay of freedom and security."[14] In this book, I am particularly interested in this interplay because it names a paradox that, I argue, continues to structure contemporary nation-sustaining projects and global market capitalism. Interplay here has a distinctly economic register, evoking circulation, exchange, and trade, but it also elicits what Roberto Esposito describes as an intersecting "double move" of vertical and horizontal power, or what Alexander Weheliye calls "assemblages of relation."[15] The interplay between security and freedom describes how population or the *dēmos* initially become imbued with an economic logic, first under Keynesianism. In the early twentieth century, we begin to see how "the people" become little more than "consumers of freedom" and where "the market must be supported and buyers created by mechanisms of assistance" that ultimately secure the freedom to consume and to work.[16] In this sense, the interplay between freedom and security is about "producing, breathing life into, and increasing freedom" through strategic interventions.[17] Security is not necessarily oppositional to freedom but is its "mainspring," exemplified with Roosevelt's New Deal, particularly the social policies that responded to the dangers of unemployment by legislating, embedding, and guaranteeing the freedom to work and consume.[18] While many see Keynesian economics to be directly opposed to neoliberal agendas, I understand these shifts in governance and economy to describe a historical movement toward increasing market violence. Neoliberalism grows out of this interplay between freedom and security.

The discourses and theories of proto-libertarian and neoliberal economists such as Friedrich Hayek, Milton Friedman, and the Chicago School of economics maintain that security and governmental intervention in the economy directly contradict the freedom of capitalist economies, decidedly against any idea of interplay. While these figures were major players in reconceptualizing governmentality and its institutional frameworks (particularly the rule of law) in the economy, Hayek's economic theories are of particular concern to me in *Visible Borders, Invisible Economies*. Although Hayek consistently questioned and opposed any governmental intervention and security in the economy, his theories demonstrate how the free-market economy begins to govern national and political enterprise, an inverse to Keynesian forms of governance. His work is also important because he weighs in on questions of citizenship that continue to shape and frame immigration discourse and practice today. Hayek warns that state-sanctioned provisions for citizens that protect them from economic risks may result in people thinking that they are entitled to the benefits of the wealthy and will lead to national groups becoming more exclusive, where "citizenship or even residence in a country confers a claim to a particular standard of living."[19] Citizenship means something very specific here. Hayek reduces "citizen" to those residing and profiting within the territorial sovereignty of a given nation, an understanding of citizenship that Inderpal Grewal identifies as coming from "a long history of the Westphalian state."[20] Hayek sees citizenship as a problem for the free-market economy that will result in various forms of political, social, and economic catastrophe, where these entitlements to wealth may lead to the "same principle being applied by force on an international scale."[21] Hayek imagines here a (near) future where people may think that they are citizens of the world—a collective humanity—entitled to international progress and wealth, an extra-national phenomenon that will still apply national forms of the rule of law and, thus, stunt unfettered market capitalism. His imagination about citizenship, here, is perhaps no longer speculative, but it has not hindered the market as Hayek feared. In fact, it has produced a neoliberal state, where neoliberalization produces a collapse between national concerns and market economics. Saskia Sassen argues that the institution of citizenship captures this collapse: markets now have the power to hold state governments accountable, a function that once belonged to citizens, which means that we are now seeing "economic citizenship" that belongs not to citizens but to "firms and markets, particularly the global financial market." These markets' ability to operate globally is precisely what endows them with this power over "individual governments."[22] I call this collapse the "neoliberal state" because, although it is an idea fraught with conflict, it explains how the nation-state and the economy cooperate, and this plays out on the level of citizenship.

In *Visible Borders, Invisible Economies*, I consider how the neoliberal state resolves the contradictions between nation-state regulation and free-market economy by producing a social order of us/them and haves/have-nots. Through citizenship, the neoliberal state can secure free-market ideals, such as individual liberty, for some and hyperregulate, exploit, or criminalize others. Hayek's later work often rationalized exceptions to his free-market fantasies, where government overreach was a necessary evil, especially when it came to immigration policy. While Hayek's theories and speculations would seem to be pro-migration, he still saw anti-immigration policy to be a necessary "limit to the universal application of liberal principles." The migrants who reside in Hayek's state of exception here are caught between the institutions of citizenship and economy. Hayek grounded this anti-immigrant necessity in a neo-Malthusianism, which I further explore in chapter 1, especially when he claims there are unavoidable "differences in national and ethnic traditions," particularly in the "rate of propagation." While "propagation" may refer to a country's rate of wealth, the term also conveys his sense of the Other as oversexual and overpopulated. Hayek proposes that these so-called differences between wealthier countries and less-wealthy countries support the regulation of borders. Of course, he explicitly admits that this anti-immigration regulation in an unrestricted market is an exception to the rule.[23] These exceptions became further consolidated under the administrations of Margaret Thatcher and Ronald Reagan and have advanced under each new administration in the United States, where neoliberalization of the market and anti-immigration discourse and policy have occurred in tandem.[24] Those who migrate, especially from the Third World to the First World, operate within this state of exception under neoliberal discourse and practice. Grewal reminds us that "neoliberal authority is based on the reconfigurations of citizen-subjects by the use of state security apparatuses" where immigration and racialized Others become an easy opposition.[25] The us/them binary opposition allows for the neoliberal state to maximize market freedom for some at the cost of others. This paradox demonstrates the interplay between (national) security and (market) freedom that permeates the social order.

While anti-immigrant ideologies are often marked by xenophobia and racism, such as "brown peril," the support of anti-immigration policy by neoliberal and proto-libertarian figures show how the national securing of economic freedom is about ordering global capital power.[26] It is no surprise, then, that a figure such as Hayek contributes to what we now see as First World–Third World constructions. His backhanded treatment of "undeveloped" and "primitive" countries, which are constantly "following" the progress of the wealthier and more knowledgeable Westphalian state, reinforces this perspective.[27] Contemporary anti-immigration discourses continue to uphold First World–versus–Third World disparities, all while eliding the way that global and international flows of political economy produces these unequal distributions of power and resources. These constructions of First World–Third World abstract and misplace the material conditions of global capitalism.[28] As Javier Duran claims, this abstraction leads to a "reconfiguration of state power into new immaterial forms such as virtual and biometric borders," but these immaterialities have violent and representational impacts "via processes of disembodiment and deterritorialization in the representation of migrant subjects and transborder communities."[29] Duran points to how the neoliberal state controls representation itself through the abstractions of security practices. Anti-immigration discourse is also deeply aligned with these immaterialities that have violent material effects. The nation-state practices and discourses that disembody migrants and transborder communities is a strategic form of economic violence that promotes us/them nationalisms to maximize the bottom line: capital.

Current forms of border fortification and resurgences of xenophobia may appear to directly contradict neoliberalizations of the market and borderless economy, but when the bottom line is maximizing capital, it becomes clear how the nation can play a very significant role in shaping the economy. US foreign policy has often been in the name of economic interests, and these same policies often create mass migration and have done so for years.[30] Major historical developments exemplifying this political and economic relationship of US interventionism in Latin America occurred throughout the twentieth century: the Bracero Program (1942–1964), a guest worker agreement between the United States and Mexico; Operation Bootstrap (1948), when the United States pressured Puerto Rico to industrialize; the Chicago School experiments in Chile (1970s), when the US-backed dictator Augusto Pinochet allowed neoliberal restructuring during post-coup instability; the US Maquila Decree (1989), which began the maquiladora system of cheap production south of the border and duty-free gains in the United States, to name only a few. In the instance of the Bracero Program, the agreement between Mexico and the United States was to fill the gap of workers fighting in World War II, a temporary labor contract enlisting thousands of impoverished Mexicans to come into the United States for predominantly farm labor and railroad building. It was so successful that the conclusion of World War II did not bring its end, and it was repeatedly extended until 1964. Kitty Calavita relates that the Bracero Program shows us a "rocky alliance" between state agendas and economic interests that ensure a migrant's labor captivity, even when contracts were made in excess.[31] What this historical system shows us is how the life and livelihood of people are replaced with purely economic interests, where only the ongoing life of agricultural and factory production matters. Life is tied not to human biology or even to labor itself but instead to an abstract ideal of production and to the economic livelihood of US industries. This agenda sharpens and becomes more specialized with free-trade agreements, where the state's role is no longer distinguishable from its economic imperatives. To call this biopolitics, then, is to describe the political *life of capital*, where politics and economics merge to reinforce the social order, but this so-called life comes at the violent and deadly expense of certain populations.

Necropolitics offers a framework for thinking about the violence and death built into this political economy, and with that, it names a profound paradox in biopolitical theory. Whereas some scholars understand this paradox to be a structural contradiction, I prefer to describe it as a series of interplays that often get deployed strategically.[32] Part of my reasoning here is that these contradictions and paradoxes are not necessarily problems but a part of the way the political economy works. As the old developer quip goes, "It's not a bug—it's a feature." Necropolitics forces us to account for the interplay whereby some peoples' lives depend on other peoples' deaths. Achille Mbembe's theories offer one way of considering how violence and death shape and structure the political economy. He highlights the strategic distributions of death that prop up the life of capital and state power. One way in which this phenomenon occurs is when politics conjoins with violence, where politics are always "the work of death" and sovereignty exhibits "the right to kill."[33] His argument in some ways suggests that we have returned to what Foucault calls the "ancient right," but this is not a sovereign monarch who regulates the people through the threat of death. [34] Instead, Mbembe describes how the contemporary and globalized political economy deploys the creation of "*death-worlds*, that is, new and unique forms of social existence in which vast populations are subjected to living conditions that confer upon them the status of *living dead*."[35] These populations are "kept alive, but in a *state of injury*, in a phantom-like world of horrors and intense cruelty and profanity," and the acts of violence, such as war, massacre, and concentration camps, are understood as "*managing the multitudes*." [36] Mbembe's project highlights the violence that is inherent to the political and economic order, a violence that delineates "who is *disposable* and who is not" and that is predicated on "who matters and who does not"; some populations must die for others to live (well).[37] Mbembe wants to foreground death in these contemporary forms of politics and economics, instead of solely invoking it as a background technology that upholds certain forms of life, as biopolitical theory often does, so that we are able to see how the political and economic order are "necessarily violent processes."[38] Following these ideas, I use "death" to describe a social order that depends on acts of violence, structures of terror and siege, histories of slavery and colonialism, and other politics and economics of cruelty. Distributions of death and violence, then, signal how the social order reproduces itself through uneven distribution, where populations are organized by us/them, by the haves/have-nots, by those who matter and those who do not, and by those who may live and those who *must* die. By foregrounding death, we see how the economy is not sustaining human life but creating more and more specialized forms of death-in-life.

Whereas biopolitics brings us to questions of nation and citizenship, necropolitics is irrevocably grounded in the histories of colonialism and slavery, particularly in forms of social death. Social death, according to Orlando Patterson, describes an institutional process of negation that requires structures of captivity, and he notes that "captive" literally translates to "living dead" in ancient Egyptian.[39] Captivity, discussed more fully in chapters 3 and 4, structures these states of (non)existence. The slave becomes the quintessential figure of the living dead here, a figure who belongs to no community, who has no social existence beyond the master, and who resides in various states of enclosure. For Mbembe, the life of the slave is "like a 'thing,' possessed by another person," and this existence makes the slave into a "perfect figure of a shadow."[40] This social death that produces the living dead is contingent on one's being a Platonic shadow of another's life and livelihood. Patterson proposes two historical conceptions of social death: intrusive and extrusive. Under intrusive forms of social death, the slave was understood as a "domestic enemy" or "permanent enemy on the inside," who is always an "alien" and who can never have a past or future in the cosmos or ancestral myths of the colonizers.[41] Under extrusive forms of social death, the slave was "symbolic of the defeated enemy" from within, a being of internal origin who has "fallen," whether from destitution or criminality, and operates as an "internal exile."[42] Both the intrusive and extrusive conceptions produce layers of violent paradox between membership and exclusion within a given nation-state or community.

These colonial-expansionist forms of membership and exclusion also have bearing on national discourse and practice, especially around citizenship. Sharon P. Holland understands social death to come from ideological nationalisms, and she describes social death as the result of a white supremacist national imaginary that sees racialized subjects as a threat and a necessary Other to the nation's livelihood: "The death of black subjects or the invisibility of blackness serves to ward off a nation's collective dread" of its own "inevitable" demise. For Holland, the nation's imagination of its own livelihood and subjectivity endures by forcing "someone else" to undergo death, absence, and disembodiment.[43] Nevertheless, Holland also argues that the disenfranchised and oppressed are "menace(s) to society" who are not anonymous "ghosts" of the nation but are actually "alive" and can "speak from the dead."[44] In a similar vein, Frances Negrón-Muntaner reads Puerto Rican colonial history embedded in the manufactured story and photograph *Seva* as also challenging nation-state structures and national ideology because it shows how Puerto Ricans "refused to give up their life for nationhood, choosing to live instead as *muertos en vida*, the living dead of national imaginings."[45] In Holland's and Negrón-Muntaner's understandings, social death and necropolitical structures are not simply about the construction of anonymous, disembodied victims who are living dead, but they also carry a politics of possibility in refusing and menacing the nation with its strictures of membership and exclusion.

However, the nation-state structure also makes itself meaningful through death. In his mapping of "necro citizenship" in American literature, Russ Castronovo argues that the us/them binaries of the nation are part of a strategic abstraction of citizenship that "exploits" mortality to "effect political death."[46] He understands political death as creating a "phantasmatic subject" who is "drawn away from a live social scene and cathected to a ceaseless hierarchal order" and is only "sustained by an apparatus of citizenship, its sublime orbit fixed by the gravity of death."[47] Citizenship, as such, ideologically and legislatively determines a social order that is always anchored by death. These phantasmatic subjects, for Castronovo, are reduced to bodies, but these bodies also "reinscribe patterns of abstraction" that typify US citizenry as ambivalent bodies that are "metaphorical yet actual, dead yet living, eternal yet decaying."[48] Whereas Holland and Negrón-Muntaner want to imagine forms of living death that challenge nation-state structures and imagined communities, Castronovo describes how nations leverage death to reinforce the social order. Nevertheless, all three understand citizenship as a politics that blurs who belongs and who is expelled and/or what gets embodied and what gets disembodied. Both Holland and Castronovo also find clarity in elements of ghostliness, evoking Avery Gordon's provocative closing to *Ghostly Matters*: "Because ultimately haunting is about how to transform a shadow of a life into an undiminished life whose shadows touch softly in the spirit of peaceful reconciliation."[49] In *Visible Borders, Invisible Economies*, ghosts and hauntings also clarify the historical and cultural arcs and deployments of death-in-life that produce these modes of indistinction.

These formulations of the living dead capture an ambivalent and indistinct state where life and death are sometimes indistinguishable. When violent market principles begin to shape and mold the political *dēmos* and the governmental sphere, life and livelihood—our membership in certain communities and political bodies and our quality of existence—are constituted through labor and consumption patterns, finance capital and systems of exchange, the careful consolidation of wealth into a few pockets, and various forms of exploitation that produce varying degrees of political, social, and slow death. This state of indistinction for the living dead may better be understood through theories of the state of exception whereby certain people are made exceptional in order to shift political, economic, and social power in certain directions. Giorgio Agamben describes the state of exception as a zone of political indistinction that consigns certain subjects into a state of "inclusive exclusion" where governments strip them of legal rights, even while they are still crucial for the political and social order.[50] The state of exception, for Agamben, becomes embodied through the *homo sacer*, who resides in a "threshold of indistinction" and whose existence disallows "clearly distinguishing between membership and exclusion, between what is outside and what is inside, between exception and rule."[51] For Agamben, these states of exception reduce bodies to bare life, which is to say an indeterminate zone where life and death lose their political meaning.[52] These indeterminate and shadowy zones are spaces and times where violent inequality plays out, a zone that Jasbir Puar argues is another form of interplay where "the deferred death of one population recedes as the securitization and valorization of the life of another population triumphs in its shadow."[53] The living dead also reside in these interplays and states of exception. In the case of the slave, this zone is a space of neither/nor: "neither human nor nonhuman, neither man nor beast, neither dead nor alive."[54] In the case of new political-economic forms of captivity, the living dead undergo a "symbolic sealing off," where they are "treated as no longer existing except as a mere tool and instrument of production."[55] To call this an exception is perhaps misplaced, especially considering that this is one of the organizing logics and norms of the social order. The ambivalent state of the living dead describes how populations organize themselves and others through distributions of death and violence where some peoples are more disposable than others and where some must occupy the margins to reinforce the centers.

Necropolitics and social death occur through the regular criminalization of the living dead. Lisa Marie Cacho, for example, ties together social death and current law-and-order state practices that deem certain populations and people ineligible for personhood and, thus, killable (often on the basis of race and class).[56] Cacho understands the social death encapsulated in ineligibility as the "threat and promise of state violence" against black, brown, and undocumented bodies.[57] For Cacho, this racial criminalization, especially in terms of undocumented subjects, is wrapped up in questions of labor: "If undocumented workers exercise their few legal rights to report workplace and labor violations, they also put themselves at risk for incarceration and deportation. [. . .] Undocumented labor enables corporations to bypass labor and antidiscrimination laws as well as health and safety regulations." Without legal recourse, migrant labor is vulnerable, but Cacho emphasizes that this condition exists *because* US law ensures this rightlessness.[58] Patterson also understands penal slavery, especially, to be in the service of labor regulation, and this collapse of criminal regulation and labor regulation has more recently been theorized as the Prison Industrial Complex.[59] There are clear racial valences to this phenomenon as well, and Cacho argues that the anxieties over undocumented immigration that arose post–September 11, 2001, ensured that "illegal" and "criminal" were no longer recognizable without bodies of color. She posits that new anxieties about the illegibility between the descriptors "illegal," "foreigner," and "terrorist" legitimized a "racially profiled threat to national security," in effect deploying various forms of social death and necropolitics.[60] Puar also maintains that this naming of particularly racialized and queer populations helps fuel the disciplining and control of said populations and generates "deflected and deferred death."[61] These are populations that must be criminalized to justify and give meaning to the life of the political economy. In this sense, migrant laborers and undocumented subjects are enclosed in a state of exception within the United States by being both intrusive (for the economy) and extrusive (as rightless noncitizens) to restore and reproduce the order of global capital.

By connecting the theories of necropolitics with the histories of social death, I mean to show how ethno-racial violence and death undergird the discourses and practices of the political economy. Whereas some scholars warn against collapsing these two distinct perspectives on the current state of the racialized social order, I rather draw a critical lineage between these concepts.[62] There is a *longue durée* of violence in these theories, and they call forth another form of death that I also consider in future chapters: slow death. Lauren Berlant defines slow death as "a condition of being worn out by the activity of reproducing life," wherein "agency can be an activity of maintenance, not making."[63] At times, slow death walks hand-in-hand with understandings of labor where one's life is measured by the ability to produce and work, a point I explore more closely in chapter 3. Nevertheless, Berlant broadens this understanding of slow death because they see it as a historical experience "where life building and the attrition of human life are indistinguishable."[64] Slow death permeates the ordinary and the common because it gets wrapped up in our epistemologies, ideologies, cultural productions, and ordering of things.[65] However, slow death also emphasizes the temporal and historical work of necropolitics and social death, a *longue durée* of violence that has elements of imperceptibility and a lack of traceability. Slow death encourages a politics of invisibility in that it relies on the expansiveness of history and time to veil the necropolitical order.

Often, necropolitics invokes eventful and momentous phenomena such as war, terror, Balkanization/borderization, incarceration, and genocide rather than slow and benevolent forms of death. Mbembe notes that necropolitics can also produce a slow "destruction of culture" that requires the slave to have "alternative perspectives toward time, work, and self."[66] The temporality of "slow" allows for great atrocities that often go unseen, especially when overshadowed by grand political events, but they also necessitate alternative perspectives. These alternative perspectives potentially open up new forms of narrative-making for living dead subjects. Echoing Holland and Negrón-Muntaner, Jared Sexton sees "the specter of captivity that haunts black experience" to be "both the condition of possibility and the condition of impossibility for the displacement of the human as such."[67] Sexton understands this temporal, historical, and racial experience to provide the conditions of human displacement. Forms of displacement under late capitalism create various oscillations between possibility and impossibility, and for Latinx and migrant subjects, who have multiple racial and ethnic experiences in the United States, displacement produces new forms of captivity and enclosures but also exposes narrative possibility. These narratives potentially reveal the underpower of ghosts, shadows, and living death.

These strategic interplays become clearer when looking at Latinx and migrant narratives. Throughout *Visible Borders, Invisible Economies*, Latinx narratives demonstrate how economic processes and imperatives depend on the social, slow, and political death of Latinx subjects through various forms of border securitization, immigration law, and racial and sexual criminalization. The desire for cheap, disposable labor and for free flows of capital in the United States facilitates the fortification of national borders, and Latinx narratives show how these seeming incongruities are necessary for free markets to maximize profits and veil unbridled economic exploitation. Latinx scholarship on borders and immigration necessarily complicates these understandings of necropolitics and this state of the living dead. Jason De León's anthropological study *The Land of Open Graves* warns that throwing in "words like *danger* and *violent*" and using war metaphors when talking about the US border often produce little more than "immigration pornography."[68] He challenges scholars of the border to present this violence as structural—where federal laws, La Migra, the desert, nationalist discourses, water bottles, and militarized technology all play active roles—giving rise to what he terms "necroviolence," whereby "modern necropolitics now extends beyond the moment of death."[69] In this sense, border violence produces bare death, a sort of photographic negative to Agamben's idea of bare life that foregrounds the inherent brutality to governing nation-state borders. Eduardo Mendieta contends that the United States' borders (with their many assemblages and technologies) have produced a thanatological governmentality. For Mendieta, the border no longer signifies sovereignty or neutral state spaces; now, it is a "security line" and a killing "machine," producing genocide and more specialized forms of discipline and punishment.[70]

I add to this scholarship by considering the economy's role in driving policy and in shaping these discourses and practices of death. I also extend this critical discussion into Latinx literary, visual, and performance narratives. In *Visible Borders, Invisible Economies*, I argue that these narratives reveal the economic logics operating behind state violence. My work, then, challenges John D. Márquez's argument that neoliberal and capitalist configurations of border violence poorly delineate the "relationship between race, sovereignty, and obliteration."[71] Márquez proposes that we think of the violence and death toll on the border through a model he calls the "racial state of expendability," rather than through capitalist labor exploitation, wherein "expendability" not only describes the actual death of crossing migrants but also the deportation, incarceration, policing and tracking, and state of illegality of these migrants.[72] He wants to highlight the violent workings of law and sovereignty that destroy racialized subjects with legal impunity, rendering these bodies the living dead.[73] In many ways, Márquez's idea of death corresponds with Cacho's descriptions of legal and juridico-political forms of ineligibility.[74] Nevertheless, his hard line between market economy and state processes elides how the economy has been woven into the very workings of the state, a central concern in this book. For *Visible Borders, Invisible Economies*, these formulations of politics and power are irrevocably imbued with market (il)logics, where the state opens borders for commodities and cheap labor agreements but closes them to ethno-racialized subjects seeking citizenship and rights. The necropolitical violence wrought through these slippages between global economics and state politics is precisely what constructs living death.

The Difficulty with Borders

This book often arrives and returns to the US-Mexico border, but I wish to keep the construction of borders in the plural. When considering multiple Latinx experiences and narratives, it is necessary to undercut the primacy of the US-Mexico border, especially since this is not the only site where borders are crossed and it problematically homogenizes the way borders operate. While the US-Mexico border is not the paradigmatic example of a necropolitical phenomenon, it is often the paradigmatic spectacle in which these processes play out, looming largely in US Latinx scholarship, in political practice, and in popular discourse. The US-Mexico border is both a geopolitical and a symbolic space. On one hand, it represents a national space that, we are regularly told, is being fortified against or breached by foreign, racialized bodies coming from the global south. On the other hand, it is a site where immigration policy like Operation Gatekeeper (1994) or the Real ID Act (2005) forces people to cross in very specific and violent ways. Nevertheless, I answer John Alba Cutler's call to conceive of a "new border," where we must reimagine the global histories, paradigms, and regimes of the many borders and borderlands that construct and affect Latinx subjects.[75] I maintain that these discourses and practices on the US-Mexico border are imbued with larger political and economic involvement across Latin America and on other borders, and while the spectacles of security and circulation focus our gaze on the US-Mexico border, the neoliberal state produces borders everywhere for those deemed living dead through political and economic violence.

When we consider the circulation of peoples in a global space, singular borders cannot capture the complex entanglements and matrices of political economy at play. Sassen considers how the push for internationalizing the economy by Western markets, as through NAFTA and CAFTA–DR, has produced an increase in cross-border circulations of people and labor since the 1980s, which major regional trading blocs have attempted to address through various initiatives through the 1990s. Agreements, such as Mercosur or Mercado Comun de Centroamerica, have both opened and closed borders among member countries, at times fostering mobile labor and at other times complicating refugee and return flows.[76] In recent times, these flows of people and laborers often enter Mexico via the Mexico-Guatemalan border with the intention of crossing into the United States to either stay or go on to Canada. To address this consequence of economic globalization, the United States pressured Mexico to create Programa Frontera Sur (2014), an agreement between Mexico and Guatemala that attempts to regulate these flows of people, which I explore more in chapter 1. This newly fortified border is now a violent precondition for the US-Mexico border and a necessary outgrowth of the US-Mexico border: these are borders that cooperate.

There are many southern borders that shape US immigration policy and US economic policy. The watery border between the United States and Cuba is perhaps the most obvious convergence between US capitalism and US immigration regulation, and the agreements and policies that shape this part of the border also imbue our understanding of the US-Mexico border in specific ways. When the "Wet Foot, Dry Foot" policy went into effect, in 1995, to address increasing Cuban refugee flows into the United States, it marked the first time when the United States agreed to repatriate Cubans who did not make it to US territory. This policy illuminates a series of entanglements between multiple countries, borders, and economic agendas. For instance, because of the large numbers of "wet foot" detainees and their overcrowding at Guantanamo Bay, the United States made an agreement with Panama to transfer and hold Cuban migrants at temporary camps, an agreement otherwise known as Operation Safe Haven and Safe Passage (1995). Panama's addition in these agreements and regulations is significant since it makes immigration policy a multinational endeavor. After the passage of "Wet Foot, Dry Foot," new economies of smuggling also arise, whereby Cubans could enter Haiti and the Dominican Republic and be smuggled across the Mona Channel to Puerto Rico to qualify as "dry foot" and remain in the United States. Also after this policy, the term "dusty foot" becomes a part of immigration jargon to describe Cubans who enter Mexico and arrive at ports of entry to request asylee status as they become added to the Other Than Mexican (OTM) population that comes through the US-Mexico borderlands.[77] "Wet Foot, Dry Foot" policy is but one instance that captures how national immigration regulation actually operates *inter*nationally, and how the hypernational understanding of a singular border, which the US-Mexico border often encapsulates, is a false and problematic image of the circulation of peoples and policies.

The US-Mexico border continues to be a central site for US discourse and practice, a symbolic singular border where fences and walls must be erected. However, the spectacle of this border obscures and mystifies the various political and economic processes that are increasingly global and produce many different geopolitical and symbolic borders. This book project does not touch on every entanglement with every Latinx experience, but I use "borders" and "economies" in the plural to signal the complicated, interwoven forms of regulation and circulation, and I underscore that these are international, multinational, and transnational phenomena, particularly between the United States, Latin America, and the Caribbean. With this, I echo García-Peña's claim that studies of latinidad force us to reposition borders within US history and require disruptions of "current temporal and geographical" understandings of race, ethnicity, and subject formation.[78]

The Entanglements of Violence and Narrative in Latinx Studies

Visible Borders, Invisible Economies diverges from a tradition in Latinx studies that often characterizes narrative modes as constructing, representing, and empowering our identities and collectivities. Many projects since the 1980s and 1990s establish the centrality of Latinx subjectivity in our cultural politics and stress the shared oppression of the different national groups that make up Latinos in the United States. As the field has developed and the critical ends have changed, some scholars have moved away from the radical nationalisms of the civil rights movements toward a politics of recognition, whereas others have refined the questions of rights and solidarity through terms like "Latinx." This focus on subjectivity promotes various forms of representation and highlights our historical absence across cultural industries, from filmmaking to literary canon-making. However, this recursive investment in subjectivity has generated some critical repetition where many of our conversations about borders, nations, and economics continually lead back to Latinx subject formation. These critical leanings sometimes homogenize ideas about Latinx identity and community, and at worst they feed the narrative, common within the US popular imagination, that all Latinx subjects are im/migrants or ethno-racially uniform. I wish to pivot the conversation away from these conclusions about identity and representation on some level. Instead, I am interested in the discursive step after this point: what Latinx representations and subject formations show us about the political economy.

Within Latinx studies, the critical discussion around political economy, especially as it is figured through literal and figurative borders, often departs and/or arrives at the centrality of violence in our experiences and narrative-making. This centrality of violence emanates from Gloría Anzaldúa's seminal work *Borderlands/La Frontera*. When Anzaldúa conceives of the US-Mexican border as "una herida abierta" (an open wound), she describes it as a space where the "Third World grates against the first and bleeds."[79] This border is both literal and figurative, and it describes the violent states of being torn, especially for mestiza subjects who straddle this border. In her investigation of feminicide in US-Mexico borderlands, specifically in Ciudad Juárez, Rosa Linda Fregoso argues that we are seeing a consolidation of power that follows a "necropolitical order." She understands that "global forces and conditions including neoliberalism, migrations, the war on terrorism, the growth of the security state, and proliferating violence are all shaping the contours of the modern world."[80] For Fregoso, the spread of violence on the border emerges with a process of denationalization and neoliberalism, wherein the state strips rights from groups deemed oppositional or disposable while it bolsters global economic entities.[81] This phenomenon produces technologies behind and conditions for an "order of power that control the border through death."[82] Nevertheless, Fregoso reminds us that these proliferations of violence are "not a closed narrative, but a contested one." She understands this narrative of violence as an "unfinished product" that she "wishes to document."[83] The language of "narrative," "product," and "document" troubles the material and real occurrences of disposability, feminicide, and dismantling of communities occurring on the border. Similarly, Nicole M. Guidotti-Hernández presents the histories and stories of the US-Mexico borderlands as "narratives of violence" or "a narrative of systematic patterns of violence."[84] For Guidotti-Hernández, narratives, stories, and histories expose the hegemonic repetitions and patterns that actively deny "violence as a foundation of national history."[85] This denial occurs in dominant and master narratives that "perpetuate national amnesia" and ask us to further consider the "obscured and shortened narratives in which minor descriptions of violated bodies are proof of an unspeakable act."[86] Both Fregoso and Guidotti-Hernández understand narrative and lived experience to occur in tandem within these investigations of violence. By linking narrative and violence, they force us to take stock of the symbolics of the border as a national space and as a space that produces wounded and dead bodies.

Within *Visible Borders, Invisible Economies*, the economic contours of this border violence are important. While much criticism focuses on the US-Mexico border and borderlands, the economy's global flows paradoxically reinforce multiple borders, both figurative and literal, for many different Latinx experiences. In her explorations of market logics within Latinx lives and neighborhoods, Arlene Dávila argues that "marketing strategies" and "commercial mass-mediated culture" illuminate how citizenship "is implicated in equities of culture, race, and gender, which ultimately determine who is or is not part of a given nation and on what grounds," especially within the "demanding new context of transnationalism and displacement."[87] Transnational flows may open up new markets of cultural exchange and representation, but they have equally produced more and more violent demands about belonging, rights, and political status. I would call this a market violence, in that it exploits and displaces ethno-racialized subjects in the name of free exchange *and* reinforces state-sanctioned border violence in the name of citizenship. Some scholars readily maintain the distinction between Latinx subjects who experience migration and immigration to the United States and those who are second-generation-plus "resident" Latinx subjects, but market violence messily and problematically interpellates all into these transnational flows and border violences.[88] For Dávila, Latinx subjectivity becomes defined and shaped by these market forces, especially in advertisements that sell intrinsic or sweeping characterizations of Latinx consumers.[89] Market violence directly influences subject formation, often exploiting ethno-racial difference for niche markets, but it also homogenizes people to construct good consumers. When this same (il)logic influences the policing of citizenship, Latinx subjects undergo erasure from numerous systems and processes of belonging and rights.

These investigations of violence often conclude on the question of subject formation, although many see it as an opportunity for new imaginations and possibilities. Raphael Dalleo and Elena Machado Sáez understand the impossibility of upending the violence of colonialism to produce new subjects: "The goal of anticolonialism is to let the dead bury the dead, to write an obituary for the colonized consciousness, and to move into a new stage of human existence. The lesson of postcoloniality is the impossibility of this total rupture; radically new men and women will always be embedded in and burdened by history."[90] For Fregoso, the cultural politics of *praesentia*, an ephemeral and spiritual practice (such as the use of calaveras) that animates an "alternative sense of presence," calls for a new politics and (re)imagining of subjectivity.[91] Much in these determinations or speculations about "new subjectivity" extends from Anzaldúa's la conciencia de la mestiza, wherein recognizing our torn and ambivalent condition ultimately constructs a new mestiza.[92] These critical turns to new subjectivity reveal something about how narratives of violence shape and form us. These understandings of subjectivity are not celebratory but instead recognize the historical, structural, and ongoing ways that violence shapes lives and infiltrates states of being.

I wonder, however, how it may look if we think about what these newly constructed and refashioned forms of Latinx subjectivity tell us about the violence, about exploitation, about the open wound of the border, and about necropolitics. In her consideration of Anzaldúa's new mestiza, Alicia Schmidt Camacho reminds us that subjectivity is also a form of narrative-making: "Unspeakable forms of violence produced new narratives of subjectivity, declarations enunciated from a border space whose political reach far exceeded the binational institutions charged with its regulation." For Schmidt Camacho, Anzaldúa's work has forced us to conceive of the borderlands, and thus our subjectivities and narratives, "at the center of global traffic." Schmidt Camacho uncovers how the distribution of violence and the critical focus on subjectivity are both productions of narrative.[93] Whether through global traffic, neoliberalism, removal of human and civil rights, or state-sanctioned elisions of history, the political economy circulates through these terms and meanings. As such, political economy imbues Latinx subjectivity in violent ways, but it also becomes a more visible and clearer phenomenon from these embodiments and narratives.

I use the term "narrative" throughout *Visible Borders, Invisible Economies* to describe many different forms, modes, and genres. I understand narrative as delineating a literary component within various forms of cultural production and within political and economic discourse and practice.[94] My use of this word also places this book into a well-established tradition within Latinx studies and its academic predecessor Chicanx studies. Notably, "narrative" in these fields describes the various cultural portrayals of Latinx subjects and experiences. Ramón Saldívar's seminal *Chicano Narrative* presents narrative language and representation as a strategy that "enables readers to understand their real conditions of existence in postindustrial twentieth-century America."[95] Narrative, for Saldívar, not only portrays Chicano lives but also connotes oppositional and ideological meanings, in that it seeks to "attain a true knowledge of society," confront the norms and imaginaries of mainstream American culture, "embody new ways of perceiving social reality," and produce new modes of interpretation.[96] Marcial González further develops this idea when he defines narrative as a "formal totality" that expresses implied social reality, whether in realist documentary style or postmodern fragmentation.[97] Saldívar and González point to how narrative mediates between the literary and the social, a process more closely engaged in chapter 3. "Narrative," in this sense, describes how imagination, fiction, performance, and story tell us something about our social world.

When we look at the understandings of narrative through the lens of Latinx studies, these theoretical interactions between the literary and the social continue but become productively complicated, and the social is a more slippery concept. Ellen McCracken's *New Latina Narrative* broadens and complicates the idea of narrative, arguing that narrative practices—from oral traditions to canciones to populist discourse to performance art—are central to enactments of social change.[98] By focusing on Latina women's narratives, McCracken conceives of collective narration that disrupts authorial individualism and transcends the diegetic borders of the "literary frame to other representations of lived experience."[99] In her exploration of the fraught spaces of Latina feminism and femininity, McCracken considers, for instance, how the Puerto Rican experience within Judith Ortiz Cofer's short stories interacts and collides with Graciela Limón's counternarratives about El Salvador's civil war. Narrative in Latinx cultural practice requires careful delineations and definitions of overlap and conversation. More recently, Ylce Irizarry utilizes narratology as a critical point of contact for Latinx literary study. She maps out four major narrative approaches in Latinx literary practice—loss, reclamation, fracture, and new memory—as ways to identify and reckon with the ongoing negotiations of meaning and the formal patterns that interact with our histories and experiences.[100] Irizarry argues that these narrative categories are "the cultural repositories for communities finding things out about themselves both through and outside the rhetoric of U.S. neocolonialism."[101]

McCracken's and Irizarry's ideas of narrative recursively define and redefine Latinx subjectivities and collectivities, even when they claim they are upsetting definition. However, they also use the term as an embodiment of ambivalence when bringing together such heterogeneous ethno-racial, migrant, gendered, and sexual experiences and perspectives. Narrative, in this sense, opens up various forms of interplay, and I would emphasize that this interplay is central in reading the political economy from these narratives.

Narrative, nevertheless, is not simply a term coming from the academic tradition. We are also in a historical moment when the only way to describe our current state of political violence and economic inequality is through what are now distinctly literary terms. Political propaganda within US media outlets is regularly called "narrative," especially when describing the rhetoric of opposing political parties. The media are inundated with accusations that the alt-right or liberals are deploying narratives, as though these discourses and rhetorics are constructing reality itself.[102] I recognize these multifaceted and problematic meanings embedded in the term: some narratives consolidate ideology, some masquerade as truth, and some challenge our social order. In this book I am interested in narratives both within Latinx cultural traditions and outside these spaces, but more importantly, narrative in this book is about strategic interplays: between national borders and borderless economies, between a Latinx cultural politics and a neoliberal political economy, and between economic theories and performance studies. To put this in practice, I engage with many different critical tracts. Part of the reason for my engagement with a large set of critical fields and narrative modes is because I see this book as a world-building and a world-shattering project. By this, I mean that I am trying to put into dialogue both overlapping and disparate conversations and texts to produce a larger picture of national fortifications of borders and global market economies. This methodology is not about imagining something new per se but about sharpening what is visible and invisible in our current political economy.

The Cultural Politics of In/Visibility

One of my principal claims in *Visible Borders, Invisible Economies* is that cultural production and texts allow us to *see* the underlying violence of the political economy. In many ways, this inquiry follows Puar's ideas that the state increases visibility around ethno-racial and queer subjects when criminalizing them and limits the visibility of those deemed outside the parameters of citizenship.[103] These politics of in/visibility are not simply a form of state violence but equally have an economic valence. Arturo Escobar argues that theories of economic development also "need to compose the world as a picture."[104] Puar's work counters and displaces "visibility politics," whereas Escobar's work questions modernity's "objectifying regime of visuality," but both understand these political and economic structures to oppress rather than empower.[105] Nevertheless, I am interested in how Latinx cultural production engages with in/visibility and exposes the shadows, both within political economy and as a social formation. *Visible Borders, Invisible Economies* maintains that the shadows have eyes. By bringing attention to these elements of visuality, I engage with José Esteban Muñoz's aim to "capture and render visible" the "queer specters" and "ghosts of materiality" that haunt Latinx cultural production.[106] This critical move in my analysis regularly draws on queer theory's interrogations of time and normativity and understands that border politics, social formation, economic flows, and history are given shape within Latinx narratives. Sometimes, this cultural politics appears in graphic and performance-based texts; other times, it forms within genres of realism and speculative fiction.

In *Visible Borders, Invisible Economies*, I bring together a range of texts—prose, photography/graphic, and performance—to interrogate market and border violence within and surrounding Latinx narratives. This book wishes to better understand the hyperfortification of US borders under free-trade capitalism. Anti-immigrant policies like Operation Wetback (1954) and Operation Gatekeeper (1994) are in tension with borderless economic policies, such as the Bracero Program (1942–1964), the Bretton Woods Agreements (1944), Operation Bootstrap (1947), NAFTA (1993), and CAFTA–DR (2004). Within these pages, I explore how Latinx bodies are pawns in this sociopolitical game, a game that directly ties back to neoliberal and (proto-)libertarian economists such as Friedrich Hayek, Milton Friedman, and the Chicago School. My interdisciplinary methodology puts in conversation written, visual, and performance narratives that cross different genres and ethno-racial, migrant, gendered, and sexual experiences. Most of these cultural productions were published or released after the 1980s and announce the growing troubles with market violence. I have chosen these narratives within this book not necessarily because they are representative of the ever-growing field of Latinx studies but because they engage with how and why border fortification is a strategic economic move: it reinstates nation and nationalisms as the organizing logic of populations to ultimately obscure the economic practices of US imperialism and market capitalism. Latinx narratives play a critical role in exposing the contradictory discourses and practices of the current global economy because such subjects are uniquely targeted within the larger immigration discourses (such as "brown peril") and because US economic policy historically influences migration from Latin America. As a result, these narratives uncover the workings of the political economy.

I have structured the book by putting three primary texts in conversation with one another within each chapter to interrogate my overarching theoretical concerns. These critical and narrative mashups allow me to consider multiple angles, genres, and points of departure/arrival. The chapters that make up part I, "Documenting the Living Dead," each tackle a single genre (the novel, the photograph, and the film, respectively). They question the role of documentary and how these narratives participate in documenting what is really happening across US borders, both performatively and ideologically. Ideally, each genre successively drives my reading of the next. This discussion sets the stage for part II because it establishes these genres as already slipping between representation and documentation. Part II, "Imagining the Living Dead," considers how Latinx narratives challenge and subvert this violence through more speculative and fantastic forms and futures. The chapters in part II mix the major genres of this book together to more readily examine the way an economy of death may close our imaginations and/or open up a politics of possibility.

The first chapter, "Games of Enterprise and Security in Luis Alberto Urrea, Valeria Luiselli, and Karla Cornejo Villavicencio," considers how the popular and political imaginary in the United States constructs a series of misrecognitions about immigration, Latinx subjects, and the global economy. Focusing on Luis Alberto Urrea's *The Devil's Highway* (2004), Valeria Luiselli's *Tell Me How It Ends: An Essay in Forty Questions* (2017), and Karla Cornejo Villavicencio's *The Undocumented Americans* (2019), this chapter interrogates how migrant bodies become synonymous with discourses about "brown peril" in US popular and political discourse, where Latinx subjects are painted as purely corporeal and racialized "hordes" who are violating national resources and/or threatening the well-being of a nation. On one level, these neo-Malthusian discourses complement US security theater and saturate state regulations of migrants in the United States. On another level, these texts reveal how these discourses deeply misrecognize the market logic behind what is happening in a security state. I argue that these literary narratives reveal how the misrecognitions of immigration strategically target racialized subjects in order to obfuscate the actual conditions of the (political) economy: exploitation, violence, and death.

Urrea's nonfictional work *The Devil's Highway* relates the story of the Wellton 26 (more famously known as the Yuma 14) and uses governmental documents, interviews with Border Patrol agents, and research on those that died crossing the Devil's Highway in Arizona to show structural violence in the name of US life and resources. The politics of misrecognition are further problematized when attached to the question of documentation, a central concern in Luiselli's *Tell Me How It Ends*, which relates her work interviewing and translating for New York City's immigration courts. The way these questionnaires write out the actual experiences of Central American children coming to the United States demonstrates how documentation and the rule of law enact various forms of exclusion and social death. Cornejo Villavicencio's *The Undocumented Americans* narrates multiple experiences of undocumentedness by Latinx immigrants across the United States, and she delineates slippage between labor resources and water resources, cultural responses to the lack of healthcare, and the aging-out of the undocumented economy. The narrative reveals how policy and economy produce experiences that must navigate the shadows in multiple ways. Together, these texts throw into question the role of documenting migration and migrant experience, especially in terms of how documents advance an incomplete picture or paint the picture of immigration in troubling ways. Problematic perceptions house a deep misrecognition of the free-market economy's workings.

The second chapter, "Documenting the US-Mexico Border: Photography, Movement, and Paradox," focuses on the narratives produced by select border photographers and photography projects: Don Bartletti (1990–2002), David Taylor (2010), and the Border Film Project (2007). Some of the images are commercial clichés, whereas others are little more than fleeting snapshots, yet this chapter shows how they produce a paradoxical narrative about the so-called immigration problem and the call for national security on the US-Mexico border. I begin with the photojournalism of Don Bartletti and the documentary photography of David Taylor, whose projects wish to record the truth of what is happening on the border but instead often capture images that produce and maintain a narrative of fear and anxiety around undocumented immigration. As Anglo and male artists who inadvertently embody a distance from their subjects, they often present a side of documentary photography that captures the borderlands as a binary space. In contrast, the photographic mission of the Border Film Project, in which migrants and Minutemen used disposable cameras to photograph their experiences, challenges and builds on Bartletti's and Taylor's visual narratives. The project documents the line between the United States and Mexico but reveals its porous and symbolic nature. As such, it breaches and upsets nationalist discourses of legal/illegal, citizen/foreigner, and us/them by offering the lived experience of the

US-Mexico border. By blurring the lines between photographer and subject, these photographs capture the not-always-visible truth about the border as an opening, both in terms of Anzaldúa's herida abierta and as a space of global traffic.

Simultaneously, the images ask us to reconsider the form of the photograph itself, as well as the questions of recognition and misrecognition raised in chapter 1. I conclude with the theoretical conversations about paradox within photography studies, where the photograph's frozen moment may still denote forms of movement and where the norms of photographic styles, such as the candid shot and the portrait, cross. These paradoxes ask viewers to pay particular attention to what Judith Butler calls the politics of recognition and lead to questions about which images are legible or illegible. Susan Sontag clarifies these paradoxes as a part of a market desire to sell very specific ideologies when it produces and disseminates recognizable and legible photographic images. I employ these theories to ultimately call us to locate the illegible and unrecognizable in border photography.

In the third chapter, "Latinx Realisms: The Cinematic Borderworlds of Josefina López, David Riker, and Alex Rivera," I consider multiple forms of Latinx realism in film and performance texts. Realism, in many ways, is inextricable from forms of documenting and documentary, and as a result, Latinx narratives that consider migration and immigration processes often utilize realism to reexamine the power dynamics behind documenting and to challenge so-called social truth. This question of realism becomes most explicit in contemporary Latinx filmmaking, largely because the cinematic genre has a very specific history of realism: from Italian neorealism to postmodern theories of the hyperreal. This chapter explores realism through three cinematic projects: *Detained in the Desert* (2012), a play by Josefina López that she later produced as a screenplay alongside director Iliana Sosa of the film collective Femme Frontera; *La Ciudad/The City* (1998), a documentary-style four-part collection of shorts written and directed by filmmaker David Riker; and *Sleep Dealer* (2008), a speculative film written and directed by second-generation Peruvian American filmmaker Alex Rivera (which he cowrote with David Riker). This chapter explores how cinematic projects position Latinx migrants and labor as the disposable lifeblood of the US economy.

López's *Detained in the Desert* presents a hypothetical situation wherein the us/them politics of US-Mexico border discourse play out in the desert between two characters. Employing what López calls "cineatro," a genre that blends cinematic elements with theatrical drama, the narrative engages realism as a response to the racial-profiling law SB 1070 enacted in Arizona in 2010. Riker's *La Ciudad* more explicitly exhibits a neorealist aesthetic to interrogate the way Latinx bodies are vital and yet made invisible within the United States. Rivera's use of speculative sci-fi in *Sleep Dealer* emphasizes how the corporeal vitalities of Latinx subjects are completely appropriated by the economy. Intertwined throughout these analyses are Jean Baudrillard's theories about hyperrealism and the symbolic economy of death, as a way to think through how realism offers us different perspectives under necropolitics and border violence. I ultimately argue that Latinx realisms, in their attempts to portray social truth, show us how the politics and economy of death infiltrate our narrative forms. Simultaneously, these narratives utilize realism as a speculative form that allows for imaginations and performances of "playing dead" that problematically empower Latinx subjects.

The fourth chapter marks a subtle turn in *Visible Borders, Invisible Economies*, one in which I trouble the genre distinctions of the first three chapters and begin to consider more pointedly the politics of possibilities within Latinx narratives. "Markets of Resurrection: Cat Ghosts, Aztec Zombies, and the Living Dead Economy" establishes how crucial the politics of death is within migrant narratives through an analysis of Judith Ortiz Cofer's understudied short story "Talking to the Dead" (1990), Francisco Goldman's canonical novel *The Ordinary Seaman* (1997), and Javier Hernandez's comic book and subsequent film *El Muerto* (1998–2003, 2007). Each of these works mediates the push-and-pull between the realities of market violence on Latinx subjects, migrants, and laborers. They also present the figure of death as a condition of possibility and revolution. Ortiz Cofer shapes this tension around death through the remembrance of her uncle's labor captivity and her abuelo's clairvoyance. By communing with the dead, the neocolonial relationships between the United States and Puerto Rico become fully realized. Goldman's narrative of illegal migrant labor is set in the nationally ambiguous space of a ruined freighter and considers how the workers are socially and politically dead when enslaved on the freighter. These working conditions cause one of the migrants to see the ghost of his cat, foreshadowing his eventual death in the face of this labor, but the cat ghost simultaneously signals the workers' salvation and upholds a celebratory potential in death as a means to resist economic violence.

I juxtapose these literary representations with Javier Hernandez's Aztec zombie superhero in *El Muerto*, where Latinx living death becomes zombified and fantastic. The figure of the zombie ambivalently produces the possibilities for Latinx power, which Hernandez hyperbolizes through his superhero. The possibility of power, nevertheless, is an empty utopian impulse. The superhero imaginary also allows for *El Muerto* to parody a market economy that exploits Latinx subjects and culture, which Hernandez and fellow comic artist Michael

Aushenker satirize through faux advertisements for the fictional corporation Tio Changos, when the market "eats" our Aztec zombie's power and replaces it with selling churros. I end on how these imaginations of resistance and power must grapple with the economic subsumption that these characters and figures navigate.

In *Visible Borders, Invisible Economies*, I am not interested in concluding on new subject formations, but I am interested in what sort of *social* formations may be possible under the violence of late capitalism. The final chapter, "Speculative Governances of the Dead: The Underclass, Underworld, and Undercommons," engages more speculative visions of Latinx social formations. What happens when these death-worlds are an underworld, governed by a shadowy organization policing its underclasses? This chapter focuses primarily on Daniel José Older's *Salsa Nocturna* (2012/2016). *Salsa Nocturna*'s fantastic and intertwining stories about a half-dead, half-alive agent for the New York Council of Dead presents forms of governance and resistance that both world-build and world-shatter. I weave in readings of Dulce Pinzón's photographic essay *The Real Story of the Superheroes* (2012) and Coya Paz and Free Street Theater's performance piece *Still/Here: Manifestos for Joy and Survival* (2019) to complement and expand the world-building and world-shattering stories in Older's work. The speculative perspectives in these three texts imagine the kinds of coalition-building and social mobilization that may occur among ethno-racial, queer, migrant, and Latinx subjects who help hold up the US social order and economy.

By thinking about speculative world-building/world-shattering, I interrogate what Mbembe calls death-worlds, or "new and unique forms of social existence."[107] To consider what the social looks like in these speculative imaginaries, I frame my readings with what Stefano Harney and Fred Moten theorize as the undercommons. For Harney and Moten, the undercommons is a shared space for primarily black subjects who live in a world requiring self-management but who are criminalized as ungovernable. While Harney and Moten describe the experience of blackness produced by this structural contradiction, their idea of an undercommons designates an ambivalent space and condition that many racialized subjects must negotiate collectively, especially when assembled as both peripheral and central to colonial and capitalist power dynamics. By unpacking these texts through theories of the undercommons, I conclude that they show us the impossibilities of imagining governance outside necropolitics, but they also present and perform ways of being together in this violence. By calling these narratives "world-building" and "world-shattering" forms, I speak to the unevenness in speculative texts that desire new imaginaries while living and dying under late capitalism. Harney and Moten's idea of the undercommons allows for a generative lens on what forms of kinship and community may look like in these death-worlds.

Last, in a short coda, "Dreaming of Deportation, or, When Everything 'Goes South,'" I consider the current state of deportation in the United States, with the uncertainties around DACA (Deferred Action for Childhood Arrivals) policy and the current encampments along the US-Mexico border. The policies and human rights violations of the Trump administration have been unfortunately a logical conclusion to a political economy that has overtly performed these necropolitics for years. The gross injustice and violence occurring within state-sanctioned institutions may be a form of security theater, but it is also one that has embraced what Agamben sees as the ultimate form of biopolitics—camps—and what Cacho describes as the state rationalizing of violence.[108] These politics, however, continue to be managed by economic concerns. For instance, when Trump commented on the Border Patrol's teargassing of Central American migrants seeking asylum in 2018, he said, "We are doing a job. We are doing what is right."[109] While this conflation between work and political ethos is a telling collapse of economic logic with political mandates, it grows out of a long history of xenophobia and policymaking designed to increase profits for the select few and to distribute death for racialized and marginalized populations. The veil over the economy of death is lifting, and the capital-centric undertones of these political atrocities are becoming more evident.

As the current political situation has stripped the United States of its beloved narrative of exceptionalism, it begs the question of how Latinx migrant narratives will change or not. The coda considers the phenomenon of celebratory deportation narratives, a problematic and speculative narrative genre. Latinx studies has historically presented deportation as a negative, and rightly so, considering the systemic and economic practices that encourage and foster migration in the first place. Nevertheless, narratives such as Maceo Montoya's *The Deportation of Wopper Barraza* (2014) or Malín Alegría's *Sofi Mendoza's Guide to Getting Lost in Mexico* (2008) provoke and disrupt the broader discourses about deportation by ambivalently celebrating the divorce from a nation that has enforced the docility of Latinx bodies and put into question the blind national love expected when living in the United States. Throughout *Visible Borders, Invisible Economies*, many of the literary and visual narratives have dreamed of so-called deportation, from *Sleep Dealer*'s Rudy in chapter 3 righteously moving further south as he flees the US foreign policy's Military Industrial Complex to *The Ordinary Seaman*'s old lobos del mar in chapter 4 awaiting with great anticipation their deportation. Instead, the narratives collectively refuse to vilify the global south, and thus, they challenge and subvert

US imperialist ideology and the normative migrant narrative that present el norte as the only future.

With *Visible Borders, Invisible Economies*, I hope to trace, outline, think about, and unravel how Latinx cultural productions and narratives show us the violent inner workings of a world organized by nations, borders, and capitalist globalization. The book does not promise to precisely locate where this violence begins or ends, and the texts I engage here do not necessarily offer solutions or future formations that may truly upend this violence. At times, I may fail to account for all the different Latinx, migrant, and racial experiences and voices, inadvertently producing problematic absences and more forms of violence. Nevertheless, Latinx narrative perhaps reminds us that the production and reading of art and culture is a form of *social*-care: it mobilizes communities who are living under atrocity, siege, and death. When Grise says, "Appear where they cannot go, head to where they least expect you," she imparts tactics and strategies for collective self-defense.[110] "Living death" may name the condition of many communities who are racialized, killed, and rendered disposable, but it nevertheless names a social formation. Latinx narrative exposes and imagines this "us."

PART I

DOCUMENTING THE LIVING DEAD

CHAPTER 1

Games of Enterprise and Security in Luis Alberto Urrea, Valeria Luiselli, and Karla Cornejo Villavicencio

When Luis Alberto Urrea writes in *The Devil's Highway*, "Like pro wrestling, there is a masked invader who regularly storms the field to disrupt the game. This, of course, is La Muerte," he presents surveillance politics between the Border Patrol and the coyotes as a Lucha Libre event on a Saturday night.[1] These security games on the US-Mexico border become campy entertainment and spectator sport, complete with Lycra face masks, shiny matching capes, and cliché hero-villain tropes. This is security theater at its clearest: highly visible performances that provide the appearance and illusion of security but instead ensure economic benefits for some and various forms of violence for others. Urrea's metaphor becomes more exacting when our luchador is death, La Muerte, who momentarily disrupts these performances and spectacles. In one sense, La Muerte connotes the unspoken and invisible pawns in this metaphor: migrants. The Lucha Libre arena often results in violence and death for migrants; they are the ultimate victims of La Muerte. Embedded in this figure of death is also another reading: La Muerte invading the game parallels popular and state discourse about migrants invading the country. Under these discourses, migrants become little more than bodies of racialized disease, plague, and peril—they are the bringers of La Muerte, constant invaders of national territory and "purity." What is profound about Urrea's metaphor here, then, is that migrants are both the resultant fatalities and the *already* living dead in these so-called games.

Urrea's *The Devil's Highway*, Valeria Luiselli's *Tell Me How It Ends*, and Karla Cornejo Villavicencio's *The Undocumented Americans* impart how national security practices and discourses shape the perceptions around migration, perceptions that conveniently neglect or elide the global economic processes at play. Whereas *The Devil's Highway* approaches the process of national security from the perspective of the Border Patrol, coyotes, and crossers on the US-Mexico border, *Tell Me How It Ends* and *The Undocumented Americans* consider the extra-state and/or peri-state misrecognitions that are reproduced through various media, nonprofit and rights organizations, and the everyday imagination within the United States. This chapter understands state and extra-/peri-state violence to enact "national security" practices and discourses that predominantly target "brown" bodies who cross borders and/or who are moving within urban and rural locales across the United States. I use the term "brown" here not to homogenize Latinx subjects who phenotypically present in many ways, whether as indigenous bodies, black bodies, white bodies, or mestizo/mulatto bodies; instead, I use "brown" to call out how Latinx and migrant subjects are homogenized, racialized, and misrecognized under multiple US imaginaries and discourses, both politically and culturally. Acts of security respond to and generate the US public's fears of invading "Mexicans," another homogenizing and deceptive categorization that incorporates all Latinx bodies coming from the global south, regardless of generational residency or country of origin.

Against these homogenizing and violent practices and discourses of security, the United States undeniably embraces a borderless economy through spearheading and benefiting from the North American Free Trade Agreement (NAFTA, 1993), the Dominican Republic–Central American Free Trade Agreement (CAFTA–DR, 2004), and other bloc trade agreements, alongside the importing and outsourcing of cheaper labor. These processes promote transnational movements of capital. This paradoxical relationship between fortifying borders but "freeing" economies plays out on the US-Mexico border in a violent collision that Urrea calls "the game." The game also infiltrates other borders, such as the Mexico-Guatemala border Luiselli considers, and other peri-state institutions, such as workers' rights organizations and health service programs, as Cornejo Villavicencio relates. This chapter maps out how discourses of fear and xenophobia, paired with practices of national security, veil the material conditions of immigration. Urrea's, Luiselli's, and Cornejo Villavicencio's narratives reveal that the problematic perceptions on immigration contain a series of deep but tactical misrecognitions in how the free-market economy works. They are also all literary narratives that purport to be a "true" story, whether housed in memoir, creative nonfiction, or investigative journalism, and yet they all understand that the story of undocumented immigration requires necessary fictions. The fictional qualities of these narratives may seem to contrast social and political facts, documents, and realities, but instead they become a necessary medium that fills in our collective knowledge about immigration policy and migratory experience. I find that this literary genre elucidates the interconnected relationship between national security and market neoliberalization, wherein some processes and discourses are hypervisible and others are in the shadows; as such, they produce counter-imaginations that potentially disrupt the false consciousness about immigration and show its bigger picture. In this sense, literary imagination holds both national narratives and migrant narratives in the same space but for different means and ends. Toward the chapter's end, I turn to the role of photography and documentary more directly to think through the tension between fact and fiction. I ultimately argue that these narratives show how political and popular anti-immigrant discourse and policy strategically target racialized subjects in order to downplay and conceal the actual material conditions—violence, exploitation, and death—of the political economy.

These politics and practices—these games—deployed on US borders within these narratives grow out of a larger history of global capitalism. For instance, when Michel Foucault maps out Friedrich Hayek's ideas about the rule of law operating in the economic order, he argues that this theory requires us to understand free-market capitalism as purely a game and legal institutions as "rules of the game." I am struck by Foucault's interpretation of the neoliberal economy as a game wherein law and government action are little more than playful functions in the service of capitalism: a "game of enterprise."[2] Not unlike Urrea's Lucha Libre spectacle of the US-Mexico border, the idea of the game elides the material violence of the economy. Foucault reminds us that, for proto-neoliberal economists like Hayek, this game should eventually "discard the whole system of administrative or legal interventionism."[3] However, I argue that these games of enterprise equally need games of security under neoliberal market capitalism. What the security theater on the US-Mexico border, in immigrant courts, and in various towns across the United States shows us is that the global economy needs legal and governmental institutions to maximize market "freedom" and to employ various forms of "security" that target undesirable populations and ultimately benefit desirable ones. National security advances capital gain.

The narratives that I consider in this chapter center questions of political documentation and security biometrics within migrant experiences. In the case of Urrea's *The Devil's Highway*, the novel relates the story of the Wellton 26, who crossed into the United States through a hostile stretch of land known as Desolation in Arizona; fourteen died (known as the Yuma 14), the largest fatality of migrants crossing the US-Mexico border at the time. This story can be told only because of the Border Patrol's documentation of the dead bodies and the few survivors, as Urrea recreates their lives and journey through the Border Patrol's paperwork, accounts, and perspectives. Similarly derived from processes within the US government, Luiselli's memoir *Tell Me*

How It Ends details her work interpreting and translating questionnaires with detained undocumented child migrants for the federal immigration courts in New York City. Luiselli's reflections, however, throw into sharp relief what can and cannot be documented under contemporary immigration policy and, thus, what the popular imaginary may or may never know about migration. Luiselli's work interweaves the genres of lyric essay and memoir, demonstrating how different forms of literary narrative and imagination become necessary to reveal the absences within political documentation and popular imaginaries. Whereas Urrea's *The Devil's Highway* is geographically set in the US-Mexico borderlands and Luiselli's *Tell Me How It Ends* never strays far from New York City's immigration detention centers and courts, Cornejo Villavicencio's *The Undocumented Americans* takes us to many different places across the United States as she visits the sites and people of major news events: the volunteers and first responders to the Ground Zero cleanup, the spurt of hate crimes against migrants in Staten Island, women's labor communities in Miami, Florida, and the water crisis in Flint, Michigan. She weaves her own experiences of undocumentedness within this collection, as she makes visible the unseen realities of being undocumented in the United States. While the narrative puts the voices of migrants over the state or political apparatus that enacts violence on them, *The Undocumented Americans* reveals how migrants must navigate anti-immigrant infrastructure and the lack of a social safety net. Together, these books present the actual material conditions of immigration in the United States: social death for those trying to navigate the legal system, slow death for those abandoned by the systems regulating labor and health rights, and/or states of exception for those who lack documentation.

As mapped in the introduction, the biopolitical paradox of economic freedom and national security frames my readings of Urrea, Luiselli, and Cornejo Villavicencio, which profoundly problematize the game. Together, these three narratives show how different forms of biopolitical discourse and fear, such as Malthusian catastrophe, misplace and obscure the political economy that causes and effects immigration. As a result, these narratives all present how "brown peril" discourses (that promote fear of the supposed "hordes" of racialized immigrants invading the United States) irrevocably imbue the political and popular imaginations about immigration.[4] These alarmist discourses largely target historically disenfranchised and disempowered populations, and they rely on primitive and atavistic Malthusian theories of (over)population. Their neo-Malthusianism produces a constant state of speculative catastrophe, which always imagines the possible destruction of the (pure) nation and gives rise to problematic policy and violent practices.[5]

The Devil's Highway, *Tell Me How It Ends*, and *The Undocumented Ameri-*

cans lay bare how perceptions of immigration—whether documented or un-documented—contain irrational xenophobia and influence anti-immigration policies and practices that intentionally misrecognize the inherent violence and exploitation at the heart of free-market capitalism.[6] As a result, the se-curing and fortifying of borders—both national and ideological—downplay and even conceal these free-market violences. Instead of seeing and acknowl-edging the national complicity in the killing of certain people for unbridled capital, state and popular discourses justify these dead bodies and subjects as threats to national security.[7] These narratives actively expose the necropoliti-cal structures at play within the ever-expanding security state.

The Making of Free Markets; the Making of Security States

These literary narratives develop from and respond to the long, complicated history of US economic and political interventionism in Latin American and Caribbean countries and regions. These two-pronged policies are most clearly seen in Puerto Rico with Operation Bootstrap (Operación Manos a la Obra), in which the US government, alongside the Puerto Rican Industrial Develop-ment Company, created and implemented numerous projects to modernize Puerto Rico into a developed industrial economy by moving it away from an agrarian system. Puerto Rico has been a US colony/commonwealth since 1898—placing Puerto Ricans' citizenship into a state of indistinction as US subjects without voting rights if residing on the island—and its industrializa-tion remains a primary economic model. Of course, Operation Bootstrap led to mass migrations of islanders to the United States, with which we see the beginnings of now established Puerto Rican communities, such as Nuyori-cans in New York's Lower East Side (or Loisaida) and Boricuas in Chicago's Humboldt Park. Such industrialization policies, prescribed by US imperial-ism, have consistently led to im/migration from Latin America. For those who stay in their homelands during such an economic shift, it becomes clear that it dismantles both the internal economies and the social stability of these locales and countries.[8] History shows us that US interventionism and imperi-alism occurs across the Americas, especially since the so-called Good Neigh-bor Policy (1933).[9]

More recently, the United States has imposed itself onto other countries with Programa Frontera Sur (2014). Luiselli describes this agreement between Mexico and the United States (whereby the United States pays Mexico to halt Central American migrants) as a contradiction between Mexico's promises to protect the safety of migrants and the reality that this anti-immigration policy makes migrants more vulnerable. She states, "Programa Frontera Sur is the Mexico government's new augmented-reality video game: the player who hunts down the next migrant wins."[10] Once again, the discourse about the state and the policing of immigration becomes synonymous with playing games, albeit less a Lucha Libre arena and more a digital wonderland. The spectacle here displays an economic backdrop to this security and violence.

The US-Mexico border has become a site where the nation *performs* violent acts on Latin American and Latinx bodies by hunting, surveilling, and arresting migrants or those profiled as migrants, and this site has become symbolic of the expansive violence on other literal and figurative borders for Latinx subjects. Interwoven with this state violence, we also find a resurgence of vigilantism, such as the Minutemen, and a nativist and populist revival for self-professed US livelihood and purity. These anxieties, practices, and theatrics on the US-Mexico border come under the broad and abstract term "security." This term is an ambiguous descriptor. On one hand, it denotes a nation-state's institutions and procedures to ensure citizen safety, which historically has been the jurisdiction of state/civil police for internal matters and the military for foreign matters in the United States. Now the term is irrevocably tied to the Department of Homeland Security and the securing of personal data, borders, and resources to counter alleged threats to civilian populations.[11] "Threat" is often paired with even more ambiguous and reductive terms: terrorism, immigrants, and hackers, to name a few. On the other hand, "security" equally signals more economic interests: securing our export-import relations through free-trade agreements, installing military bases in certain resource-heavy spaces, and most obviously, describing tradable financial instruments or assets on the stock market commonly known as "securities." "Security", then, stands in for both national and economic processes. I would posit, moreover, that this term connotes the interaction between the US nation (which secures a certain population's life) and the global economy (which freely exploits and kills Latinx im/migrant bodies).

While Hayek's economic ideals see national regulation as a direct hindrance to freeing the market as I have mapped out in the introduction, these histories show an interplay between national security and market neoliberalization. Inderpal Grewal describes this interplay by using the concept of insecurity, claiming that the anxieties and calls for greater national security have an economic utility. She argues that feelings of insecurity easily align with commodity production because "militarization and technological change will produce commodities that can in turn provide better security."[12] In this sense, national security is necessary to maintain xenophobia, which in turn produces an ever-growing economy, with new and improved security toys released each year. While the free market has caused, necessitated, and reinforced migration, and while the nation-state has responded with great fervor to the foreign, racialized bodies entering geopolitical territories, the circulation of fear and speculative catastrophe (insecurity) promotes commodity production (securities). Security theater, then, allows for a more "borderless" economy, since it requires newer and more specialized technologies, weapons, and other commodities. Significantly, these expanding securities discursively produce violence and, ultimately, make racialized migratory bodies ineligible for personhood: the living dead.

The Game in Luis Urrea's *The Devil's Highway*

One way this interaction between national security and a free-market economy becomes apparent is through what commonly is called the game. The game largely describes the spectacle of regulation by the state's Military Industrial and Prison Industrial Complexes. Peter Andreas's *Border Games* maps out how the US government specifically thinks about border security as purely a game, citing former Immigration and Naturalization Service (INS) Commissioner Doris Meissner as saying, "Think of this as one team, different roles, different uniforms, but with the same game plan—and that is to restore the rule of law to the border."[13] The different agencies during Meissner's time become synonymous with team sports, whether one is engaged in law enforcement or the military. The rule of law determines the boundaries of play, but reframing security as a game occludes its inherent violence. Urrea even notes after all his journalistic work with the Border Patrol: "The border *war* is often seen as a highly competitive *game*," a discourse that has apparently trickled down the bureaucratic hierarchy.[14] "War" and "game" collapse here, producing ambiguity and indistinctions both in practices and in discourses.

Urrea pays particular attention to the material conditions of these political indistinctions: "Texas Rangers allegedly handcuff homeboys and toss them into irrigation canals to drown, though the walkers can't tell the Border Patrol apart from the Rangers or any other mechanized hunt squad: they're all cowboys. Truncheons. Beatings. Shootings. Broken legs. Torn Panties. Blood. Tear gas. Pepper spray. Kicked Ribs. Rape."[15] The violence of this security is sweeping as it binds together chemical warfare, sexual assault, murder, and physical battery. "Homeboys" (coyotes? migrants? random racialized males?) and "mechanized hunt squads" (Border Patrol? Texas Rangers? random vigilantes?) are two indistinct organizations on the border, one playing the smuggling game and the other playing the discipline-and-punish game. The lack of distinction in the types of violence occurring and the types of actors in these games demonstrates a breakdown in the legibility and recognition of both formal and informal economies and institutions. This phenomenon perhaps alludes to the movement of the INS to three different but overlapping departments in 2003: US Citizenship and Immigration Services (USCIS), US Immigration and Customs Enforcement (ICE), and US Customs and Border Protection (CBP), all under the jurisdiction of the Department of Homeland Security (DHS). While the differentiation in departments would seem to create sharper nuance and clarity, instead it appears to have simply created more moving chess pieces for the state to enact various forms of physical and legal violence on migrant bodies and subjectivities. In *The Devil's Highway*, the state and peri-state organizations are the side of La Migra, whereas the migrants, coyotes, and/or homeboys are the ungovernable and killable. The violence of this game, which Urrea lists with the finality of periods, represents the "savage gospel of the crossing."[16] This is the inherent violence in the game that makes border security indistinguishable from border war.[17]

Urrea's narrative exposes how the game develops into full-on spectacle once the so-called crimmigrant enters the picture, an operation that Nicholas De Genova calls the "'illegality' effect."[18] Through explanations of "cutting the drag," for example, Urrea shows how the coyotes and La Migra become enlisted into a contest: "The whole game for their team is to pass by invisibly, and the team on this side is paid to see the invisible. The Coyotes score when they make it, and the Migra scores when they don't."[19] The drags are the game board, where car tires are dragged through the desert every few days to the east and the west, ideally forcing the crossers to walk over them on their south-to-north trek, leaving tracks. Not to be tracked is the goal for the coyotes and crossers. Urrea's use of team rhetoric condenses the numerous groups partaking in this game—the coyotes, the crossers, the Customs and Border Patrol (CBP), Immigration and Customs Enforcement (ICE), the Department of Homeland Security (DHS), the US military, the drug cartels, the Minutemen, to name only a few—into only two sides. Those policing borders and militarizing borders are indistinguishable, and those profiting off migrants and the migrants themselves are synonymous. However, this simplistic duality of the game is reductive, and as such, it erases the legibility of how these politics and economies work. The descriptions of cutting the drag in Urrea's narrative show the strategic deployment of "sport" as a way to elide, legitimize, and/or mitigate the (often invisible) consequences of this game: dead bodies, unbridled violence, exploitation.

Justin Akers Chacón and Mike Davis's coauthored treatise *No One Is Illegal* explores the history behind the national security practices, drawing out their economic roots. Davis, in particular, argues that many regulatory institutions in the United States historically have been constructed for private corporate armies and securities and have enacted private or peri-state violence. This violence originates from late nineteenth- and early twentieth-century geo-politics: for the Heartland, we get the Pinkertons; for the South, we get the Klansmen; and for the West, we get white vigilantes. Davis claims that we see this private violence when the "biggest industrial, mining, and railroad corporations, loathe to put their entire trust in the local state, deployed literal armies of armed guards, plant detectives, and company police," wherein "the Pinkertons alone reputedly outnumbered the regular US Army in the early 1890s."[20] This schematic of privatizing security founded in the late nineteenth and early twentieth century was deeply influenced by Reconstruction failures, the rise in industrialism, and the increase in Southern European and Asian immigration. Privatized or peri-state security is not about a state's protection of the *dēmos* or national population but about the interests of a select few. Notably, this understanding of security is still a state-sanctioned rule of law, ever more in the service of the economy.

Grewal describes this arming of both police and "exceptional citizens" (not the living dead here but state-sanctioned militias such as "slave owners, set-tlers, and white persons") in the nineteenth century as the catalyst for when gun violence and sport economies collapse. First, she argues that the making of the US nation-state comes from a "white racial sovereignty" whose mi-litias and settlers produced statehood and independence and whose armed police met runaway slaves and labor protest movements with lethal force. This history of racial and class violence has produced "mythologies of white masculinity related to guns" wherein "[s]hooting with guns became a sport [and] has remained a sport" from shooting ranges to video games. Grewal concludes that "the ubiquity and conjoining of pleasure and violence produce subjects who naturalize violence as a sport."[21] The way violence and games have collapsed in the United States, as shown in *The Devil's Highway*, dem-onstrates how racial violence becomes a state-sanctioned norm. Andreas de-scribes the "enforcement-evasion game" as economically viable on all sides. On one level, these games require migrants to hire coyotes or smugglers if they want to play the game successfully, and failure to do so increases "their likelihood of assault by border thieves and abuse by the authorities." Simulta-neously, the Border Patrol regularly fail to deter most "illegal crossings," mak-ing their enforcement "largely a ritualized performance" to meet the demands of the "numbers game": to show that they are "keeping busy" and have "politi-cal ammunition for budget requests."[22] This incredibly violent political game, then, also emphasizes Grewal's point that this so-called sport is a spectacle primarily for economic reasons.[23]

Urrea calls out these forms of spectacle throughout *The Devil's Highway*. For instance, he relates, "Of course, the illegals have always been called names other than human—wetback, taco-bender. . . . In politically correct times, 'illegal alien' was deemed gauche, so 'undocumented worker' came into favor. Now, however, the term preferred by the Arizona press is 'undocumented entrant.' As if the United States were a militarized beauty pageant."[24] Urrea establishes precisely how the immigrant becomes discursively reduced to a body that must strut and pose across the stage/border, an object for US forces to regulate and then photograph, fingerprint, and input into the system, dead, alive, or both. In a similar spectacle, at the end of the day, the Minutemen are still donning their uniforms to enact an old role-playing game in which "the immigrant" simply becomes another prop on the stage of regulation, while the real culprit—neoliberalism—operates behind the scenes. And although the deaths happening on the US-Mexico border are very real, these deaths are coming out of a desire for the *appearance* of state regulation, purely sport and spectacle.[25]

This late nineteenth- and early twentieth-century privatization of security is the blueprint for current vigilantes and nativists, such as The Minutemen Project. This project, according to Chacón and Davis, grew out of a long history of infighting between NFWA and UFWOC unions and grower-shipper teamsters ever since the end of the Bracero Program (1942–1964). The Minutemen, deeply influenced by the grower-shipper teamsters, see themselves as a group of concerned *citizens* protecting their national rights (read: economic and geographic resources) from the threat of "the Mexican hordes."[26] What is perhaps most interesting about these later formations of privatized violence is how they market their agenda through a rhetoric of nationalism, claiming to be super-patriots even while their existence is rooted in fights over labor rights. Chacón and Davis describe the Minutemen as a "theater of the absurd as well as a canny attempt to move vigilantism back into the mainstream of conservative politics" through "jabbering to the press," all while they sit in their lawn chairs drinking, cleaning their guns, and getting "sunburned and bored."[27] The Minutemen have done little in terms of securing the nation-state against "illegal immigration"; instead, they look and talk big. They are part of the theatricality of security.[28]

Urrea's own engagement with vigilante groups on the US-Mexico border remain largely in the background, as *The Devil's Highway* puts into conversation governmental documentation and the process of rehumanizing migrant bodies. When describing the "hunt" for the Wellton 26's coyote, Jesús, Urrea begins with the bodies of the survivors lying in hospital beds as camera crews hover over them: "Their features are overwhelmed by glare. They're nearly invisible in the brutal light."[29] When asked who their coyote is, the narrative moves from the survivors to the partly imagined life and journey of Jesús, a young kid with a "stupid red punk-rock haircut hanging down in front" and ample experience with manual labor in a brickyard.[30] The prospects of money and economic stability turn him to the world of human smuggling. Once the survivors describe him, however, a manhunt begins, representing the full force of the Military Industrial Complex. Urrea describes the line of law and order: Border Patrol on small ATVs, BORSTAR (Border Patrol Search, Trauma, and Rescue) rescuers, BORTAC (Border Patrol Tactical Unit) known as the Cactus Cops, the Customs unit known as the Shadow Wolves, Native American trackers, the DEA, BLM cops, and INS agents. These state-sanctioned forces are joined by "big angry white men in Jeeps, two separate groups of 'citizen' border watchers working the western desert outside of Tucson" and by self-described "patriot militias" whose trailers are "pulled into secure configurations" with "upside-down American flags and black MIA/POW flags and the occasional Jolly Roger fluttering in the wind."[31] These militias and the militarization of the border are never short of description here. The hypervisibility of state and peri-state regulation contrasts against the invisibility of migrants in hospital beds. This moment draws out a pointed critique about what is made visible in representations and discourses of migration and immigration practices and what is not. Moreover, this moment also underscores the massive theatrics and resources put into play for the hunt while the survivors are rendered nearly invisible in the spectacle.

The Rule of Law and Other Performances in Valeria Luiselli's *Tell Me How It Ends*

While security theater and anti-immigrant discourse work hard at making some processes hypervisible and other processes invisible, there are also legal practices that play a significant role in constructing this game. Luiselli's *Tell Me How It Ends: An Essay in 40 Questions*, her (re)collection of translating im/migrant children's answers to the intake questionnaire for the US immigration courts in New York City, shows how the rule of law operates as a structure that actively occludes the full economic picture of immigration. *Tell Me How It Ends* relates the incongruities between migrant experiences in the United States and narrative representations of these experiences. She recalls,

> I hear words, spoken in the mouths of children, threaded in complex narratives. They are delivered with hesitance, sometimes distrust, always with fear. I have to transform them into written words, succinct sentences, and barren terms. The children's stories are always shuffled, stuttered, always shattered beyond the repair of a narrative order. The problem with trying to tell their story is that it has no beginning, no middle, and no end.[32]

Luiselli identifies the illegibility of these children's stories and transcriptions when she must fill in answers for children too young to articulate a response to the second question on the questionnaire: When did you enter the United States?"[33]—or when she cannot include their nutritional and medical deficiencies while they are detained in the so-called "icebox" (US detention centers) awaiting processing and deportation.[34] Alongside the impossibility of fully capturing and putting together these children's narratives stands a story too easy to tell by various mainstream media:

> In varying degrees, some papers and webpages announce the arrival of undocumented children like a biblical plague. Beware the locust! They will cover the face of the ground so it cannot be seen—these menacing, coffee-colored boys and girls, with their obsidian hair and slant eyes. They will fall from the skies, on our cars, on our green lawns, on our heads, on our schools, on our Sundays. They will make a racket, they will bring their chaos, their sickness, their dirt, their brownness. They will cloud the pretty views, they will fill the future with bad omens, they will fill our tongues with barbarisms. And if they are allowed to stay here they will—eventually—reproduce![35]

Luiselli calls out a series of familiar cliché soundbites about immigrants that erase the children's ages, their stage of development, their backgrounds, their struggles, as well as the United States' own histories of meddling in Latin America and producing these struggles. These nationalistic soundbites lack a self-awareness in the complex and messy stories in which migrants are protagonists, pawns, villains, and objects. Luiselli ends this paragraph on the fear behind these mainstream clichés: the racial and foreign Other may not only invade this geopolitical space but also will reproduce in it, giving life not to the nation and its economic imperatives but to more Others. This "brown peril" discourse operating behind these fears is strategic in that it elides the "life" of the immigrant that the nation desires—cheap disposable labor—and instead makes claims that reinstate false ideologies about the nation itself: as some racially and culturally homogeneous, "pure" space of the so-called citizen.

Luiselli's vignettes of her work as a volunteer translator and interpreter for the federal immigration courts relate the ideological and methodological friction of the work. She wants the children to answer the questions correctly in order for a stronger case to be made for their asylum, but simultaneously she is unable to lead the children's answers. The children are incapable of building a legible and court-ready defense for asylum and migration as primarily Spanish-speaking and at their age (although many people would struggle with this task at any age), and Luiselli contends with her own cooperation in a legal system that upholds age difference in some instances but ignores it others. She instead looks for "more general categories for each story that may tip the legal scale in favor of the future client in a future trial—categories such as 'abandonment,' 'prostitution,' 'sex trafficking,' 'gang violence,' and 'death threats.'"[36] When asking very young children why they came to the United States and what they left behind, she must simplify the questions or find different avenues to ask difficult questions about their past.

Luiselli's vignettes describe the inevitable incoherence of a child's account, but this illegibility comes up against the importance of evidence and documentation. When Luiselli is talking with a teenage boy named Manu about why he left Honduras, he pulls out a police report he filed against the Honduran gang Barrio 18 that shot and killed his friend while they were walking home from school. He explains that the police "don't do shit for anybody like me"; he carried this report with him all the way to the United States.[37] Another boy, Miguel Hernández, has a poem about the death of his childhood friend that he also carries, and Luiselli ruminates that this "elegy" is not about remembrance but about "an obsessive conjuring of his friend's buried corpse."[38] These are both mementos of violence and trauma that are remainders, in excess and surplus, of an experience. As such, they document the experience, although the children do not necessarily see them as evidence for US immigration law within *Tell Me How It Ends*. Nevertheless, Manu's report has potential legal significance, whereas the poem can never be included in the government questionnaire. The poem is politically dead, embodying the status of these children in this political state of exception.

Manu's police report produces a glitch in this necropolitics because it gives him proof for asylee status, a legal process that Luiselli identifies and instigates for Manu. In the United States, as of 2017, applying for asylum requires those who meet refugee status and who are unable or unwilling to return to their country of nationality to "establish that race, religion, nationality, membership in a particular social group, or political opinion was or will be at least one central reason for their persecution or why they fear persecution" if they return.[39] This means that they must bring evidence of persecution and of fear. Luiselli relates how drawing out these fears from children, especially when it comes to gangas and panderillos, is "like pressing the button on a machine that produces nightmares."[40] This police report, nevertheless, demonstrates Manu's ability to prove that he deserves asylee status, so when Luiselli meets Manu again during the second phase of his deportation appeal, she notes, "But thanks to the material evidence that Manu has of his statements—the folded slip of paper—The Door [a nonprofit organization that is a part of the Immigrant Children's Relief Effort (ICARE) coalition] was able to find a large firm willing to take his case pro bono. With that kind of material evidence, it would be impossible to lose. The lawyers at The Door *transformed a dead document into legal evidence* for a case."[41] This document is dead because its original purpose in Honduras has failed, but Luiselli understands The Door as resurrecting its political life in new circumstances, much like as Urrea must do for the Yuma 14. Of course, this lawful moment in *Tell Me How It Ends* is tempered by our knowledge that this is a young child who has no reason to know the law, let alone be prepared enough to bring proof of his inability to return home. The law, in Luiselli's account, appears fundamentally abstruse.

This moment in *Tell Me How It Ends* points back to Foucault's formulation of the rule of law within the current economic order, where the law is no longer something that gives legitimacy to the state but now operates as rules of a game, with the game being driven by capital.[42] For Foucault, this neoliberal game has a concrete order, where legal institutions simply frame and supervise the way the game is played by individuals. These rules of the game allow players the "possibility of behaving as they wish in the form of free enterprise" (e.g., competition), and they now only arbitrate the inevitable frictions and crises that arise from this "free enterprise."[43] In this instance in Luiselli's account, the dead document that must be transformed into legal evidence presents a juridical strategy that allows one side (migrants) to get ahead of the other side (federal judiciary), all while ignoring the histories and politics that give rise to this document: US interference in Honduras to protect the banana industry (Standard Fruit and United Fruit Companies), US military destabilization of multiple Central American governments throughout the twentieth century, and International Monetary Fund (IMF) programs for modernization. Luiselli illuminates an epistemological limitation here: the document works only within the nation-state's legal system, but it cannot represent or know anything more than that, especially the global political economy operating beyond such state institutions. For the "undocumented," the rule of law frames immigration as purely existing within state borders, its territory, and its chess board. "Refugee" and "asylee" exist only as internal enterprises (if the document happens to be on the body when detained), even while these terms connote transnational and neoliberal developments. When Alicia Schmidt Camacho describes the "condition of being 'undocumented,'" she argues that this condition is not simply about the lack of legal protections but about the "active conversion of the migrant into a distinct category of stateless personhood" that "emerges with the contradiction between market demands for mobile labor and consumable goods and the immobility of rights beyond the bounds of the nation-state." This understanding of the undocumented condition underlines the migrant's precarity within the United States, where migrant mortality, disappearance, and departure necessarily enact "the migrant's detachment from the state, a severing of citizenship that is also a death, a death that produces."[44] Migration, then, is a fatal condition for migrants, and their undocumented existence within the US nation-state, which requires them to play certain games, produces this condition of death repeatedly. At one point during Luiselli's interview with Manu, a momentary reflection disrupts the narrative that is without agency: "Everyone was dying or going north."[45] If we understand Schmidt Camacho's point, however, then dying and going north are no different: both sever the migrant from the law and from their histories. I would add that even when a document may open the door to documented status as in the case of Manu, this legal evidence does not speak to or care about the economic histories that produce migration in the first place, and in fact this process relegates Manu to rules of law that must kill his statehood, his personhood, or both, all for the game.

Undocumentedness in Karla Cornejo Villavicencio's *The Undocumented Americans*

Within these discourses and practices of security theater on borders and in courts are questions of undocumentedness. Where documents in *Tell Me How It Ends* become the be-all and end-all of asylee/refugee status, Cornejo Villavicencio compiles the experiences, fears, and stories of those without documents who are living and dying in the United States. Her book is a work of creative nonfiction that follows the narrator-author through a series of journalistic encounters with undocumented people and their experiences in New York City and Staten Island, New York; Miami, Florida; Flint, Michigan; Cleveland, Ohio; and New Haven, Connecticut. In her introduction, Cornejo

Villavicencio notes that she feels uncomfortable putting on the "drag of a journalist" when dealing with undocumented peoples and stories, making this book "not a traditional nonfiction book" but a "snapshot in time, a high energy imaging of trauma brain."[46] The book imparts these multifaceted and overlapping stories of various undocumented people as they navigate the social death and slow death of US migrant life, whether they are exploited manual and service-industry labor, confronted with an inaccessible and callous healthcare industry, or seeking sanctuary in churches during the intolerant Trump administration. The book arguably produces a pathos of sympathy/ empathy that Urrea's and Luiselli's works also readily target vis-à-vis their readers, but the narrative also assembles a journey in which the narrator-author transports and then leaves the reader in these lives and deaths, a sort of heaving and desertion that reproduces the anxieties, inescapabilty, and realities of undocumentedness.[47]

The Undocumented Americans is also an act of exorcism for the narrator-author. She often finds herself having to confront and process her own experiences as undocumented and her own struggles and traumas with her family, who migrated from Ecuador, that often complement and collide with the collections of stories she is putting together. At one point, Cornejo Villavicencio says she is not a journalist because "[j]ournalists are not allowed to get involved," but the fact that she is also a part of these communities means she is irrevocably experiencing these same structures of social death and slow death.[48] In another moment, she notes that her need to fix problems with education means she's "drunk the social mobility Kool-Aid from college prep programs run by white people" that "brainwashed" her.[49] Her own journey through undocumented status and eventually as a DACA (Deferred Action for Childhood Arrivals) recipient infiltrates her interactions and readings of others' experiences, and she consistently acknowledges her own bias in these interactions. The book even opens with the uncomfortable confession that she had many rich benefactors throughout her education who paid for her road to Harvard as long as she wrote them letters.[50] The narrator-author understands her position of privilege, and she regularly calls out how it distances her from her subjects, even while they may share many experiences. There is a tension in the narrative with the narrator-author doing investigative journalism, memoir, fiction, testimonio, and self-reflection all at once.

When discussing the effects of lead poisoning on a baby in Flint, the narrator-author can no longer fully contain the narrative or her positionality in it. The narrative accumulates too much death and killing of undocumented migrants, and she bursts out with the full weight of it all:

The wait is torturous for Ivy. It is torturous for her mom. It is torturous for the community. They want us all dead, Latinxs, black people, they want us dead, and sometimes they'll slip something into our bloodstreams to kill us slowly and sometimes they'll shoot and shoot and shoot and shoot and shoot shoot and shoot and shoot and shoot and shoot and shoot shoot and shoot and shoot and shoot and shoot and shoot shoot and shoot and shoot and shoot shoot and shoot and shoot and shoot and shoot and shoot shoot and shoot and shoot and shoot shoot and shoot and shoot and shoot and shoot and shoot shoot and shoot and shoot and shoot and shoot shoot and shoot and shoot and shoot and shoot and shoot and shoot and shoot shoot and shoot until their bloodlust is satisfied. [. . .]. What I saw in Flint was what I had seen everywhere else, what I had felt in my own poisoned blood and bones. Being killed softly, silently, and with impunity.[51]

The forty-two iterations of "shoot" in careful refrain captures a sense of endlessness to the violence as it slowly devolves almost into meaninglessness. This passage also illustrates the narrator-author's own emotional absorption into the narrative of undocumentedness as she erupts with poetic excess. This moment in the narrative forces us to question where these lines between fact and fiction, between emotional market and journalistic imperative, and between life and death blur, disintegrate, and collapse when telling the story of undocumented immigration.

The narrative especially treads between fact and fiction not purely to produce sympathy/empathy but to present the structures at play when one is Latinx and undocumented in the United States. While Cornejo Villavicencio acknowledges that this is not "traditional nonfiction," noting that names and other identifying details had to be changed and fabricated, she keeps these fictionalizations in question.[52] At one point, she imagines the life of a day laborer that the others rarely talked about, an alcoholic who died during the Hurricane Sandy flooding.[53] She concludes this imaginary story of his life and death with a series of questions:

Did this happen?
   Are we in gangs?
   Do we steal Social Security numbers?
   Do we traffic our children across borders?
   Is this book nonfiction?
   Can we imagine that he was capable of kindness, even as he was drinking? That he was capable of courage, even as he was wounded?
   What if this is how, in the face of so much sacrilege and slander, we reclaim our dead?[54]

The fictional and the imaginary become a way to recover stories that can no longer be told or can be only imagined, but they also work as a way of locating and resurrecting the dead, who undergo a structure of doubleness: one as living undocumented and another as the living dead. She immediately moves from this fictionalization to the experiences of undocumented subjects who lived through and died from the events of September 11, 2001. Immediately following the events of 9/11, she describes how the response was first about locating survivors and *second* about locating the dead at Ground Zero. In parallel, she designates how the first responders were firefighters and EMT and the *second* responders were undocumented immigrants.[55] These classifications of who is second—the dead and the undocumented—mark a significant relationship between undocumentedness and necropolitics. There is a double bind and double invisibility occurring for Latinx subjects, especially first-generation and 1.5-generation migrants, in *The Undocumented Americans*, that chronically produce social, slow, and literal death. The narrative ensures that these fictions and imaginations are not in the service of simply producing reader sympathy/empathy but lead the reader through these cyclical structures of undocumentedness.

Caught up in these questions of undocumentedness is also the political economy of so-called resources. The discourses and ideologies around resource depletion and scarcity is a particularly common misrecognition within immigration politics, especially when migrants are perceived to be taking jobs or overtaxing social safety nets and thus become an alleged resource threat. Nevertheless, these resource fears imbue multiple discourses and imaginations about Latinx immigration in communities across the United States, and these discourses are often irrevocably tied to economy, whether through labor, health care, or Social Security. *The Undocumented Americans* beautifully and troublingly presents the way resources are distributed *or not* when one is negotiating undocumented spaces. The book primarily concentrates on two forms of resources: labor and healthcare.

In terms of labor resources, she calls out the popular image of undocumented workers wherein "day laborers seemed like an almost mythical archetype, groups of brown men huddled at the crack of dawn on street corners next to truck rental lots and hardware superstores and lumberyards."[56] This stereotypical image of undocumented Latinx migrants as always "brown" and waiting for manual labor is something she laments throughout *The Undocumented Americans*. In the introduction, she speaks to how she hates most books about migrants because "I couldn't see my family in them, because I saw my parents as more than laborers, as more than sufferers and dreamers."[57] The popular image that makes undocumented migrants synonymous with workers is something she wants to reject and yet cannot fully exorcize. At one point, she exclaims, "I almost wish they'd call us something rude like 'crazy fuckin' Mexicans' because that's acknowledging something about us beyond our usefulness—we're crazy, we're Mexican, we're clearly unwanted!—but to describe all of us, men, women, children, locally Instagram-famous teens, queer puppeteers, all of us, as *workers* in order to make us palatable, my god. We were brown bodies made to labor, faces pixelated."[58] The homogenization of undocumented immigrants with workers (and as Mexicans) within the broader discourse, however, is coupled with the way undocumented workers are exploited. Cornejo Villavicencio emphasizes that undocumented workers have no protections and no collective bargaining, which has given rise to various work centers and workers' rights organizations such as Colectiva Por Fin, Nuestra Calle, and Mujeres en Solidaridad.[59] These organizations help workers navigate their rights, find jobs with reputable contractors, and offer a sense of community in a rather bleak economy.

This idea of workers as pure corporeal resource ("brown bodies made to labor, faces pixelated") is a recurrent image within the book, but the question of resources is further complicated when the narrative considers the water crisis in Flint, Michigan, for undocumented subjects. Cornejo Villavicencio relates how the dying of industry in Flint resulted in the city's getting "smaller and blacker and browner and poorer, public services crumbled." She emphasizes that the water crisis affected undocumented residents in "disturbingly specific ways," especially since these residents could not read the English-only flyers and would not answer the door to canvassers, fearing they were ICE. These undocumented residents did not know there was a problem long after the problem was publicized.[60] When talking with Margarita, a local Mexican American immigration activist, Cornejo Villavicencio asks about the role of churches in helping these communities through the crisis, and Margarita tells her that the situation has actually made more services available to them since "[t]hey finally realized we were here."[61] Yet when these populations are living, working, and dying in a city and country that has historically ignored and/or despised them, then the city and national services are met with great suspicion. Cornejo Villavicencio asks:

> What promises can you make to a child about the world of possibility ahead of them when the state has poisoned their bloodstreams and bones such that their behavioral self-control and language comprehension are impaired? How many graves has the government of Michigan set aside for casualties of the water crisis that will end with a gunshot in fifteen years' time? We all know how cops respond to kids of color with intellectual disabilities or mental illness.[62]

The narrator-author draws out a series of tensions around resources here. First, there are undocumented Latinx and racialized bodies who are pure economic resources; when industry leaves Flint, they become useless and surplus. Second is the problem of the now-tainted resource of tap water in Flint, which is poisoning this devalued underclass. Third, once word leaks to the larger public about the Flint water crisis, public resources become abundant but are underutilized because of a lack of communication and an ingrained mistrust of public services that cannot fix the water infrastructure. Cornejo Villavicencio's questions point to the impending consequences of these resource tensions: more forms of death for undocumented Latinx communities.

The anxieties around resources within Latinx narratives and immigration discourses are not a new problem. The space of the US-Mexico borderlands is known to historically lack water as a resource, and the semidesert conditions always come with a constant anxiety about the lack of water. The US-Mexico political fights over Rio Grande water rights have been a common fixture since the Treaty of Guadalupe Hidalgo (1848). Water warriors put out water jugs for crossers, and they are often criminalized for this humanitarian act. The desert, however, is a great equalizer. Urrea portrays vacationers going into the Arizona desert only to find "[t]hey didn't carry enough water," an issue that immediately recalls his earlier description of the Yuma 14 being found with "cactus spines in their faces, their hands" and so dehydrated that "there wasn't enough fluid in them to bleed."[63] All are transitory desert tourists "killed by the light."[64] The water fear in the southwestern United States feeds the rhetoric of resource depletion on the border, and all sides are affected by the scarcity of water, compelling Urrea to write, "In the desert, we are all illegal aliens."[65] The crisis in Flint also produces a sense of shared experience by both undocumented migrants and citizens, as all are being poisoned by lead. Resources for the victims of this political blunder were abundant and dispensed without limit initially, a similar response post-9/11 with the September 11th Victims Compensation Fund, which Cornejo Villavicencio explores. The abundance of resources following the Flint water crisis and 9/11 all but disappear, however.

Contrasted with these crisis resources is the utter lack of any social safety net for older undocumented immigrants within *The Undocumented Americans*. Cornejo Villavicencio notes, "Even though half of undocumented people pay into Social Security, none are eligible for the benefits. They are unable to purchase health insurance. They probably don't own their own homes. They don't have 401(k)s or retirement plans of any kind. Meager saving, if any. [. . .] This country takes their youth, their dreams, their labor, and spits them out with nothing to show for it."[66] Her parents are a part of this demographic

that "are sick, uninsured, and aging out of work in a fucking racist country,"
resulting in her father preferring to die rather than have his prostate cancer bi-
opsied.[67] These moments in the narrative consider what it means to grow old
in a system that usually expels or kills people before they even get the chance
to reach a certain age. These moments also evoke Cornejo Villavicencio's early
reference to usefulness when she confronts how Latinx immigrants are never
allowed to be anything but useful in their labor. Age and health devalue the
undocumented immigrant as a resource and cast a bright light on the lack of
resources for undocumented immigrants.

Resource discourse is complicated in itself, but when it becomes paired
with immigration politics, it takes on specific historical contexts. Economically, one of the most famous negotiations over resources between the United
States and Mexico was over labor depletion with the guest worker agreement
the Bracero Program (1942–1964). The program was so successful (read: the
labor was so cheap) that it was extended for about twenty years after World
War II and largely marks the beginning of the perception that "Mexicans"
(regardless of their actual country or localities of origin) are overtaking jobs
and are in abundance in the United States, especially when met with xenophobic policies such as Operation Wetback (1954).[68] These perceptions often
ignore the United States' role in migration. While the Bracero Program continues to be a hypervisible example, other less visible economic histories have
also influenced migration in the Americas. Maritza E. Cárdenas reminds us
of the impact of The Central American Common Market (1960) in promoting
the United States as an economically prosperous destination that has shaped
current Central American migrations, and rarely does The Caribbean Basin
Initiative (1984) come into discussions of free-trade agreements in the Americas.[69] While Cornejo Villavicencio does not speak to any of these economic
entanglements directly, she elucidates how 9/11 irrevocably collapses state
violence and economic violence for undocumented migrants. While undocumented immigrants are already cast as the antithesis of American citizens in
popular imaginaries, 9/11 also made all immigrants suspect. This targeting of
immigrants as possible threats to national security unravels in myriad ways,
from the suspension of driver licenses for undocumented immigrants to the
management of detention centers by private prison groups.[70] Unsurprisingly,
these actions to limit and regulate this population tend to have primarily
economic consequences, where the lack of a driver license disallows some
to work, such as Cornejo Villavicencio's father losing his taxicab job, or re-
distributes taxpayer money to corporate entities, with the rise of the Prison
Industrial Complex. This national response also deeply ignores the relief work
of undocumented peoples during the cleanup of Ground Zero or Hurricane

Sandy, an elision for which Cornejo Villavicencio concludes, "Nobody will ever know you died. Nobody will ever know you lived."[71]

Nevertheless, these resource histories, both of scarcity and of abundance, have led to the much more sinister discourse of overpopulation. If biopolitics and its securing of populations is a tactic to reconstitute power to the elite few, then overpopulation rhetoric works to expel certain populations from this economic power and often points the finger at those who threaten nation-bound resources. Cornejo Villavicencio's narrative captures the way undocumented immigrants are covertly rendered dead, but it also speaks to how they are loudly targeted. At one point she admonishes, "One of the bogeymen of the right, in this country or any Western country, is the image of the sick immigrant—the supposed strain on the healthcare system, the burden of emergency rooms and taxpayers."[72] This loudness about the parasitic threat of immigrants is a part of the discourse of the "brown peril" and the supposed "hordes" of immigrants leeching off social—whether public or private—institutions. While Malthus's theories now are widely dismissed, his work has a strange afterlife in popular and political discourses about immigration, especially those that point to overpopulation and resource depletion. The Malthusian assumptions within the discourses of the "brown peril" often lead to hyperbolized, speculative catastrophe that violently targets historically disenfranchised and disempowered populations. The fear of alleged "Mexican hordes" is central to "brown peril" alarmism. In these imaginaries and discourses, Latinx migrants are problematically all Mexican, all brown, and all coming across the US-Mexico border en masse. As "hordes," they are reduced to little more than bodies of racialized disease, plague, and threat, invading the United States and violating national borders. The image of millions of bodies coming to take away "our" jobs, oil, property, and money is one of the leading appeals in anti-immigrant practice and discourse. This racialized xenophobia, when paired with overpopulation discourse, immediately alludes to various colonial forms of population control and even eugenics. We see this most prominently when governmental institutions create specific policies and actions (such as Proposition 187 in California) that target disenfranchised and subaltern populations but that also conflate these populations' qualities (such as phenotypes or class status) with quantity ("hordes").[73] This discourse also places fear on citizen/foreigner binaries (us/them), which allows this alarmism to be legitimized through nationalism rather than racism and bigotry. These overpopulation claims, thus, reduce the conversation to easily digestible ideologies and clear-cut nationalisms.

If theories of biopolitics are preoccupied with and submerged in the problem of population, as Foucault claims, then the problem of ever-growing populations (which is central to these Malthusian discourses) redefines the biopolitical project, from regulating populations in the name of life to regulating the growth of life. It is precisely this question of growth—however unsustainable—that shapes the discourses of anti-immigration sentiment. Unlike market discourses of growth, where the goal to increase profits every fiscal quarter or every year, "population growth" often takes on a negative connotation, especially when paired with "immigration." David Harvey argues that global crises provoke many to blame the underlying reason for these problems on the "runaway rates of population growth."[74] But these charges often obscure the central role of the economy, which must put power and capital in the hands of a select few. Harvey states, "Whenever a theory of overpopulation seizes hold in a society dominated by an elite, then the non-elite invariably experience some form of political, economic, and social repression."[75] Harvey's observation of the non-elite's repression renders these fears within a terrifying state of Malthusian reasoning. For instance, Malthus understood poor laws to create a "dependent poverty" that would only motivate poor peoples' population growth, leading to more misery and more poverty. He saw this domino effect as a natural law of the "labouring poor."[76] This alarmism produces a repression of the material and legally mandated conditions of migrant labor, and *The Undocumented Americans* ensures that we see exactly what is made covert. While the "bogeymen of the right" is leeching off taxpayer healthcare, Cornejo Villavicencio reminds us what the economy is doing to undocumented workers: "Let's talk shop. People think cleaning houses is easy, but it's a dangerous job. None of them [who attend Mujeres en Solidaridad meetings] have been personally assaulted, but they all know women who have been groped or raped on the job, who have had wages stolen, who have been psychologically abused [. . .] deported [. . .] have facial paralysis, [. . .] suffer from migraines, from rashes."[77] These medical ramifications of the cheap labor that is desired by so many in the United States never seem to come up in the conversation when "brown peril" catastrophe is the topic. Neo-Malthusianism produces a fear of racialized "hordes" coming en masse and violating national borders, but in this alarmism, it also produces the false sense that those migrating are disposable labor and mere numbers, masses without a story or experience. By calling this "shop" talk, Cornejo Villavicencio reminds us that this is all part of the game, and while the game is regularly disrupted with medical malady (Urrea's La Muerte, perhaps), these jobs continue to be in demand. Mujeres en Solidaridad can offer only a few resources and mostly community in the maid-and-cleaning economy of Miami.

What is being repressed in the loudness and visibility of "brown peril" discourse is the economic imperative that creates a systemic underclass of workers and migrants. Harvey points out that Malthus's solution to poverty and misery was to do nothing at all, to create policies of "benign neglect,"[78] most succinctly captured when Malthus dramatically laments, "To prevent the recurrence of misery, is, alas! beyond the power of man."[79] Harvey notes that these early views of poverty and overpopulation have stunted our ability to recognize population growth as produced by the "penetration of the market and wage-labor relationships into traditional rural societies."[80] As Saskia Sassen and Néstor García Canclini also critique, this market penetration encouraged by US imperialism has dismantled rural subsistence farming and agriculture in Latin America and the Caribbean in favor of industrialization.[81] This leads to migrations to city centers with factories, but as those maquiladoras are closed for new, more exploitable labor pools, then new waves of diaspora and migration occur. Anti-immigrant discourses, however, rarely point to these market penetrations when identifying the cause of immigration because it is much easier to blame "brown" bodies and to see these bodies as functions of a "naturally" over-reproductive Third World, a point Luiselli equally drives home.

When Malthusian discourses frame the popular and political imagination about immigration while market practices operate in the background, the question becomes, what do narratives and representations of immigration by migrant populations or those who descend from them reveal about this phenomenon? The hypervisible is "brown peril" discourse about immigration that only sees brown bodies, hordes, criminality, and plague-like invasions (often regardless of documented status or the lack of it), but there is an economy operating here that is often put into the shadows. Cornejo Villavicencio tackles this shadow economy deliberately and unabashedly. Money, in particular, becomes a recurring signpost throughout *The Undocumented Americans*. At one point, while Cornejo Villavicencio is speaking with Julián, a day laborer in Staten Island who crossed the desert four times to see his children, she asks him what he would miss if he left America, and he responds, "I'd miss the money." She agrees, and they laugh.[82] In another instance, she meets with a mambo to see if Vodou will help her recurring fears of ICE and deportation, and this being often a scam practiced by notarios, the mambo, who is possessed by the spirit Emmanuel, asks for more money during the ceremony. Cornejo Villavicencio offers her writerly currency: a recitation of an Emily Dickinson poem. She tells the spirit, "They're love poems but they're not about a boy, they're about Death." The spirit is disgusted by this offer; he just wants money.[83] And in yet another instance, at the end of the narrative, Cornejo Villavicencio speaks more explicitly about the role of money in the lives and deaths of undocumented communities, which she relates through her own experiences with poverty and her need to give money to all those she meets. Using the metaphor of buying umbrella after umbrella to walk in a hurricane, she acknowledges that money buys only a series of "cheap fixes" that provide only temporary relief when one is poor. While she currently has discretionary income, she knows it will not last. She explains, "The guilt I feel for having made it out—for now, until my own umbrella breaks—is like having been poisoned. I feel constantly disgusting, dirty, hungover, toxic unless I'm hemorrhaging money in this very specific way that I find *cleansing.*" She remembers what it was "like having my dad back from the dead" when the Latina and Puerto Rican executive assistants left him a big tip for delivering them food.[84] Money is the reason for coming to work in the United States; it is the incentive for certain forms of healing culture; and it is a constantly misplaced solution to the troubles of undocumentedness. Death often accompanies these narrative recurrences to money, where the narrator-author likens her income status to "having been poisoned" and her attempt to solve problems with money as a form of "hemorrhaging." Her father is even resurrected from the dead with large tips. Money becomes a life giver and a life taker in these moments, and it remains an element that starts and stops stories.

While Cornejo Villavicencio begins *The Undocumented Americans* with the claim that she did not "set out to write anything inspirational," she still ends on a note of possibility.[85] After bringing together the stories of Argentines, Cubans, Mexicans, Ecuadorans, and many others who are undocumented in the United States, she takes her dying father to Lighthouse Point Beach. She notes that she likes this beach because "there are always black and brown families fishing and building sandcastles there, proudly being alive, and there is something about the ocean air perfuming dark bodies refusing to die that makes me want to live another day too."[86] These dark bodies that refuse to die reject the reductiveness of "brown peril" discourse, challenge the violence of national security, and find community in these small acts of resistance. Schmidt Camacho argues that migrants live with a constant sense of their "minimal subjectivity": "*Minimal* because the undocumented have been subjected to a criminalizing discourse that renders their status abject in relation to that of the citizen; *minimal* because their *un*recognized status renders the undocumented vulnerable to an almost total abridgement of their social relatedness as materialized in actual kinship ties and communal belonging."[87] While "minimal subjectivity" describes the slippery rule of law that imposes a violent process of devaluing one's belonging, this state of unrecognizability is precisely what allows for the building of community and produces "actual kinship ties." Enjoying the beach amid one's social, slow, and literal death is perhaps an ambivalent positionality but one that counters the speculative catastrophe embedded in the United States' neo-Malthusianism and xenophobia.

The Trouble of Visibility: Photographic Documenting of the Dead

National security strategically diminishes and obscures the economic machinations of migration, but Urrea's, Luiselli's, and Cornejo Villavicencio's narratives all demonstrate the consequences of this biopolitical paradigm: various forms and figures of death. In *The Undocumented Americans*, undocumentedness means living without basic labor rights, without social safety nets, and with few resources. In *Tell Me How It Ends*, children are obsessively conjuring their dead friends' corpses as they sit in US detention centers awaiting a legal process that strips them of personhood and rights. And in *The Devil's Highway*, fourteen of the Wellton 26 are found in various states of decomposition resulting from state-sanctioned border games. These are physically, socially, and politically dead bodies, the remnants of pawn pieces that maintain a theatrical show of security. At the end of *The Devil's Highway*, the narrator describes an interaction between a possible relative of one of the Wellton 26 and an INS secretary. The relative is quite bluntly told, "He's dead. I've got him on the slab." The secretary leaves the room after this abrupt announcement, then comes back to find the woman crying: "'Oh!' she says. 'We've upset you.' She sits and says, 'Señora, you must forgive us. We deal with death so often here that we forget. We forget, you see. We're indelicate. If you don't work here, death still means something to you.'"[88] Desensitization is an inevitable consequence of the security state. This moment is framed by descriptions of the files, all "exact replicas," all about immigrants listed in death as "WHITE MALES," without any particularity or personalization, all stacked onto shelves. Not even race and sex mean anything; they are simply markers that pose as documentation for the Border Patrol within the narrative. Marking the dead bodies as "white males" does not de-racialize or give social power to these migrants in any way but instead appears to be an easy, routine practice to file away bodies into the bureaucratic abyss. Death is figured as simply part of the job. It holds little humanity when it is simply another nine to five on the border.

Urrea's *The Devil's Highway*, Luiselli's *Tell Me How It Ends*, and Cornejo Villavicencio's *The Undocumented Americans* ascribe personhood to the dead by presenting the slippages around documentation. Urrea reveals the bureaucratic processes and performances that distract from the realities of crossing.

Luiselli shows us how this state violence is legalized.[89] Cornejo Villavicencio demonstrates how these violences are actively operating in the everyday experiences of those living and dying in the United States without documentation. Significantly, they all consider the function of documentary photography—as a form of state biometrics, legal evidence, and proof of a life. Through photography's narrative possibilities and paradoxes, the still image becomes what rehumanizes the dehumanized and potentially resurrects the politically dead.

When the *New York Times* first reported on the Yuma 14 tragedy on May 25, 2001, the headline that hit the newsstands was "Devastating Picture of Immigrants Dead in Arizona Desert."[90] The picture defines the event. Most notably, when Urrea goes into a deep and grotesque description of the documents, specifically the photographs of the dead, a slippage between documented and undocumented unfolds. The narrator describes looking through public records issued by both the INS and sheriff's reports. His gaze relates the various levels of decay. Many body parts are unrecognizable, while other parts remain intact but bloated. The narrator cannot tell even the sex of the victims, although the difference would be moot since they will all be filed as "white males." The photographs all show the same thing: all the dead are stretched out naked with their skin cracking open from being baked for days by the Arizona sun. After intense descriptions of bodies, Urrea tells us, "For many of them, these are the first portraits for which they posed."[91] We are suddenly reminded that these are people, not simply dead objects in photographs. After a barrage of grotesque descriptions, this reflection works in two ways. On one hand, it reanimates the immigrants back to life by suggesting that they posed for these photographs and, in many ways, reconstitutes them as people through the act of getting a portrait.[92] Simultaneously, this moment alludes to the lack of portraiture required for passports, visas, and other legal documentation required for crossing national borders, especially since the narrator makes a point of distinguishing these photos as their *first* portraits. This moment creates conflicting paradigms within the story: on one side, the immigrant is a human being, and on the other side, the immigrant is a nonhuman antagonist to state institutional politics. In this narrative, the Wellton 26 become people only through a literary and photographic reanimation of their lives.

Urrea's treatment of photography here is in conversation with Jason De León's *The Land of Open Graves* (2015) and Tanya Sheehan's edited collection *Photography and Migration* (2018), where the photographic documenting of dead migrant bodies works as a function of state biometrics, which is to say state technologies that are aimed at mobility control. Mark Maguire describes state photography as a form of biometric security that "oscillates between knowledge of and power over populations and the securitization of individual identity,"[93] a point that Javier Duran productively complicates by arguing that the biometric system is not only about identifying and preventing "CTAs (illegal migrants, criminals, and terrorists) from entering national territories" but equally about "ensuring the efficient flow of people, goods, and services across international borders."[94] Biometric securitization, then, comes from a dual impulse to control (racialized, "foreign") bodies and to open the flow of capital. The forensic photograph of dead migrants grows out of these impulses but occupies a peripheral relationship to them as well.[95]

Like Urrea's photographs, images of the dead are documents that sit in files on an overworked agent's desk, but they also give the dead visibility and story. The photograph, thus, goes beyond simply recording identities, authorizing entrances, and controlling border checkpoints; it documents the bigger picture of what these securities do. *The Devil's Highway* summons the dead by humanizing the forensic evidence, but this goes further than simply showcasing an image; it becomes a narrative act. For instance, Urrea brings a "true story" to the Wellton 26 when he devotes an entire chapter to "Their Names" (even while having to imagine some of them). Urrea's "Their Names" introduces twenty-two of those crossing Desolation, even though we have met them on their journey in previous chapters. Fifty-six-year-old Reymundo Barreda Maruri has been laid off by Coca-Cola and must come to the United States for work. He has come to the United States before to work in a cannery in Ohio, and he and his nephew both know their coyote, Mendez, is making this journey worse and getting them into trouble.[96] Mario Castillo is one of the many who is laid off during Mexico's economic crisis, when the bottling, coffee, and citrus industries are all tanking. He imagines that picking oranges in Florida will be a reasonable plan after his previous work.[97] All that Urrea shares about Javier Santillan is that he is falling behind because the "heat was melting his brain." Javier is so far gone with heat stroke that he seems to be hallucinating.[98] Javier has no age or backstory. These vignettes demonstrate the unequal distribution of information in government databases, in fellow migrants' accounts (if they were brave enough to come forward to help with identification), and in investigative journalism. One's story seems to continuously expand, while another's lives only in the immediate moment of crossing and dying in Desolation. The names and faces of the dead give them a posthumous voice, a posthumous humanity.[99]

These vignettes operate much like how José Esteban Muñoz describes portrait photography: they are snapshots that reanimate the dead in varying degrees. Muñoz offers one way to read how photography, specifically portrait photography, "summons back" the dead. In his reading of the photographic work of James Van DerZee (as reproduced in the film *Looking for Langston* and as collected in the macabre *The Harlem Book of the Dead*), Muñoz argues that the role of photography "first gives face, then gives voice."[100] For Muñoz, the photographer produces visuals of the dead as an act of prosopopoeia, and this act gives voice to the needs and sufferings of historically repressed and colonized communities, especially those who are racialized and/or queer.[101] Nevertheless, this moves the other way as well: from visuals that give voice to the dead to voice that allows for new forms of visualization. Muñoz sees the photography of the dead as opening up possibilities for new imaginaries through communal mourning, where spectators may "visualize the past and thus enable an 'imaginary' coherence that make the visualizing of a present and a future possible," a process that works against the violence that wants us to have only disembodied fragments and parts.[102] While Muñoz is showing how photographs can become tools to confront colonial and imperial history and disidentify with oppressive social constructions, the idea that photographs of the dead may produce a full, more comprehensive vision matters to reading Urrea's photographs and snapshots of the Wellton 26 because the "true" story must be crafted from multiple perspectives and sentimentalities, must be documented and mourned, and must recognize the series of misrecognitions. If the photographs of the dead that populate the forensic databases of USCIS produce a certain type of mourning for groups under siege, then we must accept that these photographs are not simply governmental documents that gather forensic evidence for records, for data, and for international agreements. They quite literally summon the dead back, in parts, to tell the story of state and extra-state violence.

I have argued that these narratives more accurately reveal the necropolitical structures at play, but there is also a necessary spectacle of the dead occurring within this photographed violence, a spectacle that complicates the politics of visibility around immigration and security theater. Jasbir K. Puar considers how the photographs of the Abu Ghraib tortures, released through various reports from 2003 to 2006, partake in a larger narrative about the how the "united front of American multicultural heteronormativity" is performed and felt.[103] She describes how "the pictures look indeed as if the U.S. Guard felt like they were on a stage, hamming it up for the proud parents nervously biting their nails in the audience. . . . they repulsively invite the viewer to come and jump on stage as well."[104] These images of regulation, for Puar, depict "how both process (the photographing) and product (the pictures) are shaming technologies and function as a vital part of the humiliating, dehumanizing violence itself: the giddy process of documentation, the visual evidence of corporeal shame, the keen ecstatic eye of the voyeur, the haunting of surveillance, the dissemination of the images."[105] While Puar is interested in visibility and affect here, she also unpacks the economic logic at play in and around these photographs. This is perhaps why she ends her analysis with the problem of consumption:

> It is devasting, but not surprising, that the U.S. public's obsessive consumption of this story nevertheless did not result in any deep-seated or longer-term demand to know who the victims are, what they experienced and felt, and how their lives are today. The problems with the testimonial genre notwithstanding, fourteen victims' testimonies that were interpreted and transcribed in January 2004 are available in full in their original text versions on the *Washington Post* website in downloadable PDF files.[106]

Puar identifies two key features here: (1) the photographs produced little more than fleeting emotions and strong opinion that deflect from the material reality of the subjects in these images, and (2) the inherent violence in our current political and global order operates under a market logic at all times. To call this necropolitics instead of biopolitics, then, is to understand the production and consumption of these images as the "power grids implicating corporeal conquest, colonial domination, and death."[107] Photographs, then, crystallize the push-and-pull where they may offer possibilities for new imaginaries, as in Muñoz and Urrea, but can also reestablish the political economy's exploitative, colonial practices. The series of violences housed in photographs that Puar describes here also infiltrates discourse, where images often feed problematic ideologies about immigration, migrants, and racialized subjects.

Luiselli's description of how the media represent undocumented children as biblical plagues and locusts comes after she has been looking at a photograph of men and women in Vassar, Michigan, waving flags, banners, and rifles in the air while they protest a center housing "illegal juveniles" and another photograph of an elderly couple holding anti-immigrant signs while sitting in beach chairs in Oracle, Arizona.[108] These images of anti-immigrant and nationalist sentiment and spectacle centralize death. Duran sees biometric security functioning as a spectacle as well because it "gives the impression that the state is indeed in control."[109] Such "territorial anxieties" primarily "feed these public spectacles," but Duran also understands these spectacles as a tactical response for engaging in the dynamics of global capitalism. Specifically, the "creation of government technologies that have administered the immigrant problem for internal consumption" emerge to exclude "individuals incapable of integrating into a system which requires more and more financial and social self-responsibility in the face of real life insecurities."[110] People who cannot participate successfully in the economy are rendered fair game for consumer spectacle. When Luiselli tells us that the photographs of public spectacles inspired *Tell Me How It Ends*, her narrative practice then works to fill in the bigger picture of state and extra-state violence: both figurative forms of state death (deportation and/or legal states of exception) and real deaths (Manu's and Miguel's friends, for instance).

Of course, the spectacles in photographs are quite different from the security theater on the US-Mexico border. The media rarely broadcast La Migra cutting the drag, the coyotes abandoning people in the middle of Desolation, the varying states of decomposition of the crossers' corpses, or vigilante groups knocking over water stations. On the border, the viewer of these images is never fully present, and often the institutions securing borders actively disallow viewership by banning photography of agents. I mean to suggest not that security on the border is a private performance but rather that these performances are supposed to be a part of the banality of everyday life. This relationship between necropolitics and performance on the border, in other words, is not sensational or exceptional but normalized. This dehumanization of the immigrant, then, becomes simply a part of the job, another day on the llano, and just drinking beer on lawn chairs with military-grade guns pointed at the border.

The photograph becomes the impetus to challenge this structure of dehumanization in Cornejo Villavicencio's *The Undocumented Americans*. Photography in *The Undocumented Americans* operates more subtly and less explicitly in comparison with *The Devil's Highway* and *Tell Me How It Ends*. It does not become synonymous with the biometric state, and it does not become an object that can decide one's fate under the rule of law. Instead, the photograph flits into the narrative here and there illuminating character types, history, and/or proof of existence. In one instance, the act of taking photographs describes the narrator-author's mom's "taste outside her means."[111] In another instance, when interviewing Leonel Chávez, a forty-five-year-old Ecuadoran man who was in sanctuary in a church in Connecticut, Cornejo Villavicencio recalls Leonel's interest in Kevin Carter's Pulitzer Prize–winning photograph of a vulture approaching an emaciated child in Sudan in 1994, during the famine. Carter committed suicide not long after taking the photograph, and Leonel states, "That photo cost him his life." Cornejo Villavicencio notes that Leonel does not understand how someone can see such suffering and not do anything to change it, even though Leonel experiences that same lack of aid and comfort each night when churchgoers easily turn their backs on him as they leave mass.[112] These moments in the narrative are radically different, with one a sign of being too bougie and the other marking how documentary photography places us in compromising and inhumane positions. Nevertheless, the photograph captures a sense of humanness and humanity, a direct challenge to the dehumanization that photography performs for state and legal institutions.

The Undocumented Americans, however, also presents the photograph as a significant form of proof, one for undocumented peoples to document their existence and worth. At the end of the narrative, when Cornejo Villavicencio's father is dying of cancer, he begins to text her photographs of the waiting room while waiting for work at a job agency. They are snapshots of other people waiting for work, and the narrator-author describes their clothes and facial expressions. Her father calls these photographs "*[f]urther proof that we're not a burden.*" The connection between a photograph and proof of usefulness implies that documentation is required in varying degrees. Even when one is undocumented and aging out of the labor industry, proof becomes one of the few ways of making visible what is always invisible. When she asks him who says he's a burden, he responds, "*It's hard to see men like that not get jobs. We're invisible . . .*"[113] Her father does not need anyone to tell him he is a burden because the politics of visibility and the economy of invisibility are already a part of his everyday experience of being undocumented. These are not sensational spectacles of immigration but normal commonplaces that her father struggles with seeing, living through, and dying from; the photograph documents this unbearable norm.

These figures of dead immigrants are a narrative response to the troubling realities on US borders, in US courts, and in labor agency waiting rooms. They allow the dead to rise, at times, but ultimately they demonstrate the violence inherent within biopolitical formations that uphold some populations (and their capital livelihood) over other populations. These figures of dead and dying immigrants reveal the problem of documentation housed in stories of immigration. Even while Urrea pointedly subtitles his book "A True Story," there are limitations to this truth when Border Patrol records and documents are incomplete and many of the names of the Wellton 26 are unlisted and unknown. Even while Luiselli's essays describe her experience translating for the US immigration courts, she must still figure out how to untranslate the legal system's inhumanity. Even while Cornejo Villavicencio is producing creative nonfiction, she must imagine and fictionalize to fill in what is invisible and to protect those who must remain invisible from deportation. These narratives impart the trouble of undocumentablity. Cacho remarks, "For all legally uncertain populations, the law punishes but does not protect, disciplines but does not defend." Cacho describes these populations as "dead-to-others" and made criminal.[114] Documenting the dead, then, lays bare the material violence that migrants undergo because of the economic demands that incite the crossing and the national securities and political imaginaries that deem them less than people, without legal personhood. Documenting the dead ultimately reveals what it means to be living dead.

Bleeding Money: A Conclusion

Immigration fears and brown peril in the popular and political imagination have produced various forms of security theater and violent spectacle. *The Devil's Highway*, *Tell Me How It Ends*, and *The Undocumented Americans* show how these imaginaries and policies obscure a fundamental truth about the global economy: the life of capital is more important than the life of racialized and foreign people. To call these necropolitics is to understand that political and social practices and discourses under global capitalism are inherently violent against those who are rendered the living dead or dead-in-life. Urrea at one point imagines the Wellton 26 preparing to walk across Desolation, with the coyotes changing their prices and each step of the journey looking more and more like a scam. He relates, "Fifty pesos here. Fifty pesos there. They were just bleeding money."[115] This moment directly contrasts with Urrea's descriptions of how the dead migrants are found in the desert, so decomposed by the sun that they do not have "enough fluid in them to bleed."[116] These graphic images paint migrant blood—their livelihood, their ethno-racialization, their *bios* and *erōs*—as merely a drainable resource, bled for money. Similarly, in *The Undocumented Americans,* Cornejo Villavicencio finds herself hemorrhaging money to quiet her guilt at having relatively "made it" in spite of undocumentedness.[117] I want to distinguish here between the many literary readings of "blood money" and the Latinx figure that "bleeds money." Criticism on "blood money" describes race, nation, and family as structured by and/or mirroring economic processes, such as business, transaction, or exchange.[118] In distinction, "bleeding money" describes how one's life must be extinguished for capital. The migrant who must die does so for the life of capital. When human life is replaced with capital life, we get a dead immigrant in a photograph on some overworked and underpaid ICE agent's desk.

Bleeding in *Tell Me How It Ends* becomes a descriptor for narrative-making itself. Luiselli relates, after interviewing dozens of detained children, that she is unable to keep the children's stories separate after a while: "The stories they tell me bleed into each other, get confused with one another, shuffle and mix. Maybe it's because, though each story is different, they all come together easily, pieces of a larger puzzle. Each child comes from a different place, a separate life, a distinct set of experiences, but their stories usually follow the same predictable, fucked-up plot."[119] Bleeding narratives, like bleeding money, perhaps tells us "how it ends." Narrative is not lifeblood here but a structure of death and violence that overwhelms our imaginations and becomes normalized in migrant experience. Cornejo Villavicencio also finds bleeding to become caught up in the act of telling these stories. At one point, she talks about her ulcer, an open wound that she can feel "spasm and bleed" and that just "keeps bleeding" as she reads and writes these stories. She exclaims that undocumentedness has led to a public health crisis where "[w]e're all fucking *sick*."[120] This moment in *The Undocumented Americans* captures how these stories and experiences directly affect bodies, through stress, through trauma, and through a lack of resources. Bleeding money, bleeding narratives, and bleeding bodies all occur in tandem.[121]

Although these Latinx and migrant experiences potentially resurrect the dead, the narratives make visible the often invisible processes that kill or confine people without states and people without personhood. In many ways, this pointed critique of the security state within these narratives echoes Hayek's warnings that all government action is coercive and is thus, irrevocably, against so-called liberty.[122] Hayek imagines an individual and economic liberty that will unburden an individual from political and civil players who render "him a bare tool in the achievement of the ends of another."[123] Yet, securitized nation-states and liberalized economies are not in opposition as Hayek forwards. Narrative conflations of bleeding and money uncover their beneficial relationship, which occurs at the expense of Latinx, racialized, mobile bodies. *The Devil's Highway*, *Tell Me How It Ends*, and *The Undocumented Americans* reveal that the popular and political discourses of immigration—brown peril, xenophobia, hypernationalism—operate as a distraction from the material conditions of migration and actively elide the disposable populations that the economy produces. These stories present the strategic misrecognitions that let certain populations live and make others die. Bleeding money, bleeding narrative, and bleeding bodies become central descriptors for this necropolitics.

Hayek's economic theories about market liberty may seem far afield, but my reading of select Latinx migrant literature in this chapter questions what the freedom of the economy means amid national security politics. I return to Hayek because he calls for celebrating individual liberty over social responsibility, which has deeply influenced current free-market ideology.[124] This celebration of the individual over a more altruistic social worldview is precisely the ideology that allows us to enjoy cheap products and cheap labor while ignoring the dead bodies in the desert. This division between individual self-interest and social justice also allows for a security state to sow insecurity and deny personhood to so-called surplus bodies. Those who benefit from this market logic do so by way of racialized, sexualized, and erasable others who can never benefit from it. The documenting and narrating of the living dead, nevertheless, upend the workings of this political economy by exposing the strategic misrecognition of the social world necessitated by global capitalism.

CHAPTER 2

Documenting the US-Mexico Border: Photography, Movement, and Paradox

One of the most famous photographs by Don Bartletti, *Interstate Pedestrians*, captures about twenty Latinx women and men racing across a southern California highway in front of oncoming traffic (fig. 2.1; plate 1). They run headlong as a group. Headlights and billboard signs punctuate the image, framed by chaparral-covered hills; this telephoto view emphasizes the foregrounded people. Bartletti uses a low-contrast black-and-white grade, making the grays dominate. This photograph, published in the *Los Angeles Times* on September 2, 1990, motivated the California Department of Transportation to create the iconic yellow warning signs that once peppered the freeways: large horizontal rectangles depicting a man, woman, and child running, using the same form as crossing/warning signs for deer or other animals. Bartletti recalls, "Hundreds were killed and maimed. The yellow signs . . . helped reduce the carnage."[1] *Interstate Pedestrians* meant to document the actual immigration process: groups climbing over walls and rivers, trekking through deserts, and running for their lives over freeways. Yet, once it inspired the yellow warning signs, the photograph took on new meaning, warning us of impending "hordes" and painting immigrants as "wildlife." As explored in the previous chapter, these images reflect what Justin Akers Chacón and Mike Davis describe as the ongoing representations and discourses about the "brown peril": the constant appearance and threat of "Mexican hordes" crossing into the United States. This image paints the foreign subject as invading and infesting the nation. An element of plague and disease accompanies these images and discourses, often creating a dystopian sense of the border.[2] Leo Chavez argues that the media especially depict immigrants as hordes or invaders so that immigration can be "interpreted as a hostile act, even an act of war."[3] Playing out behind this xenophobia are also fears about resource depletion, from jobs to water to money. However, as Peter Andreas succinctly quips, "The popular

Figure 2.1. *Interstate Pedestrians,* by Don Bartletti. Published August 21, 1990. © 1990 *Los Angeles Times;* used with permission.

notion that the US-Mexico border is out of control falsely assumes that there was once a time when it was truly under control."[4]

From sensational news headlines to magazine covers to traffic signs, the image of the US-Mexico border produces anxieties about so-called unauthorized immigration and national security. These anxieties demonstrate photography's role in constructing national imaginations and documenting national politics, what Chavez describes as the "interplay of denoted and connoted messages" in a reproductive or imitative art like photography.[5] Nevertheless, I wish to turn from chapter 1's questions about documenting national imaginaries to the question of documenting the paradoxes of these national imaginaries in the era of globalization. I am especially interested in how this occurs within documentary photography, a medium that professes to represent the realities of Latinx and migrant experiences as truthfully as possible. Where Latinx literature exposes the politics of misrecognition at the heart of necropolitical violence, photography troubles these questions of recognition and visibility. In this chapter I consider how photography, both professional and nonprofessional, produces a paradoxical narrative about the so-called immigration problem and rising national security on the US-Mexico border. By specifically looking at the works of Don Bartletti, David Taylor, and the

Border Film Project, I bring together the different faces of documentary photography: photojournalism, formal art, and snapshot. First, the chapter examines Don Bartletti's photojournalism and David Taylor's photography. These two artists both have their own distinct approaches to photography, but they both wish to truthfully record immigration and border security. Traditional bastions of truth—newspapers, educational institutions, museums—publish, exhibit, and house these photographs, but this seeking of truth is imperfect. At times, the photographs produce narratives of fear and anxiety around immigration, from capturing and publishing images of migrants running across highways en masse (as seen in *Interstate Pedestrians*) to focusing on the US Border Patrol's games (as in some of Taylor's work). Moreover, the images often cannot capture the totality of these border phenomena, especially the unbridled economic and political violences at play, whether these be the pulsing effects of free-trade agreements, the exploitation of maquiladoras, or the dead bodies in the desert. The visual discourses within Bartletti's and Taylor's photography presents largely national(ist) narratives of immigration—the border patrol's surveillance tactics, the construction of the wall, and people crossing nation-state boundaries—instead of obviously global economic or necropolitical ones. As a result, this documentary photography participates in selective ideological constructions of Latinx and migrant bodies.

In the second part of this chapter, I consider the Border Film Project, which gave point-and-shoot single-use cameras to members of the US vigilante militia on the border known as the Minutemen Project and to migrants crossing the border to visually archive their two perspectives. The photographs included here capture both the migrants' and the vigilantes' distinctly authorial points of view; these are shots of what they see and face in the US-Mexico borderlands. The Border Film Project's photographs blur the line between photographer and photographic subject, allowing the images to upset and transcend the narratives of Latinx migrants as purely objects of documentation. Consequently, the images make visible to viewers what cannot be seen in most border photographs: the lived experience of the border. According to Rebecca M. Schreiber, the migrant images counter the sensational and spectacular portrayal of immigration by mainstream media and the "spectacle of surveillance" within the Minutemen's shots.[6] Nevertheless, I see these photographs by both migrants and militia to be building a bigger picture about the border, rather than reenacting the dissonance between these two groups. Together, they show the uneven narratives, enigmatic aesthetics, and porous, fluid geopolitics of the US-Mexico borderlands. Alongside the photojournalism and art photographs of Bartletti and Taylor, the Border Film Project's snapshots make the conflicting discourses and practices of immigration even more visible and legible. The project at times challenges and disrupts what Bartletti and Taylor cannot capture from their distant position—as photographers rather than photographic subjects who carry the weight and consequences of crossing or fortifying borders—but the snapshots also bolster those professional projects by highlighting the border as a space of constant movement and discursivity. The Border Film Project reveals the border's porous nature and thus breaches and upsets nationalist discourses of legal/illegal, citizen/foreigner, and us/them. The amateur photographer–subjects present us with the not-always-visible state of the border in the age of globalization: it is always porous, no matter how many walls, border patrols, or militias attempt to close it.[7] Simultaneously, these photographs also keep invisible what is not explicitly photographed and disseminated: the violence inherent in securing borders and in the economic eradication of borders, whether it results in dead migrants or produces more insidious forms of living dead.

The theoretical stakes for examining the tension between fortification and permeability are two-pronged. On one level, border photographers wish to authenticate the truth of the border, which the photograph arguably does by freezing a moment of the real.[8] On another level, a photograph complicates the line between visibility and invisibility, between what can and cannot be represented within the photograph, and between what is and is not recognizable/legible.[9] Although I am more concerned with the photograph's role in producing and engaging ideology than with the photograph's ontology, Roland Barthes's observation remains in the background for this chapter: "Whatever it grants to vision and whatever its manner, a photograph is always invisible: it is not it that we see."[10] I am using the concepts of visibility and invisibility to explore what these photographers and artists document on the border and how they do so. Engaging Susan Sontag's *On Photography*, I end by interrogating the medium of photography itself. I propose that the conflict between securing and breaching the border plays out within the medium itself. The photographic form reproduces a state of movement and migration while simultaneously halting it. In this sense, border photography is always a photography in (frozen) movement.[11] This question of movement and migration is central to understanding these paradoxes. Throughout the chapter, I also draw on Claire F. Fox's work on border art, which investigates how photographers, writers, videographers, and mass-media artists represent the border through conventional images of the fence and the river, concluding that border art reveals a "conflation of national and corporate territories" and the mutability of the border.[12] I extend Fox's idea of the US-Mexico borderland's ever-changing and dispersed spatial structure by bringing it to a more pointed paradigm about recording truth and making narrative that is specific to documentary photography. While the terms "visible" and "invisible" describe what a photograph documents or elides, they also delineate the ideological legibility and misrecognitions of the US-Mexico border. In this sense, these projects build a larger geopolitical narrative about migration and national security. I argue that the tension between visibility and invisibility in these border photographs embodies the paradox between the border as a space of national fortification and the border as a porous zone, full of movement, between the United States and Mexico.

Images of Immigration and Security

A *Los Angeles Times* photojournalist from 1983 to 2015, Don Bartletti is a prominent documentarian of immigration on the US-Mexico border, winning the 2003 Pulitzer Prize for Feature Photography. His early 1990s oeuvre in the *Los Angeles Times* (later collected and exhibited by the Oakland Museum and published in 1992 in *Between Two Worlds*) includes a series of black-and-white photographs showing various forms of border crossing.[13] These images made him "a voice for immigrants," especially for southern California's newspaper-reading population, and he captured unprecedented shots. *Too Hungry to Knock*, a photograph of migrants crossing the Tijuana wall in 1992, provides a glimpse at these often unseen, unseeable movements, as men jump to climb the wall at the right moment undetected (fig. 2.2; plate 2). Bartletti recalls how he was almost unable to take this shot when the men stole his camera:

> I set a tripod on the U.S. side of the 10-ft-high border fence with Tijuana. Through slits in the steel planks I bantered with men who admitted they would jump over when the moment was right. I stepped away for a few minutes when a passing Border Patrol stopped nearby. When I returned to the tripod 10 minutes later, the camera was gone. "Chingaderas," I yelled through the cracks. "I can't believe you guys would do this! You've taken my heart, my soul, my livelihood!" "We didn't see who did it," they said. "Okay," I argued, "Keep the camera, just give me the film." "We don't know who did it." God, I was frustrated. I offered one guy $10 bucks [*sic*] to help me. He countered with $40. "Olvida te!" I said. Forget it! Then I countered with $15. We settled on $20. In a few minutes, an arm appeared through the iron barrier with my Nikon FM2. As I grasped the camera I considered keeping the $20 bill. In spite of my humiliation, I passed the money through, preferring to end the standoff on a positive note. I

ditched the tripod but hung around. At 1am the time was right and I made the image titled, *Too Hungry To Knock* with the same camera.[14]

The camera is crucial here: it becomes synonymous with the photographer's life, with power for the powerless who use it for economic advantage, and with seeing the unauthorized operations that should be unseeable if the migrants want to avoid persecution and deportation.

The often high-contrast black-and-white style of many of Bartletti's early photographs plays an important role in framing the way immigration looks. It is startling. It is binary. It appears as a black-and-white issue. Only us/them exists on the border. Claire Fox argues that US-Mexico border art stages the "extreme polarizations" of our national imaginary,[15] and Bartletti's black-and-white medium, while a frequent feature of newspaper printing, hyperbolizes this effect. This polarity in the photograph, then, mirrors the polarities of immigration discourse. Chavez claims that alarmist and negative images of immigration became the norm for representing the border on magazine covers in the 1980s and 1990s. He attributes this to both a rising discourse on the immigrant threat to the nation and the implementation of public policies,

Figure 2.2. *Too Hungry to Knock,* by Don Bartletti. Published June 18, 1992. © 1992 *Los Angeles Times*; used with permission.

specifically the 1986 Immigration Reform and Control Act.[16] Saskia Sassen theorizes that the black-and-white medium potentially "unsettles meaning," primarily because it lacks the specificity of color and thus "produces knowledge beyond the actual visual contents."[17] She further argues that this sort of "universalism" works only when photographic images "dislodge mobility and globality from the *entrapment of geographical* movement."[18] Although Bartletti's *Between Two Worlds* presents moments of kinship that are not obviously about the geographic border, such as the endearing moment caught between a father and son in *Filial Devotion*, his early work in the *Los Angeles Times* often documents the geopolitical problems of immigration (fig. 2.3; plate 3). I should note, then, that *Filial Devotion* is not only different from much of his other early work but is also one of the few photographs in *Between Two Worlds* that was not previously published and is not under copyright with the *Los Angeles Times*. While Bartletti has never posited a political agenda in his photography, his early work for the *Los Angeles Times* is irrevocably part of a historical moment when there was a media impulse for hypernationalist discourse, often resulting in extreme polarities and xenophobia.[19]

Bartletti's later work, however, captures a less anxiety-producing polarity. Instead, as the news industry has moved into more digital venues, his images

Figure 2.3. *Filial Devotion,* by Don Bartletti (1992). © 1992 by Don Bartletti.

are more often in color and focus on smaller groups or on individuals, creating a more humanist pathos. Bartletti's photo essay *Enrique's Journey* documents Central American migrants coming through Mexico by train (known as La Bestia) and then entering the United States, widening our purview of immigration to more than a US/Mexico dichotomy. His project collaborates with and develops alongside Sonia Nazario's book of the same name that tells the story of Enrique, who makes multiple attempts to cross the Honduras-Guatemala border, the Guatemala-Mexico border, and the Mexico-US border to find his estranged mother in North Carolina.[20] The *Los Angeles Times* special report from September 29 to October 12, 2002, wished to give a face and story to the number of children (often unaccompanied) crossing the border via La Bestia. Many traveled to join already migrated family members or to escape political and economic destabilization at home. This trend increased throughout the early twenty-first century, becoming quite controversial and divisive in the summer of 2014 with the detention of thousands of unaccompanied Central American children. Bartletti's images introduce us to many of these kids as they navigate trains and avoid or join gangs. Regarding one photograph, he describes: "As dawn breaks near Mexico City, Jorge Velasquez Felipe, 15, center, and his brother Juan Carlos, 16, right, huddle near a fire aboard a speeding freight train. Unprepared for the night ride from Veracruz through cold mountain tunnels to Mexico City, they desperately burned trash and scraps of cloth to keep warm" (fig. 2.4; plate 4).[21] His caption evokes viewers' emotions as we witness the young subjects taking a dangerous journey for which they are unprepared. The images and their captions emphasize "the child," a figure who embodies hope and inspires reproductive futurism. Furthermore, these captions individualize migrants, contrasting Bartletti's earlier images of "hordes." In *Simple Pleasure*, Bartletti shows the brothers in more innocent repose as they clasp hands and shout into a tunnel to hear their echoes (fig. 2.5; plate 5). The image begs viewers to identify and empathize, at least momentarily, with these kids as we gaze upon their hard journey.

This liberal humanist aspect of the images and their captions, however, also engages a more complex political picture. By focusing on Central Americans, the content of Bartletti's photo essay disallows audiences' attempts to collapse the experiences represented into a simplistic US/Mexico binary.[22] Simultaneously, the formal aesthetics of the shots magnify the complexity of immigration through their implication of motion: the trains racing through blurred foliage capture the movement of people and goods from Central American countries through Mexico. Ideally, these photographs also expose the wars, social unrest, economic interventionism, and political persecution that give rise to these immigrations through subtext. For informed viewers,

Figure 2.4. *Shivering,* by Don Bartletti. Published October 4, 2002. © 2002 *Los Angeles Times*; used with permission.

Figure 2.5. *Simple Pleasure,* by Don Bartletti. Published October 4, 2002. © 2002 *Los Angeles Times*; used with permission.

these images recall the US-sanctioned Programa Frontera Sur, which Luiselli's *Tell Me How It Ends* names as producing the groundwork for a violent and brutal crossing, as explored in chapter 1. For those thinking about undocumented status, the photographs evoke how these subjects must remain hidden from a legal standpoint once in the United States. Invisibility is necessary and mutually beneficial. Peter Andreas reminds us that historically the "illegal nature of the labor flow benefited both employers and the state. For employers, the illegal status of the labor force assured compliance and low wages: lacking public support and state protection, illegal immigrants were less likely to organize or complain. [. . .] For US officials, the very fact that the workers were in the country without formal invitation helped reduce the appearance of direct government complicity."[23] Thus, the ongoing tension between visibility and invisibility—between what is represented and what is not—becomes part of the photograph.

Bartletti's photographs document moments in immigration that, even though they try to capture the border's realities, often feed xenophobia within the United States. In the 1990s and early 2000s, these images gave rise to calls for fortification and demands for more border security. More troublingly, post-9/11 sentiments made it easy for political leaders to manipulate national fears by equating immigration with terrorism, as Tom Tancredo did during his congressional campaigns and reforms in Colorado, while the image of the border became synonymous with the image of security.[24] While Bartletti's early and later work catalogues more conventional and problematic images of the border and immigration, *Enrique's Journey* at least disrupts well-entrenched discourses about the border as solely a space of national binaries. In a similar vein, David Taylor's photography project *Working the Line* wishes to "move away from a simplistic binary portrayal of the border as something 'illegal' and 'legal' and into a narrative that is more nuanced and complex."[25] While Bartletti's work is produced largely for commercial photojournalism, Taylor's work is less in the service of for-profit institutions. As such, Taylor does not need his work to appeal to the masses in the same way, potentially allowing him to refuse the sensationalism of newsworthy documentation. Yet both photographers wish to *publicly* document the truth about the border.[26]

When visiting Taylor's *Working the Line* exhibit in 2010 at the Museum of Contemporary Photography at Columbia College in Chicago, I was struck by his attempt to reach and photograph all 276 obelisks, installed between 1891 and 1895, that mark the US-Mexico border (fig. 2.6; plate 6). These obelisks, according to Hannah Frieser, have witnessed the people who cross the border and the people who patrol it throughout the markers' long history.[27] In Taylor's 2017–2018 exhibition at the Museum of Fine Arts in Houston, he

Figure 2.6. *Border Monument No. 184.* In David Taylor, *Working the Line.*
© 2010; courtesy of Radius Books.

imparted his reason for documenting these 276 obelisks for over a decade: "Most battles over border politics are fought in the theoretical realm, as if discussing the logistics of a board game without real-life consequences. But along this 2,000-mile boundary every legislative decision impacts people and landscape in concrete ways. Within the discussion of border politics, little consideration is given to what the actual border looks like."[28] From El Paso/Juarez to San Diego/Tijuana, Taylor's project captures these landscapes, both topographically and politically. His panoramic shots of the border present an arid and unforgiving landscape, one seemingly defined by the line (fig. 2.7; plate 7). These historically rich photographs are only half the project, however. The other half of his images focuses on the often unseen labor happening on the border to maintain this line, specifically policing, militarization, and surveillance. As explored in chapter 1, policing the border requires games in which death and violence are commonplace. It is unsurprising that Luis Urrea and Taylor regularly shared sources and stories after meeting at The Cup in Tucson while Urrea was researching *The Hummingbird's Daughter.*[29] Urrea's descriptions of "cutting the drag" in *The Devil's Highway* are in dialogue with

Taylor's images of La Migra and their games. While Taylor captures various strategies that they employ to detain migrants, his image of "cutting the drag" displays how these necropolitical strategies depend on movement (fig. 2.8; plate 8). The shot shows a Border Patrol SUV dragging car tires east or west through the desert. Often, they drag these tires for many miles every few days, forcing the crossers to walk over them on their south-to-north trek, making their journey traceable. The photograph does not simply suspend the act of "cutting the drag" on the glossy paper of *Working the Line*, however. Instead, the SUV leaves our field of vision in a specific way, where the shot captures the vehicle exiting the frame from this particular angle, as though the SUV is in motion. By reproducing the movement of these games, Taylor captures surveillance practices as always "in play." While Taylor's shots capture the historical changes of the border, especially from obelisks to fences and lines, his images of security theater produce a sense of ceaselessness, games without end.

Peter Andreas in *Border Games* sees border policing as a spectator sport, one in which calling these security techniques and strategies "games" draws

Figure 2.7. *U.S.-Mexico Border, Looking east toward El Paso/Juárez.* In David Taylor, *Working the Line.* © 2010; courtesy of Radius Books.

Figure 2.8. *Drag, New Mexico.* In David Taylor, *Working the Line.* © 2010; courtesy of Radius Books.

out the performative nature of the interactions.[30] According to Andreas, these games show how the Border Patrol or La Migra must "maximize the appearance of control" and look like it is "winning."[31] Andreas observes that the line between policing and militarizing the border is no longer easily distinguished: "Technologies and equipment originally developed for military use have increasingly been adapted for border enforcement purposes. Magnetic footfall detectors and infrared body sensors, many of which were first used in Vietnam, are deployed along the border. . . . The Border Research and Technology Center established in San Diego continues to facilitate the conversion of defense technologies."[32] Taylor, too, documents everything from the seismic sensors (once a technology for natural disasters and now a technology to track foot and vehicular traffic) to the armories, highlighting this lack of distinction between militarizing and policing. While the term "games" may counter the metaphors of war attached to these actions, the photographs leave viewers with little else to conclude. Jason De León's ethnographic work on photography and migration on the US-Mexico border unpacks how different forms of technology establish the border as a space of warfare on both sides.

Whether it is La Migra's night-vision goggles and gun rooms with the "fun stuff" or migrants' dark, camouflaged clothing and "sneakers with carpeted soles" to decrease visibility, such technologies/tecnologías are instrumental in the strategic violence taking place in the borderlands, where immigrants *must* be killed.[33] Taylor's images display the increased weaponizing of the La Migra, whose technological toys allow them to play the game in newer, more specialized ways.

Taylor, nevertheless, juxtaposes these images of games and equipment alongside the banal, everyday work of the border, as in his compositionally striking *Office Work (Shared Desk), Texas* (fig. 2.9; plate 9). This image frames a single agent performing the decidedly nonsensational work of government bureaucracy. She sits at a desk typing on a box computer. Paperwork litters the wood-paneled walls behind and beside her, some of it apparently filled with data and some with a child's drawings. Paperwork also overflows her desk, dominated by a large Rolodex. Her expression is vaguely annoyed with whatever is showing on the computer screen. *Office Work (Shared Desk), Texas,*

Figure 2.9. *Office Work (Shared Desk), Texas.* In David Taylor, *Working the Line.* © 2010; courtesy of Radius Books.

stands out among the surveillance-heavy work that dominates Taylor's shots because it captures what is happening behind the hypervisible violences practiced on the border by La Migra. It allows a peek into the work that keeps the theater alive. These disparate images of La Migra's work problematize what the United States is actually doing on the border: Regulating immigration? Enacting war? Destroying terrorism? Firing military-grade rifles on border crossers? Working nine to five?

Taylor's photographs also document a commitment to the nation, as both an imagined community and a state structure, when capturing the border. As a result, his images expose how the border is wrapped up in hypernationalist baggage: xenophobia, nativism, and exclusionary ideologies. As a crafted discourse, hypernationalism intentionally conceals the economic influences driving immigration. In this sense, border security works as a (violent) smoke screen that obscures the numerous economic processes producing inequality both inside and outside the nation. The use of nonsensical equipment to stop migrants, while money and goods cross the border easily, paints these activities as little more than theater. Wendy Brown describes fortification on the US-Mexico border as "staging" sovereignty: the wall "is an icon of the combination of sovereign erosion and heightened xenophobia and nationalism," even while it is an "ineffective bulwark" to the violence of neoliberal globalization.[34] Brown questions whether fortification keeps out encroaching globalization or whether it shuts people in, imprisoning citizens and confining them to only "hunkering and huddling."[35] Yet cheap labor is a constant desire—especially in view of historical US economic initiatives such as the Bracero Program (1942–1964), the US-Mexico Maquila Decree (1989), the North American Free Trade Agreement (NAFTA, 1993), and the Dominican Republic–Central American Free Trade Agreement (CAFTA–DR, 2004)—and thus border fortification ostensibly contradicts US economic desires. As Claire Fox describes, it was intended that the maquiladora industry would absorb migrant workers left jobless at the end of the Bracero Program while opening the door for more explicit free trade.[36] The Maquila Decree grants the exportation of labor and production to Mexico, where factories manufacture everything from clothing to firearms, and the products can come into US sister manufacturing plants duty-free. As a result, sister cities with twin plants have emerged: McAllen/Reynosa, San Diego/Tijuana, Brownsville/Matamoros, Laredo/Nuevo Laredo, Nogales/Nogales, and El Paso/Ciudad Juarez. In each case, the US plant benefits from cheap manufacturing in Mexico (now extended into Central America and Latin America), securing end-product selling power without the economic burdens of taxes or work visas. The United States keeps the labor "over there" while reaping the benefits, thus fulfilling the contradictory desires for cheap privatized labor and a (seemingly) homogeneous national population. Simultaneously, the exploitation of these economic systems creates political unrest and a working class who often need to migrate to survive. This social, political, and economic transborder phenomenon conflicts with the reinforcement of the border and the desire for national divisions.[37]

These economic practices and understandings may not be at the forefront in images of the border, but they inflect and encode the shots of surveillance and fortification with more violence. Bartletti's and Taylor's photographs glance at this tension between national fortification and market neoliberalization. Bartletti's image of freight trains, for instance, connotes the transfer of commodities, while the main gaze of his photographs—bodies/people/children—captures subjects who often must move because of uneven development. Taylor's obelisks, meanwhile, represent the demarcation of the US-Mexico border and bear witness to its porous history and geography. These photographers, whether intentionally or not, produce narratives about migration and immigration that often align with the narratives evoking fears over resources and inciting calls for more wall construction. Simultaneously, fortification is a symbolic, razor-wired, and surveilled curtain that the government promotes to obscure how the US political economy produces border crossings.

The Porous Border and Lived Experience

Processes of immigration and border fortification have created transborder structures that foster innovative technology and security theater but also inspire new aesthetic production and cultural mobilization. Fox sees the binational exchange of art and culture as a phenomenon parallel to the industrial parks along the border, arguing that the heterogeneity produced by economic systems (like maquiladoras) establishes border art as another exportable commodity.[38] Economic violence often undergirds transcultural production. While these cultural exchanges may not resist and challenge larger types of economic violence, they bring into focus what can and cannot be seen on the border. Documentary photography, in particular, desires to make practices and events visible in sometimes invisible or hard-to-see places. The Border Film Project shows us something about so-called documentary that Bartletti's and Taylor's work cannot on their own: the images collected in this project capture and document the paradoxical state of the border and show how such documentation must happen from multiple social, political, economic, aesthetic, and technological perspectives. A photographic undertaking such as the Border Film Project complicates this tension between visibility and invisibility and puts into question the conflictual crossing and fortifying of borders.

The Border Film Project is a collaborative endeavor that gave disposable cameras to undocumented workers crossing the US-Mexico desert and to the US Minutemen militias trying to stop them. To date, the project has received seventy-three cameras from thirty-eight migrants and thirty-five Minutemen, gathering approximately two thousand photos. To recruit migrant photographers, project representatives went to shelters in Mexico, explained the project, taught basic camera usage, and gave participants a Walmart gift card that would be filled with money once the camera was returned. To recruit Minutemen, the Border Film Project gave them Shell gas cards as incentives to participate. Giving migrants a Walmart card and Minutemen gas cards exacerbates their differences, which the project claims to be challenging, although the collaborative does not explain these choices.

In the case of the migrant shots, viewers are presented with many candid group photographs that capture fraternity and friendship. We see travelers eating together and enjoying one another's company during their journey (fig. 2.10; plate 10). In one instance, migrants walk single file through the chaparral, watching their companion take the snapshot (fig. 2.11; plate 11). They carry jackets and bags, visibly sweating as the sun is either just rising or just setting. The image documents the act of walking in the great open spaces of the US-Mexico borderlands, as the subjects almost seem to be moving out of the bottom left corner of the frame, much like Taylor's SUV cutting the drag. These photographs document the migrant journey, and the fraternity of the subjects comes across in rest and in movement. It is also notable that the subjects in the photographs are mostly men, painting this journey as a gendered and masculine experience, although that is perhaps more indicative of the manual labor that US companies have historically sought from undocumented migrants. Of course, the project's migrant photographs also include images of women, children, the landscape and encounters with wildlife, and the physically brutal experiences of crossing, such as graphic blisters.

In contrast, the Minutemen's photographs highlight their political ideologies, featuring clichéd patriotic objects that draw the eye: military surplus, military trucks, and the American flag. The shots, while also candid and sometimes group photos, often represent their nativist border politics, hyperbolized with national symbols and quite literally spelled out at certain moments. For instance, one shot is a handmade sign on private property that states, "Minuteman / Keep Out / go to 'Canada'" (fig. 2.12; plate 12). The sign announces the political beliefs of those who live in the house on the edge of

Figure 2.10. Camera 169, Juan Carlos (29). Camera distributed in Agua Prieta. From *Border Film Project* (2007).

Figure 2.11. Camera 501, Eduardo (33). Camera distributed in Chihuahua. From *Border Film Project* (2007).

Figure 2.12. Camera 10, Wayne (55). Camera distributed in New Mexico. From *Border Film Project* (2007).

the shot and gives a clear message, although it presumes an English-speaking audience. The sign uses "Minuteman" to announce who resides on the property and to establish a threat to so-called foreigners, making explicit the resident's nativism. Furthermore, the sign appears to be hastily thrown together, with "go to" squeezed in as an afterthought, almost as though the sign was created and hung abruptly for this snapshot. This image occurs alongside images of vigilantes posing on the job and patrolling. For example, Tim's photograph from Camera 51 poses a vigilante in an expensive white leather coat that mimics and appropriates (the idea of) indigenous clothing, with a matching white cowboy hat (fig. 2.13; plate 13). He has a large hunting knife holstered in one of his indigenous-esque leather tracking boots. He smiles at the camera as he points at some "tracked" trash in the dirt. The costuming and posing present a subject who has spectacularly confused "playing Indian" and practicing violent Anglo nativism, but the image also demonstrates how this vigilantism is purely spectacle. The Border Film Project states that they included the perspectives of the Minutemen to offer a more nuanced picture of the vigilante instead of the media caricature. The project editors maintain that many are concerned citizens and retired veterans who want to make the United States a safer place, and many are warriors. Their political position, nevertheless, reads as racist, nativist propaganda. Chacón and Davis argue that Minuteman propaganda appeals to a "disaffected middle class" that blames immigrants for its tottering class position, concealing the real cause: the corporate elite.[39] These vigilantes, nonetheless, are part of the border's visual narrative.

Neither group used (D)SLR technology, nor did any of the members necessarily know the basics of photography, let alone its aesthetic principles; these photographs are not Taylor's skilled art or Bartletti's award-winning commercial photojournalism.[40] Nevertheless, their amateurish and low-tech quality captures movement in a significant way. This movement is literal in that it lacks tripods, proper lighting, and planned timing, making the photographs less sharp, grainier, taken by unsteady hands. These are *snapshots*, taken on the move and producing fleeting, ephemeral documentation.[41] This photographic form documents the border in a constant state of movement: migrating people and bodies, shifting discourses and ideologies, importing and exporting labor and goods, and changing landscapes. Consequently, through inexperienced photography, viewers can more effectively see the experience of the border. Similar to Bartletti's *Enrique's Journey*, the Border Film Project's

Figure 2.13. Camera 51, Tim (39). Camera distributed in Twin Peaks, California. From *Border Film Project* (2007).

documentary photography evokes humanism by comparing these two lived experiences: "Migrants and Minutemen have very different backgrounds, yet they share one profound belief: at the end of the day, both sides would agree that they are documenting a situation that should not be happening. US border policy is broken and needs to be fixed."[42] The project's website includes a page dedicated to identifying the photographic similarities between the Minutemen's images and the migrants' shots, as though this juxtaposition demonstrates how these two groups are not so different in what they see and document, even while one hunts the other.[43] Thus, the project wishes to unify values and norms: all sides understand the problem of the border; all document the border through photography; all see strikingly similar things and live strikingly similar lives on the border.

When Schreiber discusses the Border Film Project, she understands the migrants' photographs to challenge the vigilantes' images, and she reads the "Similarities" portion of the website to instead "emphasize [their] different 'ways of seeing.'"[44] For Schreiber, the project's framing of the two groups as similar or as sharing a vision of the borderlands is misleading. Instead, this discourse of similarity conceals the two groups' differences and partakes in the problematic tradition of documentary photography that depoliticizes under the auspices of recording truth.[45] Documentary photography, as Paula Rabinowitz establishes, traditionally reproduces and makes us all complicit in the "construction of the social order."[46] For both Schreiber and Rabinowitz, this class consciousness imbuing documentary photography is often directly tied to the captions and narratives of the images. In Schreiber's analysis, the captions fabricate the vigilantes as ethical subjects and the migrants as unethical, whereas Rabinowitz considers how captions (specifically in James Agee's work) conscript the viewer in "a process of self-recognition" and false identification.[47] While the captions become a form of narrative-making that imparts these power dynamics, both scholars understand the photographs themselves to also contain and order the social world through compositional elements and subject matter. Of course, these criticisms on some level presuppose that documenting enacts an empirical view of the subject matter. Instead, we may consider how the Border Film Project captures and exposes the truth about the social. The social here is not the tidy division of nations, the so-called order of class difference, or fear-inducing discourses about the failed securing of these divisions and differences. Rather, these photographs display a borderland where these divisions and differences blur, move, and get called into question. This does not necessarily result in the polar opposite, reducing these divisions and differences to "similarities" (even if the project's collaborators claim so); instead, the photographs capture a moving ambivalence around these hardline distinctions.

By putting the Border Film Project in conversation with Bartletti's and Taylor's work, I mean to demonstrate how the paradoxes of the border become more visible through multiple and overlapping techniques, perspectives, and viewpoints. Both the professional and the nonprofessional camera eye, the formal shot and the candid shot, the carefully crafted shot and the snapshot, and the striking shot and the banal shot present this larger narrative. The Border Film Project especially complicates this larger narrative by adding in the lived experience of the border. Photographer, subject, and viewer lose distinction, and the categorizations of migrants and vigilantes are not always legible. The border is less a line between states and more a fluid, porous phenomenon.

Paradox and Photography

Of all the art coming from the US-Mexico border, I keep returning to photography because this visual medium produces a paradox around movement. The camera eye halts and fixes our vision in time and space; it freezes moments, yet some formal choices still capture movement, as we have seen with the three projects in this chapter.[48] Border photography always is in this state of tension, both through the photographic medium and through its representations of secured yet porous geopolitical spaces. The aesthetic paradoxes parallel the narrative paradoxes. When photographs present racialized bodies crossing the desert, some will see invading "hordes" to stand against, while others will see the problematic flows of capital and exploitation. Simultaneously, some of these photographs make visible what wishes and/or needs to be invisible, such as the militarized equipment of the Minutemen, the Border Patrol's games, or the undocumented migrants who must live in the shadows in the United States. These visual documents trace the conflicting discourses and practices of immigration and security.

One of the underlying assumptions in this chapter is that the photographers and viewers imbue these images ideologically. Photography's narrative tension develops from the way photographs discursively construct the photographic subject, the audience, and the photographer. The paradoxes of border photography, then, presuppose that photography works on a social as much as an aesthetic level. Pierre Bourdieu claims that photography structures our social relations and social classes. Accordingly, he challenges the position that art can and should be removed from the social and political discourses embodied within it.[49] He argues that photographic forms, especially those that capture and pose people, entangle aesthetics and social norms.[50] For instance, when photographers pose subjects or frame a photograph, they are governed by social norms of how things should look (as is the viewer).[51] This normative impulse is a problem when the photograph hopes to document some sort of social truth. Susan Sontag articulates the different role of photographers in this social contract, wherein they are aesthetic eyes and objective recorders who recycle reality with their "machine-toy."[52] For Sontag, the photographer produces a contradictory and incompatible set of attitudes—"the aesthetic and the instrumental"—about the subjects and objects in an image, and the latter becomes problematic when it constructs our vision of the world in the service of power, surveillance, and narcissism.[53] In describing the Farm Security Administration (FSA) photographers Walker Evans, Dorothea Lange, and others, she points to their countless frontal shots of sharecroppers as they tried to capture the right facial expression on each of their poor farmer subjects. According to Sontag, these precise expressions were less about a "mirror of reality" and more about the photographers' own ideas about "poverty, light, dignity, texture, exploitation, and geometry."[54] She interlaces class ideologies with aesthetic concerns here, demonstrating how they inform and complement each other. As a result, documentary photography captures not a mirrored truth of its subject but the truth of social relations.

In the case of Bartletti's *Enrique's Journey*, the boys on the train are candidly captured, and many are not looking at the camera. Bourdieu might question these shots for their seemingly natural posturing because it is difficult to determine how much the photographer's attention to angle and composition strategically staged the shot or how much the subjects were inadvertently reacting and posing because they were being photographed. Bourdieu considers any natural shot to be an illusion since there are too many unconscious ideologies and expectations imbuing and producing a photo's composition, from the photographer to the subject to the audience. The illusion of a natural shot conforms to and produces "cultural ideals" about how the subject "must appear."[55] For instance, Jorge Velasquez Felipe and Juan Carlos burn paper on the end of a train car, one sitting and staring down at his hands and the other hunched on his feet and ready to move, staring out at the passing landscape (fig. 2.4). They do not look up at the photographer, whose position above them consolidates his own authorial power in this relationship, makes his subjects inferior by the angle, and naturalizes them as part of the train. Simultaneously, the candid naturalness also humanizes these subjects, as we glimpse into their lived experience. This shot becomes a microcosm of Sontag's claim that photography is the "central activity that [reflects] all the complexities and contradictions and equivocations of this society. . . . [T]his activity, by which I mean both the taking of and the looking at pictures, encapsulates all those contradictions."[56] Whereas Sontag totalizes all photographic forms and contents into "contradiction," the two images of Jorge Velasquez Felipe and Juan

Carlos capture a specific, shifting power dynamic between photographer, subject, and audience. This dynamic is unsettling, because it is potentially subversive yet simultaneously normalizes the social order.

In contrast to the "natural" shot, the amateur photographers of the Border Film Project's participants often present "posed" photographs with subjects smiling directly into the camera eye. Certain aesthetic norms are at play in these images, norms that Bourdieu identifies as requirements for posed shots: subjects look directly at the camera, often smiling, and are pressed against one another in happy familiarity, almost always in the center of the picture.[57] These compositional elements produce the visual equivalent of standard social values, such as fraternity, familia, and community. Of course, these values are not always posed. Bartletti, for instance, captures candid fraternity with his photographs of Wilfred Ramirez, aged fifty-five, shaving his eighty-seven-year-old father, Emiliano, in *Filial Devotion* (fig. 2.3), and of Jorge Velasquez Felipe and Juan Carlos holding hands as they go through a tunnel (fig. 2.5). Notably, both Bartletti and the Border Film Project always name their subjects or photographer-subjects when they are able to do so, helping to construct a sense of humanism in the images themselves. Taylor, on the other hand, does not capture these fraternal, familial, communal values in his shots and does not name the subjects in his images. When he does include human subjects in his images, they are rarely posed in any traditional sense and do not evoke viewers' empathy or identification; instead, he presents the seemingly natural regulatory structures that have become part of the landscape itself, where the border is purely a space of labor and lines. These are social relations that tread in theatrics and bureaucracy. The photographs of Bartletti, Taylor, and the Border Film Project make visible the push and pull of social relations and norms on the border through their various forms and styles.

These professional-candid and amateur-posed images create a politics of what Judith Butler has elsewhere called recognition and/or misrecognition.[58] In particular, Bartletti's professional-candid shots operate as so-called truth givers about immigration, as though they capture authentic moments that truly express the migrant journey. For instance, the beleaguered faces of Jorge Velasquez Felipe and Juan Carlos trying to stay warm on a speeding train appear to authenticate migration in a specific way (fig. 2.4). Bartletti's shot maintains a normative image of crossing, a picture of hardship and struggle. In contrast, the point-and-shoot image of Juan Carlos's Camera 169 resembles a family-album photo, recording a happy moment in the lives of two buddies (fig. 2.10). Outside the context of the Border Film Project, we might not even know that his image documents migration. The photograph presents friendship and laughter and, thus, unsettles our visual expectations of the adversity faced when crossing the border. As singular shots, they both consolidate and challenge normative narratives about immigration processes and national security. When it comes to narratives of im/migration, Juan Carlos's photograph perhaps does more work than Bartletti's because it subverts the normative visual expectations of (undocumented) migration. It forces us to confront what Butler calls the politics of recognition/misrecognition. In her recent work on assembly, she maps out this political paradox: some are recognized as human whereas others as nonhuman, when in fact the latter are simply illegible humans and, as such, necessarily misrecognized.[59] For Butler, this politics of recognition/misrecognition is a mode of power that normalizes and upholds racism, anthropocentrism, and the definition of who matters, becoming a "vicious form of logic" for the subject-objects who are constructed as illegible and who must struggle to dismantle these norms.[60] This logic forcibly returns us to *Interstate Pedestrians*, Bartletti's photograph that inspired southern California road signs that in turn constructed migrants as little more than infectious "hordes" and wild animals (fig. 2.1).[61] If these road signs are the *necessary* misrecognition of (undocumented, in-flight) migrants as nonhuman, then they function to define citizens alone as legible, and thus it is citizens alone who matter. This politics of recognition/misrecognition and legibility/illegibility, in other words, produces a necropolitical violence.

I have turned to the politics of recognition/misrecognition because it encapsulates the question of visibility wrapped up in these ideological constructions of performance (what we literally see) and reception (what is represented and interpreted). Conventional border photography has maintained a social order predicated on us/them and citizen/foreigner dynamics. However, these social relations also necessarily obscure the networks, economic exchanges, and family ties that perpetually breach the border. The border can no longer be recognized as simply a fence and a river, as Fox once interrogated, and citizens and vigilantes cannot actually identify who belongs and who does not. This uncertainty around the border materializes not simply through the photographic subject but through the medium itself. Sontag unravels the social order surrounding the photograph, accusing documentarists of being well-off voyeurs who desire to document and revel in social misery. These images of misery come from photographers in comfortable positions as omnipotent and detached authorities.[62] In this sense, the power dynamics within photography, where the camera lens becomes a glass border, automatically produces an us/them opposition.[63] This voyeuristic dynamic between photographer and subject-object also extends to the viewer. Photography produces distance from its subject, so viewers are always gazing at the Other in some fetishistic form. We at times see this effect in Bartletti's and Taylor's images, as they capture ("illegal") migrant movement or La Migra's labor (figs. 2.8 and 2.9); these images remain removed from the lives and livelihoods of the viewer and the photographer and offer a safe, sterilized space from which to look. Even when these shots produce identification, it often reads as empty humanism: viewers have momentary empathy for children on a train before moving on with their lives. From this perspective, the power dynamic stays firmly in place.

Joseph Entin calls this "documentary humanism," a liberalism that arises in traditional documentary photography (particularly the FSA project) to fulfill the clichéd signifier of "universalized common humanity."[64] In the case of Entin's example, the production of so-called universal humanity hoped to bridge the inequalities of US social life at the time. Now, this humanism often problematically supplants and elides the violence of exploitation and the growing gap between the haves and have-nots on a global scale, the very political and economic inequalities that help to produce and solidify metaphorical and geopolitical borders. However, universal humanity also performs a strategic misrecognition. For Parvati Nair, this humanism is a result of documentary photography's "crucial role in mediating otherness" on the border. She argues that the witnessing of border violence in photographs—"the suffering, metaphorical and real, of human lives and bodies, the practices of exclusion, and the violence of non-belonging"—generates a responsiveness in viewers that "can override divisions of class, race, or ethnicity, even if always confronted with the inequality and violence of national borders." For Nair, this empathy may be optimistic and problematic, but it is crucial in changing the "equation of power."[65] I see these tensions within documentary photography's humanist production to parallel the tensions around the border itself. If the border is a national space to secure *and* an economic space to open, then these photographs must reveal how these paradoxes are a part of the lived truth of the border. In the case of the Border Film Project, this becomes even more complicated, since the social order constructed by the photograph is often indistinct. On one level, the photographer and subject overlap, blurring the line between an objective viewing distance and a lived experience. On another level, it both consolidates and upends the normative narratives of la frontera.

Photographing Borders in the Era of Globalization

Because the Border Film Project breaches borders on multiple levels, I would like to end with a discussion of how these photographs potentially represent the border in a state of globalization. Peter Andreas argues that border security is a performance that promises a "bigger and better show," thereby increasing the visibility of policing but decreasing the visibility of "illegal crossings."[66] Wendy Brown adds to Andreas's critique by arguing that walls, especially those securing nation-state borders, create an image of the state as protective and self-determined. Simultaneously, according to Brown, this image is simply spectacle, an illusion that attempts to counter fears about terrorism and distract from the practices of unregulated, neoliberal capitalism.[67] The border photographs included at the beginning of Andreas's *Border Games* (images of the fence provided courtesy of the US Border Patrol) and in the first chapter of Brown's *Walled States, Waning Sovereignty* (Marc Silver's and David McNew's shots of the US-Mexico border, in sequence with images of the Israel-Palestine wall, the India-Bangladesh fence, and the India-Pakistan fence) are mere accessories. For Andreas, the introductory photographs function as an opening historical anecdote about immigration processes' evolution, whereas Brown never directly discusses her collection. Nevertheless, both scholars argue that the *image* of a fortified border is normalized.[68] I, however, prefer to emphasize border photography's significant role in the production, maintenance, and disruption of these representations and spectacles, where the medium of photography gives us a formal foundation for exploring the tensions embedded in these images.

Lurking in the subtext of these images are the complex economic interactions that often produce immigration and that arguably consolidate the social order. Sontag pinpoints how the image operates as an economic form:

> A capitalist society requires a culture based on images. It needs to furnish vast amounts of entertainment in order to stimulate buying and anesthetize the injuries of class, race, and sex. And it needs to gather unlimited amounts of information, the better to exploit natural resources, increase productivity, keep order, make war, give jobs to bureaucrats. The camera's twin capacities, to subjectivize reality and to objectify it, ideally serve these needs and strengthen them. Cameras define reality in the two ways essential to the workings of an advanced industrial society: as a spectacle (for the masses) and as an object of surveillance (for rulers). The production of images also furnishes a ruling ideology. Social change is replaced with a change in images.[69]

Sontag positions photography as the principal form of consumer capitalism. Invoking Guy Debord's foundational concept of spectacle and image, she argues that the image now operates as pure commodity, devouring our subjectivities as it demands more and more images. Photography becomes a perpetual mechanical reproduction of image-commodities.[70] From this perspective, the market arguably depoliticizes the photograph or commodifies its politics in safe, clichéd packaging. In many ways, this understanding extends from Walter Benjamin's theories on the reproducibility of the photograph. For Benjamin, photography's reproductive medium makes it no longer anchored to a certain historical moment and divests it of "authenticity," and this means the photograph is less about artistic ritual and more about politics. Benjamin sees this politics as putting into motion viewer identifications with the camera, distracted masses who absorb art rather than are absorbed by it, and a fascist aestheticization of politics.[71] The medium of the photograph, in other words, enacts a violent and exploitative political economy that subsumes photographers, subjects, and viewers.

Nevertheless, the photographic projects that I have linked in this chapter, when considered together, often push against normative and ordered market desire, and they underline a deeply ambivalent politics that is at play on the border. When we look at Bartletti's image of Jorge Velasquez Felipe and Juan Carlos clasping hands and yelling into the abyss of a train tunnel, we are not necessarily being sold a recognizable and prepackaged image of immigration, even if the photo was taken for commercial purposes (fig. 2.5). When Taylor captures the Border Patrol's banal everyday work in *Office Work (Shared Desk), Texas*, we are not mindlessly celebrating security and consuming standardized hypernationalist discourse (fig. 2.9). In other words, these professional and artistic photographs are illegible in productive ways. When coupled with the lived experiences documented in the Border Film Project, these images show the shifting paradoxes of what is happening on the border. These photographs are not depoliticized or wholly spectacle; they partake in a complex narrative about the troubled condition of the border. They illuminate a transitory understanding of the US-Mexico border: dehumanizing elements come up against humanizing shots, nationalistic desires to secure the border materialize alongside social and economic relations in the age of globalization, and professional and amateur shots blur the line between legible and illegible. Border photography constructs, engages, and questions the conflicting narratives and ideologies at play on the border. The layers of paradox begin to show the border for what it is: a state of perpetual movement. We see migrants functioning as little more than excess commodities on freight trains, La Migra doing bureaucratic paperwork, vigilantes flaunting their military surplus, fleeting moments of kinship and hardship, and the ever-shifting frontera.

CHAPTER 3

Latinx Realisms: The Cinematic Borderworlds of Josefina López, David Riker, and Alex Rivera

Leaving aside rape or murder, leaving aside the bloody catalog of oppression, which we are in one way too familiar with already, what this does to the subjugated, the most private, the most serious thing this does to the subjugated, is to destroy his sense of reality. [. . .] It comes as a great shock to discover that Gary Cooper killing off the Indians, when you were rooting for Gary Cooper, that the Indians were you. It comes as a great shock to discover that the country which is your birthplace and to which you owe your life and your identity, has not, in its whole system of reality, evolved any place for you.

JAMES BALDWIN, DEBATE AT CAMBRIDGE (1965)

La Ciudad (*The City*) opens with an aerial shot of the city, the only movement coming from a freight train slowly cutting through the haze of gray buildings. The camera cuts to a vacant single sidewalk, angled obliquely on a photo store, advertising one-hour photos for "loteria de visa & aplicaciones." Our gaze, as the camera eye, enters the photo shop and sees portraits being taken of individual people: the Latinx men and women pose against cliché panoramas of pretty nature scenes, photographs decidedly not for visas or applications. A young man combs his hair carefully and appears excited. This artistically striking opening in black and white crumbles when later in the film the young man dies during grueling, invisible day labor, and we discover this portrait was meant to be sent home to his wife. In chapter 2, the photographic portrait signals both the question of political documentation and the documenting of one's life. In *La Ciudad*, it is but a trace of a life that undergoes economic death. I argue in both chapter 1 and chapter 2 that documentary photography complicates what is visible and what is invisible, especially within various borderlands and through multiple medium-specific paradoxes. Most significantly, documentary photography slips between capturing or recording the truth of our current realities and staging or manufacturing strategic discourses, misrecognitions, and narratives. These paradoxes in documentary photography, nevertheless, trouble how narratives mediate between the real and fictional representations of border experiences.

Documentary proper, with its desire to capture social reality empirically, is not always enough and cannot always attend to the ideologies, imaginaries, and enclosures around migration and Latinx subjectivity in the United States, although it draws attention to absences or misrecognitions. "Realism," instead, may better describe the complex and uneven narrativization of the real.[1] Ramón Saldívar argues that Chicano narrative is an "authentic way of grappling with a reality that always transcends representation, a reality into which the subject of the narrative's action seeks to enter, all the while learning the lesson of its own ideological closure, and of history's resistance to the symbolic structures in which subjectivity itself is formed."[2] This is not the simplistic understanding of realism as naïve and vulgar mimesis, the seemingly pure reproduction and replication of reality, but a definition of realism that includes narratives that try to capture lived, multilayered, subjugated experiences and consciousnesses. Marcial González describes realism, specifically in the Chicano novel, as a logic of formal contradictoriness that is "consistent with the structural limits of late capitalism" and "offers the possibility of elucidating the specific historical circumstances and social processes within which Chicano novels have been produced and to which they are a response."[3] For Elena Machado Sáez, realism is a pedagogical tool of anticolonial and diasporic fiction that fills historical gaps and recenters the excluded stories and lives that have shaped Western, especially North American, culture and politics.[4] For Machado Sáez, some of this fiction also responds to and subverts the market's or audience's "desire for realism," a point that suggests realism pervades our social, economic, and cultural relations.[5] This chapter, then, extends from the limitations of documentary and arrives at this question of realism. Furthermore, I want to think of "realisms," plural, as a multifaceted and variable concept and form. I also move from photography to film in this chapter because, while both mediums involve visuality, cinema further complicates how performance constructs Latinx subjectivity under global capitalism and why the violence of this political economy often remains invisible. I am especially interested in those films that produce a sense of *cinema verité* and reside between documentary and fiction.[6]

This chapter specifically considers how Latinx cinema uses different forms and conceptualizations of realism to navigate, understand, and challenge the political and economic structures that govern and imbue Latinx lives and deaths. I focus on Josefina López's adapted *Detained in the Desert*, David Riker's collection of shorts *La Ciudad*, and Alex Rivera's science-fiction film

Sleep Dealer, all employing the medium of cinema to explore and confront the realities of Latinx experience. These three films all engage forms of realism even though they utilize divergent styles and approaches and would be categorized in different genres. For instance, the film *Detained in the Desert* is adapted from López's play of the same name, which employs a form she calls "cineatro." Two storylines intersect in the Arizona desert: one about a right-wing talk-radio host whose vitriolic rhetoric instigates xenophobic and racist violence against immigrants and who eventually is abducted and tortured for it, and the other about a Chicana college student who is detained by ICE when returning home for a term break and refuses to show any documentation proving that she is a US citizen. These two people meet in the desert when escaping their respective imprisonments, and the ghosts of dead migrants lead them to a savior of sorts, Ernesto Martinez, who is based on a real-life water warrior, Enrique Morones, the founder of Border Angels. López notes that she wrote her play *Detained in the Desert* to "show the ridiculousness" of Arizona's 2010 SB 1070 law, which allows police to racially profile people suspected of being undocumented migrants. Developed from López's frustrations with the "hate talk" that continues to shape the law, she wonders "if the men at the forefront of this 'hate talk' [. . .] are aware that they have blood on their hands."[7]

In contrast to López's cineatro style, Riker's *La Ciudad* presents a neorealist representation of migrant life in New York City. The four shorts—"Ladrillos"/"Bricks," "Casa"/"Home," "Titiritero"/"Puppeteer," and "Costurera"/"Seamstress"—are filmed in black and white and show a glimpse into different Latin American migrant experiences in New York City. Since the two shorts that bookend and frame the collection are specifically about migrant labor and economic exploitation, I focus mainly on them in this chapter. Riker sees his vignettes not as a documentary but as something more that may show the world in its true skin: "As a direct result of my documentary work [. . .] I did not want to make a didactic film anymore, [. . .] it was not as effective, [. . .] it closed the discussion before the discussion could even begin. By that I mean I didn't want to start with the agenda. I wanted somehow to bury it. I wanted it to come out organically from the dramatic story."[8] In utilizing a neorealist sensibility, the film wishes to show an authentic image of the global city and migrant life (or lack thereof), wherein there are ever-new discursivities and enclosures.

Alex Rivera's *Sleep Dealer*, cowritten with Riker, is the least obviously "realist" text among these films and is often categorized as science fiction or speculative fiction. It presents a near-future world where US-based multinational corporations control all the water and factory labor in Mexico.[9] The story follows Memo, a young rural farmworker who travels north to Tijuana to get nodes implanted into his circulatory system so he can operate robotic labor in the United States via virtual reality matrices. The film interrogates and challenges the corporate presence in securing the borderlands and its resources. While speculative about the future ramifications of border security, Rivera argues that the film emerges from "the reality we're all going to live in, the surveillance we'll all live under, the way we'll be treated legally, or the rights we'll have, those are all tested first on the border . . . the entire concept of rights, it's first torn apart in the borderlands."[10] For Rivera, the current realities of the border are already writing our futures.

I offer these contextual summaries to show each film's differing approach to capturing Latinx social reality, especially the realities surrounding US immigration policy and neoliberal marketization. I focus on cinema and drama in this chapter because these forms offer structures of embodiment, visuality, and performance different from the literary prose and photography of previous chapters. Alicia Arrizón understands Latina performance as a complex "interaction of 'self' and 'other' centered on the struggle to find a voice within silences" that positions the Latina body as a "witness, spectator, and protagonist of the silence and suppression her body speaks against."[11] Performance, then, constructs a corporeal mode of revealing and countering histories of suppression. Leticia Alvarado argues that Latinx performance "tells us something of abjection—of the connective sinews of coalition across minoritized populations as represented by performers, the queer politics for understanding its offerings, the fecund possibilities of its political implications, and finally the textile limits of the heuristic fabric."[12] For Alvarado, Latinx performance potentially "uncover[s] unknown routes to world making."[13] Gad Guterman similarly argues that performances of "undocumentedness"—a state of legal nonexistence—is a productive strategy for subjects to be "reborn" within new national contexts.[14] All three scholars confirm what Frances Aparicio describes as the "embodiments of the colonial conditions of US Latino/as," a public condition for performing Latinx bodies.[15] Simultaneously, they also imagine the radical possibilities of performance, and they establish how performance allows for migrant and Latinx subjects to apply a different critical lens to the violent conditions of globalization from their position of subalternity. The cinematic performances in *Detained in the Desert, La Ciudad,* and *Sleep Dealer* present critical gazes on how free-market capitalism encloses certain populations in death-worlds, a world-making that attends to the spaces and times of absence, negation, and exclusion. Specifically, I am interested in how these films and performances reveal the systemic underpinnings of this ethno-racial and economic violence.

While Arrizón, Alvarado, and Guterman see Latinx and migrant performance art as challenging various subjugations of bodies and subjects, Jean

Baudrillard's idea of hyperrealism returns us to how cultural productions are produced and reproduced within the very systems that they may resist, what we might identify as a structural foreclosure of possibility. For Baudrillard, the hyperreal describes when "reality itself, entirely impregnated by an aesthetic that holds onto its very structurality, has become inseparable from its own image."[16] I turn to Baudrillard's idea of hyperrealism because I am concerned with what cinematic performance opens and closes through realisms. While less interested in Baudrillard's collapse of reality with simulation and simulations of simulations, I find his ideas around the economics of realism apropos. "Hyperrealism" describes an economic system of exchange and commodity that requires the perpetual reproduction of so-called reality in cultural objects, images, and narratives in order to graft the structure of capitalism onto our everyday perceptions of reality, history, and social relations. According to Baudrillard, this cultural phenomenon leads to reality's eventual demise into the symbolic, propagating various forms of slow and social death. Death itself begins to structure our social and cultural relationship to reality. Latinx cinematic narratives complicate the production and reproduction of slow and social death and allow for a deeper consideration of the structures of death in our political economy, not simply because these films replicate and/or represent Latinx realities within literal and figurative borderlands but because they embody and question the multiplicitous, illegible, and uneven forms of these realities and the violences underneath them.

In this sense, I use the terms "realism" and "realisms" as a broad stroke, defining a variety of storytelling modes and narratives that wish to expose the social truth for Latinx migrant subjects across time and space. Thus, I do not adhere to the strict differential line that Fredrick Luis Aldama and Ralph E. Rodríguez maintain between realism (as a generic mode that merely depicts Latinx realities and identity politics) and metafiction (which creates self-reflexive and transcendent narratives).[17] I acknowledge the difference between literary realism (largely defined through the novel form) and cinematic realism (emerging from the histories of *cinema verité*), but I understand these different forms and narrative genres of realism to collide and merge within and across this Latinx cinema. As a result, these films expose how the political economy requires various structures of death wherein some populations live and thrive because others are made disposable and commoditized. These films employ realisms to confront the multiple structures of death for Latinx subjects. "Realism," in this chapter, describes the desire to illuminate the embodied conditions of misrecognition, undocumentedness, and violence of Latinx lives and deaths, thereby unmasking the necropolitical truth of the violence at the center of the political economy. Moreover, they present the push-and-pull between a necropolitics that renders Latinx subjects disposable and a necropolitics that imagines possibilities and resistance.

Naïve Realism to Social Realism

The idea that realist texts replicate reality as objectively as a mirror comes from a Western literary history that Erich Auerbach maps from antiquity to modern literature in *Mimesis* (1946). While Auerbach differentiates mimesis across disparate literary styles and narrative objectives, the term "mimesis" often operates as a catch-all for what González describes as an "unmediated reflection" of reality.[18] Mimesis, in this sense, hinges on a confidence in a text's ability to document and represent events, subjectivities, and lived experience empirically. Many scholars call this empirical principle "naïve realism." For Rodríguez, the "rubric of realist and social realist fiction" must employ "mimetic fidelity" to representing "life in the barrio, farm work, migration, and immigration," a convention that depends on an idea of "the [real] world we think we know and that we inhabit."[19] Aldama has a more ambivalent understanding of realism. On one level, he agrees that realist narrative devices have no "material power" to "change the world," but on another, he cannot deny the power of fiction, even if it can only "reflect" and "represent" our "own sociality."[20] Raphael Dalleo and Machado Sáez offer the idea of "lowercase Latino/a realism," which describes an indirect and veiled representation of Latinx politics, but this idea assumes an uppercase and direct realism that may present and represent the Latinx world straightforwardly as it is.[21] These are definitions of realism proper, what we may identify as a singular and tidy naïve realism.[22] This understanding of realism is predicated on a representation's ability to authentically mirror the social, the historical, and the political.

López's *Detained in the Desert* arguably wishes to perform naïve realism in that both the play and film want to reflect the true realities of life in Arizona after SB 1070, with its legalization of racial profiling. The narrative has a singular goal in representing the political reality of this law, and it never strays far from it. In parallel, the characters embody a naïveté that reflects the pervasive social naïveté about border politics. The main characters—Sandi Belen and Lou Sanchez/Becker—must misrecognize what this law means in their everyday lives at first, and their two storylines rely on this initial naïveté. Sandi is a second-generation Chicana who impulsively decides to withhold her identification when local Arizona police question her and her gringo boyfriend, who is ironically an undocumented migrant from Canada, on the side of the road. In the film, she understands a little Spanish, while in the play, she does not speak any Spanish. In both, she believes her lack of accent and her obvious Americanness will protect her, but this means she is ignoring the magnitude of the political climate she is in, a world in which police are legally allowed to racially profile anyone. Lou, on the other hand, is a "portly, Anglo conservative talk show host" whose last name, "Sanchez," productively confuses this description.[23] If he is an Anglo with a Spanish last name, then he is assumably Americanized, a güero who denies his chicanidad or latinidad. We learn in the play, however, that he adopts this last name purely for his radio show, to appear to be a Chicano who is anti-immigrant and, thus, to justify his audience's xenophobia. This appearance is further complicated when he is abducted and tortured for his hate talk, disclosing that his "wife is Mexican-American . . . but like third or fourth generation" and that he is a legal immigrant from Canada who got his papers through marriage.[24] His confessions during his abduction reveal that his xenophobic politics are merely caricatures that appeal to his audience and validate their hatred. Throughout the abduction, he denies that his rhetoric has any real world consequences: "Listen, I am not responsible for what drunk white teenage boys do to illegals—[. . .]I don't tell anyone to go kill Latino people."[25] He truly believes that his job (and thus his rhetorical misrepresentation of migrants) is simply nine to five, without anything beyond it. Both characters deeply misrecognize the reality of the political environment and their places within it, and this naïveté leads both characters to be held captive in the desert.

Sandi's and Lou's reductive understandings of SB 1070 mimic individualist perspectives about racist and xenophobic laws, as though they do not affect everyone. To call this naïve realism, then, is to identify the misplaced ideas around a law like SB 1070. The characters' naïveté reflects these misperceptions and misunderstandings, but as the performance continues, this larger social relationship becomes exposed for both the characters and the viewers. Their respective captivities and eventual escapes allow their storylines to converge, and this convergence opens up a social consciousness that moves beyond a vulgar mimesis into what I would more readily identify as social realism. Through a Lukácsian lens, González argues that realism produces a sense of social totality: "Realism resists the extreme fragmentation and rationalization caused by elaborate systems of commodity production and exchange under capitalism by aspiring toward a kind of representation that implies a determinate relation between events and their causes, emphasizing historical continuity rather than discontinuity."[26] Realism, in this sense, captures a social totality as it elucidates "specific historical circumstances and social processes" that shape and construct both our subjectivities and our literary forms, even when these histories are invisible, absent, contradictory, and/or "imperfect" in the narrative.[27] *Detained in the Desert* enacts this recognition of history and social process in its second half, when Sandi and Lou meet in the middle of desert, physically and mentally broken and dehydrated. Sandi has escaped an ICE detention center after talking with a migrant woman who may have been a specter, and Lou has escaped his abduction not knowing that he is being intentionally released to die painfully in the heat of the desert. Both are running to the same point of contact, and once they meet in the desert, they are visited by another migrant ghost. The presence of ghosts in López's play and film lead the protagonists to social transformation.

Artemio and Milagros, two dead migrants, visit Sandi and Lou to bring them together and to help them fully transcend their naïveté as they see the bigger picture of migration. Milagros appears to Sandi in detention and prophesizes her escape, and when confronted with the possibility that she may be a ghost, Sandi exclaims, "I don't believe in ghosts. . . . She was real."[28] When Sandi and Lou meet in the desert, the ghost of Artemio visits them at the moment when Lou believes that they will die. In the play, Artemio speaks Spanish, making Sandi reemphasize that she does not speak Spanish, but she understands enough to identify that he is begging them to tell his wife "that he was detained in the desert and that he is still waiting there."[29] Sandi and Lou find his remains and ID only a few yards from a vandalized water station. When Ernesto, the water warrior, finds them, they are able to bring to light Artemio's death, which Sandi identifies as a murder, and disseminate this knowledge to his wife and to Lou's right-wing listeners. Sandi and Lou's encounter with these ghosts upends the systemic erasure of migrant death, and from this, they are able to see more clearly the world and how they can affect it. The ghosts open their eyes to the reasons for and costs of migration for Latinx subjects.

Both the play and the film engage in what Saldívar describes as a "complex interaction between 'mythic or magical consciousness.'" For Saldívar, Chicano narrative is not always identifiably traditional realism but bleeds into romance and myth as an "allegory of the repressed space of the worlds of work, of history, and of protopolitical conflict."[30] He understands that these narrative conventions and contradictions have ideological implications where subjects recognize themselves in an "imagined reality" and in the "pathos of imaginative life."[31] This mythical, magical, and imagined reality is not necessarily synonymous with magical realism but opens up the possibilities of social consciousness.[32] While González emphasizes the role of history in producing social realism, Saldívar expands this by allowing for the imaginary and speculative to also play a significant role in forming realism. *Detained in the Desert* arrives at this imaginary through the figures of ghost migrants.

Ghosts of the forgotten, lost, and erased revive the absent, invisible, and imperfect realities of border politics for Latinx and Chicanx subjects. Elizabeth Jacobs argues that the presence of Artemio and Milagros in *Detained in the Desert* is part of a narrative tradition that must represent "hidden or unseen histories as hauntings." For Jacobs, the presence of ghosts refuses a border politics that wishes to "erase the political presence of undocumented people, and restrict them in categories that stress their anonymity." While Jacobs sees this narrative device as decidedly "nonrealist," I would argue that ghosts pointedly embody a violent social condition for many Latinx and migrant subjects. [33] If realism captures social totality, then the dead coming back to life does more than solely uncover hidden histories and recover invisible experiences. The (un)dead show the very structures of the social order that produce various states of (non)existence, making their presence potentially transformative.

If realism is the narrative vehicle for understanding and revealing Latinx and migrant social experience across space and time, then the question of form and genre plays a role in establishing how the narrative encompasses what González identifies as social totality. I am not a champion of formalism, but I recognize that the vessels in which narratives are distributed matter. Rodríguez argues that Latinx literary criticism has traditionally neglected a close consideration of form and genre because of the excessive attention to identity formations and to critical race and ethnic studies.[34] I do not share the same lament about this critical neglect, but in López's work, form becomes quite central because her drama employs what she calls "cineatro." "Cineatro" describes a form that mixes elements of cinema and elements of theater and that ultimately "positions its audience to bear witness to the impact of anti-immigration activities."[35] López's mixture of cinema and theater is why the play and film must be examined simultaneously; these respective forms and productions overlap and converse with each other on multiple levels. On one level, cineatro enacts social experience, what González describes as a dialectical move where "the social relations within a particular mode of production establish the formal limits of narratives internally."[36] On another level, the idea that cineatro allows audiences/readers to bear witness interprets this form as a window to reality. Bearing witness, Marta Caminero-Santangelo argues, is integral to Latinx migrant narratives.[37] The mixing of drama and cinema captures how form navigates the contours of what can or cannot be seen about the social.[38] In one mode, we bear witness to how figures of authority, whether Lou as a talk show host or the legal existence of SB 1070, can paint reality in very specific and violent ways, but Lou's discursive opining or the creation of racist policy largely elides the reality of racialized and migrant subjects in the

United States. *Detained in the Desert* also confronts how this erasure of Latinx subjects is a strategic part of this world-making. The performance makes visible this structural erasure not simply as a historical depiction but as a way of uncovering and giving voice to who is invisible.

However, there is a significant difference between the play and the film that tells us something about the way migrant death and erasures are normalized. The major difference between the play and the film is the conclusion of Sandi's storyline. Both genres have Sandi and Lou finally meet at one of Ernesto Martinez's water stations only to find the jugs emptied by Border Patrol bullets, and both have the pair visited by Artemio's ghost. Sandi and Lou find the migrant's bones and ID nearby, but they have nowhere to go and have no idea how to escape the desert. In the play and the film, while making his everyday rounds, Ernesto finds them by the water station. In the play, Sandi survives with Lou, and they become changed people who better empathize with undocumented immigrants and who come to terms with their roles in the social order. Sandi even decides to join Ernesto and become a water warrior. In the film, however, when Ernesto arrives, Lou awakens to find that Sandi has died from dehydration and heat in the night. Ernesto must rip Lou away from the blistered corpse of Sandi. Lou is unhinged by how he did not notice her death while he lay next to her. There is an ease with which death happens in the desert that is hard for Lou to process. Through all this, the viewer knows Artemio's remains are steps away. The play gives a social transformation predicated on meeting with and recovering the dead, but the film presents the surprising banality of death within this borderworld. The dead become commonplace for the characters and the viewer in this space and time.

Ernesto becomes a water warrior because he sees these deaths so often. Without major policy reform, water stations are one of the few ways these deaths are avoided. Policies, in contrast, have been drafted and executed precisely to *instigate* Latinx and migrant death. Whereas Operation Wetback (1954) established xenophobic immigration policy, Operation Gatekeeper (1994) is a more sinister realization of this anti-immigrant sentiment. Caminero-Santangelo reminds us that Operation Gatekeeper and Operation Hold the Line (1993) produce enforcement strategies (as also seen in chapter 1 with Luis Alberto Urrea's *The Devil's Highway*) that drive migrants to take more dangerous routes through the desert. As these policies "took effect, the death toll began to rise sharply."[39] In this way, death has become legalized and constructed into the reality of the border. The film's ending demonstrates that, while death in the borderlands is not hypervisible, it is nevertheless normalized into the landscape and into the everyday life of the United States, manufactured to be unnoticed and ignored. This erasure is strategically constructed as banal, and it shapes the necropolitical social relations that produce and reproduce laws and policies like SB 1070 or Operation Gatekeeper.

The Question of Captivity and Enclosure

While Lou and Sandi's respective captivities awaken their social conscious-ness, the Latinx and migrant workers in "Ladrillos"/"Bricks" in *La Ciudad* are captives sealed off from the city, from legal recourse, and from basic rights, whose labor conditions occlude any possibility of social transformation. In many ways, *La Ciudad* adheres to a strict form of cinematic neorealism whereby its mimetic qualities (re)produce authentic historical representa-tion.[40] "Ladrillos"/"Bricks," in particular, organizes its scenes, cuts, and im-ages to create more than a topical story or character type; it crafts an aesthetic form that wishes to faithfully perform historical and social representation.[41] The short presents structures of captivity and enclosure in both its story and its form. For instance, when the opening cuts of *La Ciudad* leave the photo shop described at the beginning of this chapter, the frame explodes with about twenty men jostling one another on a sidewalk. They shout for work at the passing camera. The camera is so close to what appears to be a small mob— again, the recurring motif of racialized, immigrant "hordes" appears—that it is difficult to see where the crowd begins and ends. During this scene, though, the camera is still strangely removed from the crowd, because the camera is the boss whom the men are begging for work. How the camera becomes an actor within the film, and specifically an actor that is so obviously in a posi-tion of dominance, illustrates José Esteban Muñoz's idea of cinematic auto-ethnography, a form that occurs within documentary-style film, where the camera can be understood only in "colonizer's terms." For Muñoz, this form does not reproduce the binaries of colonizer and colonized but "disrupts the hierarchical economy of colonial images and representations by making vis-ible the presence of subaltern energies and urgencies *in* metropolitan culture." Muñoz sees the camera as taking a hegemonic role that cannot operate with-out its opposite. Continuous shouts of ¡A MI! in this scene puncture *La Ciu-dad's* violin soundtrack, perhaps validating Muñoz's claim that this technique of "metropolitan form" requires the "power of subaltern speech" and "needs the colonial 'other' to function."[42] This scene, however, is not a celebratory dia-lectic; instead, it hyperbolizes the social order at play by making the camera *el jefe*, which immediately subsumes the viewer into the position of both one who feels sympathy as a removed spectator *and* one who is the authoritarian target of this begging. In other words, the film interpellates viewers into this social order, viewers who are always positioned against the subaltern (even if they *are* the subaltern). Alvarado argues that "interpellative performance" does more than ask audiences to reflect on social violence: it has them replicate it.[43] In this sense, the camera and its relation to the eye of the viewer shape the aesthetic and mold it to the political power dynamic, enclosing the viewer, the camera, and the "hordes" into a rather violent and repulsive experience.

The scene moves from this homogenizing, totalizing experience to an image of the actual boss selecting ten Latinx day laborers, promising them fifty dollars per day for unspecified work, and driving them into the middle of a dilapidated nowhere land. When we get to the construction site, it is no more than an old factory with fallen walls of brick covering every square foot of visible land. This destroyed Fordist image lacks any sign of what we might call civilization.[44] This is the waste and ruin of industrialization, the necessary past to the contemporary perks of global capitalist advancement, a history encoded in terms like "civilization." Nevertheless, this ruin contains structures of visibility and invisibility for migrant labor. Saskia Sassen describes the relationship between low-wage immigrant labor and the city as a "mode of incorporation" that "renders these workers invisible, therewith breaking the nexus between being workers in leading industries and the opportunity to become—as had been historically the case in industrialized economies— a 'labor aristocracy' or its contemporary equivalent."[45] The incorporation of an invisible migrant labor force, in other words, shuts down possibilities of social mobility for these workers, reinforcing broader inequality. These incorporations of invisibility operate in tandem with Sassen's more recent ideas on expulsion, a state of existence that comes from extreme systemic concentrations of wealth. Expulsion describes when those at the bottom are removed and displaced from a "life space" through incarceration, labor, and war, while those at the top exit their "responsibilities of membership to a society."[46] I would emphasize that expulsion also constructs a central discourse for anti-immigrant nativism, such as calls for deportation or inhumane immigration policy. Indeed, this expulsion discourse arises when peoples, nations, and corporations are confronted with their violence against those who migrate. In "Ladrillos"/"Bricks," this space of industrial ruin, thus, encloses and incorporates the Latinx and migrant workers into an invisible, veiled labor, hidden within the (global) city, because if there is visibility of their presence or of the economic processes that lead to their deaths, it is often met with discourses of expulsion. This structure is central to understanding the fundamental violence of the political economy. It both incorporates the worker as an economic necessity and excludes the worker from citizenship and rights.

Riker describes the five-year making of *La Ciudad* as attempting to capture the stories and enclosures of "uprooted workers" from "the inside out," through the migrant perspective. For Riker, capitalism produces and reproduces various forms of expulsion and enclosure:

> [A]s a navigating compass, I look at what's happened since 1973 as a process of enclosure very similar to the enclosures at the birth of capitalism 500 years ago in Europe. That is, that it's essential for capitalism to develop [and] to actually produce this uprooted proletariat or working class. And that what we've seen since the mid '70s, on a global level, are new enclosures, which are as important in their consequences as the original ones. . . .
>
> So now in the year 2000 we find ourselves in a world in which a huge percentage of workers are actually an immense distance from their place of origin, from their home. . . .
>
> *La Ciudad* is an attempt to describe not only what it feels like to be one of those immigrants but also what the consequences are, politically, what the consequences will be.[47]

According to Riker, the displacement of workers creates these enclosures, which are not particularly new, although they now have a more entrenched global market logic. For instance, the Bracero Program (1942–1964) nods to these future neoliberal enclosures because its policies ensured a *lack* of state regulation of illegal labor practices, a strategic necropolitics that produced disposable populations. Kitty Calavita maps how the committee in charge of the program contract provided little regulation of the program it created, placing the power of regulation on the farmers and contractors who had called for more workers.[48] So, although this began as an intergovernmental contract, the individual worker contracts eventually were controlled by independent farmers' associations and farm bureaus. This created a wide range of wages and working conditions, since it changed from farm to farm and depended on grower-bracero contracts, which allowed for (1) various forms of labor captivity through the threat of deportation or visa cancellations, (2) a piece-rate system of payment, and (3) contracts for longer or shorter periods of time.[49] While braceros remain essential to the functionality and operations of certain labor industries in the United States, especially farm labor, the enclosures and captivity are now intensified and bureaucratic. Seth M. Holmes looks at the segregation of the farm now, where different labor hierarchies enable ever–more specialized forms of exploitation and necropolitics, with the introduction of managers, supervisors, administrative assistants, and executives. Holmes calls this hierarchal structure "conjugated oppression."[50] The bureaucratic structure allows for those in charge to remain continually removed and absent from those they exploit, while those at the bottom have little to no recourse for rights or demands. *La Ciudad*'s narrative of labor enclosure elucidates how global capitalism needs disposable and captive subjects and produces this social order.

The boss's control in "Ladrillos"/"Bricks," then, is more oblique and comes from holding all the financial cards, a power increased by his absence. For instance, once at the site, the boss changes the verbal contract and tells the workers they will get only fifteen cents per brick that they clean and stack.[51] He then leaves them in the middle of this apocalyptic rubble without water or amenities. In this situation, there appears to be no regulation. The old factory is unstable; the site is obviously not safe; and the men are placed within it as though they have no rights but to hard labor. Unsurprisingly, one of the factory walls collapses on one of the workers, and the other workers attempt to save him, madly digging out his arms. The camera captures only the hands and limbs of both the fallen and the men removing the bricks. They are disembodied parts, incomplete bodies in labor, in death, and in rescue. They are removed from the city and placed in ruin, but more, they are constructed as disposable, disassembled body parts, whose wholeness the camera negates. Once dug out, the crushed man is barely breathing, and another calls out "Yo llevo un ambulancia," but there are no phones nearby, no cars, and no ability to contact "civilization." The fallen worker inevitably dies, while the rest can do nothing but go back to work. The dead subject is the same man we see getting his portrait taken at the beginning of the film. His death works as a striking and poignant symbol of the many lacks that structure this labor: lack of a boss, lack of recourse, lack of phones or ambulances, and the lack of humanity in this political economy. This scene elucidates how migrant Latinx labor is placed into various structures of social, slow, and symbolic death. The switched contract, the collapsed geography, the incorporation into an exploitative labor market, and the exclusion from so-called civilization while cleaning up its waste all produce layers of invisibility and absence, showing the viewer how death becomes part of the job.

Slow Death: A Critical Interlude

La Ciudad asks us to think about the relationship between migrant labor and death, both in reality and in narrative. First, migrant labor, especially undocumented workers, fulfill the capitalist desire for cheap labor socially and historically, reinforcing the uneven distributions of wealth, establishing livelihood for those profiting from these workers, and rendering workers disposable. According to Jean Baudrillard, this relationship between labor and death is one of slow death, where "labour power is instituted on death," where laborers undergo "slow death," meaning workers live in a state of "death deferred," in which their lives are worthy only through their labor.[52] Baudrillard understands that production and labor power have significant material and symbolic involvement in life and death, but economics regularly masks these real structures of power.[53] Slow death, or death deferred, also describes what Lauren Berlant defines as the "condition of being worn out by the activity of reproducing life."[54] For Berlant, slow death permeates the ordinary lives of persons of certain populations, rather than purely the life of the worker.[55] In effect, slow death is the maintenance of docile bodies and the status quo, but for Baudrillard, this docility is deeply tied to an economic system that requires workers to ultimately convert "death into a wage."[56] The workers of *La Ciudad* return to work after the death of a fellow migrant because not even death can interrupt the advancement of global capitalism.

Second, in parallel, there is a narrative and textual equivalency to this social and historical experience that Baudrillard calls "hyperrealism." Baudrillard understands realism (and its aesthetic offspring surrealism, irrealism, and neorealism) as establishing a process that destroys our ability to distinguish an object from a representation of an object. Reality is recycled and reproduced through commodity forms ad nauseam, commodities that ultimately swallow all our knowledge about what is real. Like the workers whose activity is to reproduce the life of production as their own lives slowly drain, reality too is drained by its narrative reproduction. Realism, then, defines the beginnings of a slippage between the real and the imaginary.[57] "Hyperrealism" simply describes a more advanced stage of this line's effacement, a stage wherein fictional narratives and imaginaries are no longer separate from reality, and vice versa. To call this a sort of death is to identify the problematic relationship between reality and fiction under global capitalism. Notably, "hyperrealism" does not describe naïve realism but a larger culture industry phenomenon. In terms of the film industry, Bill Nichols reminds us that documentary-style realism closes the metaphorical relationship between film and historical reality and instead opens a more metonymic representation of reality. By this, Nichols distinguishes between the cinematic illusion that realist film resembles the world and an aesthetic form that puts the actors, filmmakers, and viewers on the same plane of this historical reality.[58] Reality and narrative thus operate in tandem. *La Ciudad* reveals this reality while also being shaped by it, meaning the death of the migrant worker functions as a metonymic device for these greater economic and cultural processes that produce and reproduce various forms of social and slow death.

Third, the structural invisibility and disposability of the racialized labor force exposes an interplay between free-market economy and state politics. When the US government calls for a border wall, performs violent security practices, and lauds patriotism in the name of citizen "life," it simultaneously supports economic policies that boost migration and capitalist globalization, such as the Caribbean Basin Initiative, NAFTA, CAFTA–DR, and the maquila system. These government-backed economic programs work overtly, sometimes through a lack of regulation, and are often countered by hypervisible policies that wish to impede migration. There is a historical resonance here, too. For instance, during the height of the Bracero Program, the United States initiated Operation Wetback, which aimed to stop the illegal immigration that the Bracero Program had instigated. Operation Wetback appeared to counter the Bracero Program, but because of Operation Wetback, the Bracero Program implemented harsher forms of captivity: new legislation to stop illegal immigration *by law* bound braceros to given crops and employers, and for this reason some have seen the program as a form of legalized slavery; braceros were not free agents.[59] Calavita relates that the Bracero Program was not demonstrative of economic citizens' puppeteering the state but instead showed a "rocky alliance" between state agencies', growers', and ranchers' interests to deal with the fine line between legal/illegal and to maintain economic interests that I am inclined to describe as reproducing the life of capital.[60] Life is tied not to the human but to labor and commodity production. This reproduction is at the expense of workers, who undergo various forms of death. Free-market economy and nation-state policy align on this front.[61]

There is a seemingly deep contradiction here: states are codifying their lack of presence in migrant labor economies by handing over contracts to employers and corporate bureaucracies, even while they are the administrative centers for responding to xenophobic discourse, drafting international treaties, and instigating immigration policies. This logic of contradiction returns us to González's ideas on social realism, specifically that these narratives explicitly employ formal contradiction. González unravels how Chicanx writers "reveal via their contradictory ideological positions the class contradictions implicit in the politics they critique and the losses they lament."[62] These class contradictions also function as a way to enslave laborers as living dead. In a similar vein, Gad Guterman suggests that narrative form, specifically performance, "manages contradictions," but for Guterman these contradictions are not caused by the critical division between identity politics and social class proposed by González. Instead, this condition of contradiction is "caused by legal nonexistence" for migrant subjects.[63] Lisa Marie Cacho describes this legal condition as a form of racial criminalization and social death: "If undocumented workers exercise their few legal rights to report workplace and labor violations, they also put themselves at risk for incarceration and deportation. [. . .] Undocumented labor enables corporations to bypass labor and antidiscrimination laws as well as health and safety regulations." Without legal recourse, migrant labor is vulnerable, but Cacho emphasizes that this contradictory condition exists *because* US law ensures this rightlessness.[64] I must add that the contradictions are implicit precisely because the political economy operates through the varying forms of absence that are necessary for maintaining the social order.

Nevertheless, I am wary of continuing to call this relationship between the nation-state and the neoliberal economy a "contradiction" because these two processes often require each other in order to work. The strategic interplay here makes certain features of migration and labor visible; others, invisible. Berlant identifies how the critical "melodrama" of "crisis" shapes what we see about a given event in that it follows the "logic of visible effectuality, bourgeois dramatics, and lifelong accumulation or fashioning." But crisis also distracts us from the "fact of life" for many disposable populations that takes place in the banal, normative, and deemphasized spaces of the ordinary.[65] Slow death, Berlant warns, has been normalized, and crisis discourse misrepresents this "political administration of life":

> Often when scholars and activists apprehend the phenomenon of slow death in long-term conditions of privation they choose to misrepresent the duration and scale of the situation by calling a crisis that which is a fact of life and has been a defining fact of life for a given population that lives it as a fact in ordinary time. (Etymologically, crisis denotes a crisis in judgment, which is to say that at the heart of a crisis-claim is not the quality of the object in question but the condition of a spectatorial mind.) Of course this deployment of crisis is often explicitly and intentionally a redefinitional tactic, a distorting or misdirecting gesture that aspires to make an environmental phenomenon appear suddenly as an event because as a structural or predictable condition it has not engendered the kinds of historic action we associate with the heroic agency a crisis seems already to have called for.[66]

By calling slow death a "fact of life" for disposable populations, Berlant emphasizes the structural conditions at play here. Crisis is a hypervisible "gesture" and "tactic" that ignores these long-term, historical, and systemic features of the political economy and misdirects our gaze from the necropolitics of our everyday lives. *La Ciudad* does not allow migrant death to be a crisis event, where ambulances come and mourning occurs. Instead, the film's narrative takes part in the very social realities it exists in, and everyone simply goes back to work.

The Allegory of Death and Latinx Speculative Realisms

The hyperreal does not necessarily connote a total erasure of reality; instead, it signals an absence or a trace of the real within the narratives, objects, and/ or art pieces. Garrett Stewart in his consideration of photorealism and the rise in 3-D art claims that new object art "advertises a technological grounding in some photographic original" but one that is always potentially "photoshopped" out or saturated beyond recognition. Stewart argues that this form of hyperrealism hinges on the *potential* that elements of the original— "extraneous and disenchanting stain, blot, excess, technical recess"—may remain. As a result, the original is always "haunting canvas after canvas."[67] Baudrillard argues that, through reproductive media (such as film, photography, and literature), hyperrealism becomes an "allegory of death" reducing the real to a fetish for something lost, where it is "no longer an object of representation, but ecstasy of denegation and of its own ritual extermination."[68] Being able to see this denegation means the real is discernible enough for us to perceive its slow demise. By calling this a "haunting," Stewart directs our attention to how hyperrealism and the allegory of death grow out of the same predication of absence that González identifies in Chicanx realisms or the photographic trace of the dead migrant worker that opens and closes *La Ciudad* or the transformative possibilities of ghosts in *Detained in the Desert*. Alex Rivera's *Sleep Dealer* also employs ghosts of a sort, albeit in a much less fantastic way than *Detained in the Desert*, and the film's hauntings enact Berlant's call for a critical gaze that sees the historical and normative structures of social and slow death.

Sleep Dealer's protagonist, Memo Cruz, and the military drone pilot Rudy Ramirez are haunted throughout the film by their memories of Memo's father. Memo comes from a farming community that thrived until the Del Rio Water Corporation—a Coca-Cola–like entity that utilizes US military resources— secures the water rights, dams the river, and causes the entire ecosystem to become a desert. Memo's father, who has farmland, maintains a milpa and must buy water from the corporation's heavily fortified dam. Memo, who wants to be a hacker instead of a farmer, despises this life and spends all his extra time building and playing with a satellite receiver. When he hacks into a private US military line, he is marked as a terrorist. The US military proceeds to trace and bomb his house, using a remote-controlled drone (operated by

Rudy). Memo's hard-working, innocent father is brutally murdered. Without the patriarch to run the farm, Memo migrates to Tijuana to make money for his family by becoming a node worker in the virtual reality factories called infomaquilas or "sleep dealers." Memo's experiences as a node worker on the border intertwine with memories and flashbacks of his father, the milpa, and the dam. Rudy also cannot forget his final eye contact with Memo's father before killing him, a memory that haunts him until he leaves the United States to find Memo and seek redemption. Through a series of connections, both virtual and real, Memo and Rudy eventually meet and join forces to bomb the dam, forever connected by these hauntings.

The ghosts of memory that spur Memo and Rudy forward contrast with the futuristic cultural phenomenon of selling memories through the online consumer platform TruNode. The character Luz, Memo's love interest, sells her memories of Memo to Rudy. For Luz, TruNode is work similar to being a writer, even while it monitors her truthfulness in retelling her testimonios and regulates her creative liberties to ensure the memories are "real." The program, with its requirements and enforcement of an ostensibly authentic and truthful composition, presents a world where naïve realism is an unquestionable and uncomplicated possibility. Amy Sara Carroll describes TruNode as "cyber-circuits of betrayal, an arena in which creativity is evacuated from process" because it "corrects text on the basis of affect, demanding transparent truths, a facsimile of documentary."[69] These traces of memory, in the film, are commodities that can be substituted for the so-called real according to this memory market. In many ways, the platform appropriates Luz's creative power as a producer or author of this content and, as a result, sells these memories as a (theoretically) untainted thing for consumers. For Baudrillard, the allegory of death describes capitalism's uncoupling of one's production from consumption.[70] These memories and hauntings become commodity dreamworlds for the global north to consume.

This consumerism requires and lauds what Baudrillard and Berlant describe as the slow death of the producer or the worker, who are always removed and/or kept at a distance.[71] *Sleep Dealer* imagines a near future or a future history wherein slow death and labor are inextricable. Memo's and Rudy's labor occurs through corporeal nodes that operate distant robotics. Because the nodes are implanted into the circulatory system and access the laborer's DNA, being hooked up can lead to a worker's dying from electrocution or eventually going blind. The node work causes Memo to lose his grasp on reality at times and to slip into his memories, especially when he overclocks his labor. This always results in the sleep dealer computer docking his pay for his momentary inactivity. Memo's production is both completely removed from

Plate 1. *Interstate Pedestrians*, by Don Bartletti. Published August 21, 1990. © 1990 *Los Angeles Times*; used with permission.

Plate 2. *Too Hungry to Knock*, by Don Bartletti. Published June 18, 1992. © 1992 *Los Angeles Times*; used with permission.

Plate 3. *Filial Devotion*, by Don Bartletti (1992). © 1992 by Don Bartletti.

Plate 4. *Shivering*, by Don Bartletti. Published October 4, 2002. © 2002 *Los Angeles Times*; used with permission.

Plate 5. *Simple Pleasure*, by Don Bartletti. Published October 4, 2002. © 2002 *Los Angeles Times*; used with permission.

Plate 6. *Border Monument No. 184.* In David Taylor, *Working the Line.* © 2010; courtesy of Radius Books.

Plate 7. *U.S.-Mexico Border, Looking east toward El Paso/Juárez.* In David Taylor, *Working the Line.* © 2010; courtesy of Radius Books.

Plate 8. *Drag, New Mexico.* In David Taylor, *Working the Line.* © 2010; courtesy of Radius Books.

Plate 9. *Office Work (Shared Desk), Texas.* In David Taylor, *Working the Line.* © 2010; courtesy of Radius Books.

Plate 10. Camera 169, Juan Carlos (29). Camera distributed in Agua Prieta. From *BorderFilm Project* (2007).

Plate 11. Camera 501, Eduardo (33). Camera distributed in Chihuahua. From *Border FilmProject* (2007).

Plate 12. Camera 10, Wayne (55). Camera distributed in New Mexico. From *Border Film Project* (2007).

Plate 13. Camera 51, Tim (39). Camera distributed in Twin Peaks, California. From *BorderFilm Project* (2007).

Plate 14. "El Muerto versus El Cucuy." From *Comics!* by Javier Hernandez. ©
2013 Javier Hernandez; courtesy of Javier Hernandez.

Plate 15. "El Muerto in 'The Ghost Pirate!'" written and illustrated by Michael Aushenker. From *El Muerto, the Aztec Zombie*, by Javier Hernandez. "The Ghost Pirate" © 2002 Michael Aushenker; courtesy of Javier Hernandez.

Plate 16. *Mr. Elastic—Sergio Garcia*, by Dulce Pinzón (2012).

Plate 17. *Captain America—Roy Acosta*, by Dulce Pinzón (2012).

Plate 18. *Catwoman—Minerva Valencia*, by Dulce Pinzón (2012).

the systems of consumption that profit from his labor, and this production is quite literally slowly killing him. The film's virtual labor, Javier Duran reminds us, is a form of borderization, a "biopolitical, technologically propelled act that mediates between the 'developed' north and the 'poor' south," that both "affects the ability to remember" and turns "the past into a commodity."[72] This virtual labor is removed, taking place through robots in the United States performing construction, nannying, and service work, while simultaneously, this labor causes Memo's gradual biological failure. Memo's virtual alienation from his production satirically does not negate the material consequences of his labor. His slow death is hypervisible through the technological medium of his labor. According to Duran, the film visualizes movement between reality and the virtual, so the viewer sees the blue neural fluid that Memo embodies every time he connects, crosses, and envisions the "versions of mnemonic experience" that Luz undergoes while she selects images to "create the virtual stories" in TruNode.[73] I see this less as a border crossing between the real and the virtual, however, and more as the virtual becoming entangled with and inseparable from the real, especially since the characters' virtual labor directly alters and exhausts their biology, bodies, and emotions. Furthermore, this entanglement reinforces the increasingly ubiquitous market logic in our everyday lives. Whereas the milpa represented an ever-expanding future for Memo's father, node work is instead the ever-enclosing present of global capitalism for Memo, wherein slow death is the only possibility for a wage.

According to Sarah Ann Wells, "*Sleep Dealer* has had a relatively long afterlife for a science fiction world whose contours are increasingly mimetic realism: a world of drones and militarized video games, of increasingly patrolled borders in the name of neoliberalism."[74] For Wells, this timelessness of the film disrupts the future as something beyond our presents or pasts; instead, "the future it imagines is designed to reflect upon a *longue durée* of violence."[75] We may call this "speculative realism" in that the science fiction and speculative fiction of the film show us more about the present and history than about future possibility. By calling this "speculative realism," I do not mean to invoke the philosophical movement of the same name per se.[76] I use this term to allude to what Saldívar describes as fictions that link "fantasy, history, and the imaginary" to interrogate social hierarchies and social justice. I, however, do not see these fictions producing "alternative" understandings of the "contemporary world."[77] Instead, *La Ciudad*'s speculative realism is neither a reflection on nor an alternative imaginary to this "*longue durée* of violence"; it is *a product of* these pasts and presents that shape migrant labor. The historical function of speculative realism parses both the visible and the invisible processes that produce these violent entanglements of the virtual and the real. Baudrillard proposes that the *longue durée* of slow death follows the "genealogy of the slave."[78] As I mapped in the introduction, Mbembe also sees necropolitics as growing from these histories and conditions of slavery, wherein "slave existence appears as a perfect figure of a shadow."[79] "Shadow" alludes to a Platonic allegorical enclosure where a shadow is but an impression of the real; but part of what makes shadows so important when we draw on these genealogies of the slave is how they describe a state of existence for those deemed disposable commodities. This state of (non)existence is one of enclosure and captivity: Baudrillard's hyperrealism must "lock the real up in pure repetition."[80] In parallel, Mbembe's slave is in a "state of exception" and a "state of siege" where the slave symbolically undergoes a "sealing off" and no longer exists "except as a mere tool and instrument of production."[81] These descriptions of captivity—"lock up" and "seal off"—describe enclosures that strip certain populations of life and existence.

For Latinx cinema, the colonial and neocolonial pasts and presents of the Americas inform these narratives of violence and captivity that shape many of our stories and existences. A. Gabriel Meléndez describes Chicanx cinematic realism as drawing from these historical shadows, where the film "remains a window onto a history of livelihoods that today are the stuff of memory." For Meléndez, this is not a nostalgic or distant recall but an element of a film's veracity.[82] His ideas on documentary and (auto)ethnographic cinema arrive at the question of direct cinema, research filming, and observational cinema. He argues that these methods of *cinema verité* produce a "(re)witnessing of occurrences that have long faded from individual memory," a (screening experience that does not simply verify lived experience but asks us to ruminate on shared experience with our "third eye."[83] As a result, the audience partakes in these constructs of realism. If these realisms are allegories of death, they give form to the spaces, times, and subjectivities that occupy the shadows. Machado Sáez argues that postcolonial, diasporic realist fiction "forms a part of a recuperating-silenced-histories approach," and these narratives must partake in an ethical historical revisionism that recenters excluded, peripheral, and muted experiences, events, and subjectivities into the fabric of the political economy.[84] When these are Latinx speculative realisms, the conditions of the past and present rush into the future imaginary as well.

Openings and Closings of Possibility

These narratives reveal the slippages between what is visible and what is invisible, between what is a part of the national conscious and unconscious, and between who gets to live and who must die within the economic order. While

I more fully explore the question of possibility and resistance in the next chapter, I would like to end this chapter by considering how these films and performances produce openings for possibilities that close in on themselves. All three imagine ways of counteracting the violence and structures of death that pervade their narratives, but these counteractions never seem to fully operate against the structures that enclose them. *Detained in the Desert* relies on the socially transformative visitations of ghosts, but Artemio's ghost is a product of the very forms of violence that Sandi and Lou have had the privilege to ignore until they are confronted with their own deaths. The fact that they must come in contact with the dead to transform is slightly off-putting. *Sleep Dealer* brings Memo, Rudy, and Luz together to blow up the dam that has stolen Memo's family's future. Rudy plugs in and uses his body to hack into the security drones operated by his former military corporation and bomb the dam. The bombing of the dam envisions a revolutionary response to the abjection and subjection of Latinx and Latin American peoples under global capitalism, even while it uses the same means of production—the body—to achieve this end. More, this revolutionary act does not open the possibility of returning home for Memo. Instead, Memo stays in Tijuana, and the ending shot pans out to show him growing a new milpa next to the weaponized border wall. *La Ciudad* offers perhaps the most troubling imagination of resistance that closes in on itself. In the final vignette of the collection, "Costurera"/"Seamstress," the workers stop all work, performing a symbolic and immediate death of production. I consider this short more closely in the coming paragraphs, as it attempts to disrupt slow death through forms of sacrifice and martyrdom.

Mbembe describes invisibility in two ways. On the one hand, it's the brutal and orchestrated forms of "conquer-and-annex" that deprived peoples of income or enact a "sealing off."[85] On the other hand, it is the suicide bomber whose body must operate as a "mask" for "invisible" and "soon-to-be detonated" weapons.[86] Mbembe shows us the two-headed monster of this political economy: the absolute brutality of slow death, social death, and literal death inherent to necropolitics and a system of martyrdom and resistance that only reproduces it. The suicide bomber is a problematic figure here. A person who willingly sacrifices their own body to perform acts of mass violence is a clear ethical challenge from a humanist perspective, but as Jasbir Puar argues, this figure embodies the deteriorating and decomposing nations and peoples who have been deemed unworthy of life by the world order.[87] Mbembe does not linger on this figure, but he explores how self-sacrifice gives the body value and power because it is a "process of abstraction," a "sign of the future," and a "supremacy in which the subject overcomes his own mortality."[88] Puar also describes the suicide bomber as indicative of a politics of death, where the body is a "queer modality," a "pastiche of oddities," and an "assemblage of organic [flesh] and inorganic [metal]" that produces death of both self and other.[89] Neither Mbembe nor Puar celebrates the suicide bomber, but both make sense of the way the body is both disruptive and eruptive. Baudrillard also maintains that there are only two positions for the laborer under capitalism, the slow death of labor and the immediate death of sacrifice; we are irrevocably living and dying in the abjection of the former.[90] For Baudrillard, the only opposition to an economy sustained by death deferred is through sacrificial immediate death, a disruption to an economy that needs slow death. Imagining resistance to slow death often relies on and reproduces the same economic structures that produce the living dead.

La Ciudad's last vignette, "Costurera"/"Seamstress" enacts this tenuous interplay between slow death and sacrificial death. It centers around the Fordist corollary of the sweatshop. From the fallen, post-apocalyptic ruin of Fordist factories in the beginning of the film, the last vignette revives the factory as an ongoing model of illegal labor practices.[91] With at least thirty women sewing in rows and a handful of men ironing in the back with billows of steam obscuring the windows, the sweatshop looks cramped among the yards of fabric and steam in an approximately three-hundred-square-foot brick-walled space.[92] The short tells the story of a young woman, Ana, who sews clothing for the ready-to-wear stores of New York City. A Chinese couple run the shop. By casting Chinese bosses with solely Latino workers, Riker's sweatshop demonstrates a multi-migrant process where Latinos perform the hard labor and the Chinese find themselves one notch above as the managerial overseers. The stereotype of Chinese bosses speaks to the way that the sweatshop encapsulates these global exchanges and keeps them hierarchical. At one moment, an unidentifiable white woman briefly enters as the commanding figure of the whole process, but she talks only to the Chinese bosses and barely glances at the workers. The bosses refuse to pay the workers until the job is done and fire workers for small mistakes, a practice that Ana docilely chooses to overlook at first when talking with the other ladies: "no me meta en esto." This top-down representation strategically racializes these tiers of class, while the principal boss remains absent: consumers and their desires for cheaper apparel. Instead of seeing the centrality of consumption in this space, the viewer is distracted by interracial rivalry, a long-standing discourse and practice in which the white hegemony pits racialized and migrant groups against one another.[93] How consumption drives this narrative and yet is invisible within it demonstrates a deep problem with how labor becomes separated from its products, a problem that becomes even more actualized in the futuristic world of *Sleep Dealer*. My reading gestures to Marx's idea of the "hidden abode of production," further emphasizing how these class disparities—producers of product, management of labor, subcontractors of the product or the labor (or both), consumers of the product—separate and often conceal these processes from each other.[94]

When Ana finds out her daughter is ill back home, she begins a desperate search for four hundred dollars that she needs to send back home quickly. In final desperation, Ana refuses to work without being paid immediately. What results from this refusal is the Chinese man's continuously prodding and shoving her shoulders while shouting "¡Trabajo!" He tells her to get out when she continues her tearful begging. In response to being fired, she hugs and holds on to the commercial sewing machine. This action exposes her corporeal dependency on the labor of sewing; her only protest is to lock her body around the machine that she works on. The machine is no longer a source of income since she has not been paid in weeks. Instead, the machine is an extension of her body. To think of Ana and the sewing machine as being extensions of each other is to put Ana's body into a troubling position.[95] This scene also interpellates viewers into this troubling position as our eyes become appendages of the camera machine. Nevertheless, the relationship between the body and the machine tells us something about this protest. By turning off the machine, Ana turns off her own body. In this sense, both are made dead. If the machine is not working, neither is Ana. If Ana refuses to work, so must the machine. Ana's protest, however, goes beyond this metaphor because it produces a bigger revolutionary imaginary. Everyone in the sweatshop stops working. All noise stops. All machines and bodies die. This silent protest is a social mobilization that is possible only through the violence of globalization. This moment is the antithesis of action or of living; it is precisely nonaction. This scene demonstrates a troubling juxtaposition wherein the nonactive, dead body actually does more political work than an active, living body.[96] For Arrizón, the power of performance is in mimetic representation that tells us something about subject formation and self-representation.[97] But *La Ciudad* disallows this performance of nonaction to be about Ana's sense of self. Instead, this scene figures Ana within a larger *social* paradox. Ana represents the way the living dead are not simply the result of the exploitative political economy but also the possibility for mobilization against this exploitation. Death takes on a dual meaning here: it is the violent structure and effect of the political economy, and it is also the disruption to this violence.

The conclusion to this protest is never given. We are left without any clue to whether or not the refusal to work *actually works*. Dalleo and Machado Sáez argue that realism disrupts the utopian vision that "the struggle will end or that [an anticolonial] goal will be achieved." Instead, it organizes a politics around the idea that there may be no *telos*.[98] However, when the narrative is about labor, the lack of a strike's ending means that no commodities are being produced ad infinitum. The nonworking body halts both commodity production and the narrative. There is a power in this (non)act. This silent resistance, nevertheless, seems to be the only answer for the film's ending, a passé light of hope in a rather brutally ominous film. As the camera zooms out from this moment, our gaze falls on the window of an old industrial building with many more windows, bringing us back to the urban and global city that both encloses and expels these migrant workers into various structures of death.

Baudrillard would not read the ending of "Costurera"/"Seamstress" as a form of resistance at all. For Baudrillard, resistance to the economy of exchange "is not free time, or non-labour, it is sacrifice" because "every death and all violence that escapes the State monopoly is subversive."[99] Nevertheless, from a narrative perspective, the immediate shutting off of the body opens up an imagination for alternative possibility, even while it reproduces other forms of death. If the new enclosures of global capitalism compel exploited subjects to construct "alternative perspectives toward time, work, and self," as Mbembe argues, then we need to think together the destructive and the constructive. For David Harvey, revolutionary and transformative shifts under global capitalism require these two forces. He argues that the circulation of variable capital "operates as a constructive/destructive force" on bodies in the workplace and the consumption sphere.[100] Harvey asks,

> If, for example, workers are transformed, as Marx suggests in *Capital*, into appendages of capital in both the work place and the consumption sphere (or, as Foucault prefers it, bodies are made over into *docile bodies* by the rise of a powerful disciplinary apparatus, from the eighteenth century onwards) then how can their bodies be a measure, sign, or receiver of anything outside of the circulation of capital or of the various mechanisms that discipline them? Or, to take a more contemporary version of the same argument, if we are all now cyborgs (as Haraway in her celebrated manifesto on the topic suggests), then how can we measure anything outside of that deadly embrace of the machine as extension of our own body and body as extension of the machine?[101]

Harvey further argues that these occlusions often and incorrectly paint bodies as "passive entities occupying particular performative economic roles," but actually, this slow death can lend itself to "transformative processes" that allow for "resistance, desire for reform, rebellion, and revolution."[102] If Ana's body is an extension of her sewing machine, her "deadly embrace" may reduce her to another "passive entity," but the film's refusal to give *telos* to her refusal to labor opens up the possibilities of the narrative to continue and turn ad infinitum, at least within the audience's or reader's imagination. While this non-ending may nod back to Baudrillard's concept of the hyperrealism that forever reproduces, it also establishes a speculative force only available through the constructive/destructive forms of narrative-making.

If these cinematic and theatrical borderworlds of López, Riker, and Rivera are realisms, then these narratives perform the visible and invisible conditions that Latinx subjectivity embodies. Latinx realisms reside in the gaps of history, interrogate the political discourses and governances that enact violence and death, and sacrifice themselves to the overt economics that subsume our ethno-racialized bodies. To understand this through constructive and destructive forms of narrative-making is to identify an interplay between the imaginary and the real that shapes Latinx narratives. Realism in this sense does not negate vulgar mimesis or the aims and desires of authentic documentary, nor does it per se occlude imagination, myth, or magic. Instead, it forces us to consider these forms and attempts at reflecting and representing the social, historical, and political as a part of a bigger conversation about lived experience, storytelling, and imaginations of social conditions and social possibilities.

I end, then, on the real and the imaginary. González and Saldívar understand Chicanx realisms to intersect these two modes of world-making. For Saldívar in particular, Chicanx narrative realism requires nonunitary and differential narrative form in order to represent and bring to light the complexities of the social order.[103] I extend these ideas into intersecting Latinx subject formations, as well, because they productively complicate the narratives of borders, migration, and US policymaking. Differential narrative form becomes the only way to capture different Latinx experiences, constructs, and so-called realities. Further, these narratives ultimately open up the possibility to challenge the structures that enclose these realities. Baudrillard, on the other hand, sees the imaginary as subsuming reality. For Baudrillard, narrative artifacts or objects can only reproduce reality endlessly, rendering it into a commodity that only fetishizes our experiences and realities. Baudrillard states, "Today, where the real and the imaginary are intermixed in one and the same operational totality, aesthetic fascination reigns supreme: with subliminal perception (a sort of sixth sense) of special effects, editing and script, reality is overexposed to the glare of models."[104] While the real and the imaginary are deeply opposed from a political perspective, I would argue that the cinematic borderworlds of *Detained in the Desert*, *La Ciudad*, and *Sleep Dealer* demonstrate that these are two ends of the same struggle. These narratives find themselves torn between the desire to recognize and challenge the social order and the structural reproduction(s) of these social relations.

PART II

IMAGINING THE LIVING DEAD

CHAPTER 4

Markets of Resurrection: Cat Ghosts, Aztec Zombies, and the Living Dead Economy

Judith Ortiz Cofer begins her short story–memoir "Talking to the Dead" by defining two forms of clairvoyance: "*Santería*, like voodoo, has its roots in African blood rites, which its devotees practice with great fervor. *Espiritismo*, on the other hand, entered the island via the middle classes who had discovered it flourishing in Europe during the so-called 'crisis of faith' of the late nineteenth century."[1] We can see a racial and class difference between these two forms of talking to the dead, and this disparity matters in the narrative because, as we learn, "refined matrons" prefer to see Ortiz Cofer's grandfather, who is a Mesa Blanca spiritist, instead of the "rowdy *santeros*" who practice only "spectacle."[2] Here, European middle-class magic and clairvoyance are more sophisticated and civilized, whereas African-derived magic and clairvoyance are vulgar and purely for capital gain. This racialization and economization of Santería recalls Cornejo Villavicencio's experience with Vodou as discussed in chapter 1, where the line between Haitian healing culture and notarios looking for quick money blurs. I begin this chapter with Ortiz Cofer's story because it sets up a tension between Latinx cultures of death and the free-market economy. Specifically, the story highlights how the figures of death, embedded in acts of clairvoyance, assemble slippages between an economy that desires exploitation and the cultural expressions that sometimes challenge and sometimes reproduce this violence.

This chapter argues that constructs of death expose an interplay where Latinx bodies are both in line with and disruptive to market violence. First, I briefly examine Ortiz Cofer's story, which presents a broader picture of this ambivalence and upsets the ideas of freedom in the market, and then I turn to Francisco Goldman's *The Ordinary Seaman*, where I consider how the novel negotiates immigration processes, labor captivity, and resistance. The relatively hopeful endings of Ortiz Cofer's story and Goldman's novel produce a cultural politics of possibility around death primarily because they show the power of resurrection. The idea of resurrecting the dead leads me to Javier Hernandez's *El Muerto: The Aztec Zombie* and its film adaptation, *The Dead One*, which play with the historical and cultural power of zombies but also show how the market subsumes this power through consumption. These narratives produce tensions around death and resurrection where the Latinx, migrant body is a site of exploitation and social death but simultaneously a vehicle for potential revolutionary acts. Following a significant thread sewn into each narrative, I end the chapter on questions of sexuality, gender, and futurity in which these stories complicate what it means to have what I call a "dead future." Figures of death show us the invisible violence of the economy but also offer us moments of future possibility within this violence. While this possibility is often subsumed back into the market, especially in the case of our Aztec zombie, the dead or living dead body lays bare these recursive processes.

The three narratives I explore in this chapter are all Latinx in the sense that they depict what it means to come to the United States from south of the border and/or to live and die in the United States as ethno-racialized subjects. Nevertheless, they offer vastly different perspectives, experiences, and cultural politics, from Puerto Rico to Central America to Mexico. Ortiz Cofer's short story primarily remembers her abuelo's romantic, spiritual, and artistic approach to the world in Homigueros, Puerto Rico, and she traces her grandparents' relationship conflicts. The story spotlights a moment in her family's history when her uncle gets a free ticket to work on a farm in the northeastern United States and becomes lost and held captive within imperial structures of labor captivity. The story centers on how her abuelito's visions and conversations with the dead ultimately locate his son and save him. Negotiating questions of culture and economy, the story demonstrates how death shapes the Puerto Rican experience on multiple levels: as Spanish colonial legacy, as African-derived spirituality, as the social death of labor, and as reclamation of the lost. Goldman's *The Ordinary Seaman* constructs a fictional account of fifteen undocumented migrant workers from Central America who are shipped and held captive on the Brooklyn docks, under instructions to fix a freight ship called the *Urus*. The novel tells of the men's plight, and it ends on an ambivalent note, where the men either succumb to a political economy that exploits and kills them or find power in their social death. Javier Hernandez's *El Muerto: The Aztec Zombie* comics and film adaptation, *The Dead One*, tells the story of Diego de la Muerte, who becomes a superhero Aztec zombie after an encounter with the Aztec gods of death (Mictlantecuhtli) and destiny (Tezcatlipoca). Following comic book conventions, El Muerto fights many villains and monsters, and I am particularly interested in Hernandez's use of Diego's superpowers to sell Mexican churros in faux advertisements for a fake corporation. The genre trope of the comic advertisement demonstrates a subsumption of history and empowerment into the market. All three of these narratives reveal varying levels of market violence on Latinx bodies, capturing the structures of social death and necropolitics at play. Simultaneously, they also lay the ground for a politics of possibility within these constructs of death. As such, they reveal an interplay in which Latinx bodies both advance and challenge market violence. On one hand, death embodies economic processes that strip these migrants, captives, and commodified bodies of power, while on the other hand, certain forms of resurrection offer the possibility for resistance, humanization, and subversion: visions from the underworld for Ortiz Cofer, cat ghosts for Goldman, and Aztec zombies for Hernandez. Together, then, they show us the ambivalent push-and-pull of market violence.

My readings in this chapter are entangled with theories of social death. In particular, I am interested in theories of social death that engage with the conditions of a racialized im/migrant labor force and consider what it means to be legally rightless. Under these ideas, racialized im/migrant labor is both inside and outside state juridical systems, both hypermobile in the global economy yet contained in various states of captivity. When Lisa Marie Cacho considers social death for Latinx im/migrant labor, she describes paradoxes and states of exception that play out through law and rights. This politics of death, often produced through multiple borders, is not divorced from economic concerns as John D Márquez wishes. Márquez believes "dead workers" cannot be exploited because they are in effect dead.[3] However, in this chapter I consider how the dead can undergo forms of resurrection, whether through necromarketing or in states of death deferred and death-in-life. Often, these figures of death in contemporary American literature represent the socially destructive forces of specific economic processes that necessitate a rising from the dead and a logic of revenge.[4] Ghosts and zombies, for example, provide a socioeconomic critique of the inherent violence of a market economy. Death and the living dead in these cultural productions also allow for imagining possibility, celebration, and revolution. While this possibility is often unable to truly counter state and market violence in these Latinx narratives, it leaves behind not decomposing subjects and bodies but continuously resurrected ones.

Visions from the Dead and the "Freeing" of Labor

In the case of "Talking to the Dead," Ortiz Cofer gives us a story about how clairvoyance, a source of both income and culture, mends her grandparents' relationship and saves her uncle from labor captivity in the United States. This Puerto Rican family is caught between their indigenous, African, and colonial legacies and their current subjugated situation in a US commonwealth. The first part of "Talking to the Dead" unravels the grandmother's practical, skeptical, frustrated view of her husband's spiritual visions with the invisible and the otherworldly, and she regularly takes these frustrations out on her husband. The abuela is reacting to her husband's lack of financial sense in his practices. The narrator-author relates that her abuela finds her abuelo's poetry writing and visions as "the thing that kept him from making a fortune."[5] Her grandmother's ideas and expectations of success are built around capitalist participation, and the grandfather's romantic and spiritual practices are seemingly antithetical to these economic concerns. The narrator-author describes her abuelo's reaction to her abuela's mistreatment: "He could have rebelled against the situation: in Puerto Rican society, the man is considered a small-letter god in his home. But, Papá, a gentle, scholarly man, preferred a laissez-faire approach."[6] The narrator-author describes her grandfather's decision to be a spiritist as anti-patriarchal, which is also a source of frustration for her grandmother. Nevertheless, to describe his cultural and economic practices as laissez-faire is a significant choice of terms for this positionality. "Laissez-faire" does not immediately connote clairvoyance or its role in constructing Ortiz Cofer's family's gender dynamics. "Laissez-faire" is a term that evokes libertarian capitalism and the desire to have an unregulated privatized economy, so when it becomes a term to describe her abuelo's anti-patriarchal approach to family and economics, it is initially jarring. Simultaneously, this metaphor calls out the long history of US involvement and interference in Puerto Rico's economy, such as Operation Bootstrap (1950s), which dismantled the puertorriqueña agricultural economy in favor of an urban-centered industrial one and which ensured duty-free taxation of imported materials to the United States, which would initially appear to be antithetical to a laissez-faire approach. These interferences with the economy produced displacement, expulsion, and migrations, upsetting both the economy and the culture of Puerto Rico while allowing for the US "free" market to infiltrate, take over, and de-diversify Puerto Rico's economy. Ortiz Cofer's representation of a wife who wants a practical, good capitalist husband and a husband who is supposedly laissez-faire in his spiritism, then, shows two sides of the same coin: both are products of economic strategies imposed by US interventionism and of a cultural politics that normalize this market violence.

The story's narrative turn resolves the conflict between the grandparents; talking to the dead becomes the very device that bridges their differences. This turn occurs when the narrator-author's uncle, Hernán, gets a free ticket to the United States when he is recruited as a laborer. He disappears, and his father immediately has visions of his son's enslavement and torture. In one instance, the grandfather sketches out one of his visions, which conjures the grandmother's own visions and premonitions. Papá draws a field with unripe fruit surrounded by a tall fence with bright lights in the distance; the description blurs the line between a farm and a prison. This vision then forces the grandmother's mind into a "map of memories," and she remembers that her sister's son also was recruited for labor in the United States and may know where Hernán is being held. The nephew, who is settled in Buffalo, New York, tells them he will look for Hernán at what everyone calls "the farm."[7] "The farm" becomes a figure for all the illegal practices of mainland growers on a racialized migrant labor force, even those with US citizenship, a place where farmers keep the Puerto Rican workers "ignorant to their exact whereabouts," set up a system of debt slavery, and produce a sort of labor prison.[8] Hernán is safe but has been violently exploited and is ready to "lead the exodus."[9] This story about Ortiz Cofer's uncle leads to her grandmother finally respecting her grandfather's clairvoyance and visions and paying tribute to his abilities by embroidering a cloth with the drawing of his vision.

This narrative turn is significant because it draws out a series of tensions and anxieties between political-economic processes and ethno-racial cultural practices. First, the story of Hernán deeply troubles the terms of class and race in the beginning of the story: we initially see how spiritism hails from European (read: Western, white), middle-class sensibilities, allowing Papá to be a more refined medium in Puerto Rico, but this falls apart when Hernán goes to the United States and is reduced to a racialized, disposable laboring body who is far from middle class and is stripped of basic rights. Also troublingly, in the beginning, Papá's approach to his work and family dynamics is synonymous with free-market ideology. These free-market desires are mirrored in Hernán's free ticket to northern commerce, but this economic model with its celebratory claims of freedom quickly falls apart in the narrative. In this case, it results in exploitative and dehumanizing labor practices that hold captive the supposedly free laborer. And these narrative tensions influence the grandfather and grandmother's relational turn, from one of disregard and scorn to one of mutual respect.

Some scholarship on Ortiz Cofer decodes her multi-genre and language-fluid work, arguing that it shows colonial structures of alienation, while other scholars present her fluctuating and alternative modes of national and transnational identification.[10] Maya Socolovsky in particular argues that Ortiz Cofer's transgressive strategies in her writing allow her to address "the limits between history and the present moment, the narrative of the US mainland

and the island, fiction and autobiography, and between different kinds of nar-
rators," whereas David J. Vázquez tells us that Ortiz Cofer's narrative strategies
highlight the characters' "exclusion from normative culture."[11] While these
readings identify the possibilities of Ortiz Cofer's work, they largely conclude
on its representations of Latinx culture and subjectivity. Instead, "Talking to
the Dead" exposes the broader political economy that is often hidden from
public view and not (initially) for mass consumption, but it utilizes the otherworldly to upend this political economy. On one level, death portrays global
capitalism's erasures and exploitation of racialized and laboring bodies, but on
another level, it becomes the very mechanism to enact and imagine possibility
and revolution against this erasure and exploitation. The construct of death
and particularly the living dead is at once both destructive and celebratory.

The Revolutionary Potential of Dead Labor

While Ortiz Cofer's story is particular to the Puerto Rican experience, especially as it relates to the United States as a commonwealth, Francisco Goldman's novel *The Ordinary Seaman* further deepens the Latinx experience in
the United States by featuring Central American histories, experiences, and
perspectives. While Puerto Rico is colonially still tied to the United States
and residents can more easily migrate to the mainland, those hailing from
Honduras, Guatemala, El Salvador, Nicaragua, Costa Rica, and Panama are
caught up in a less-visible, less-codified colonial relationship with the United
States.[12] For instance, the Contras-Sandinistas conflict during the Nicaraguan
Revolution (1978–1989) is a backdrop in Goldman's novel, coming out only
in fragments here and there, yet it deeply informs much of the plot and the
way the political economy operates behind the narrative. As a war heavily
funded by the United States under Ronald Reagan's administration, the war
appeared to be another Cold War artifact, reduced to communist/capitalist
binary discourse, but many read the war as a strategy to create social instability primarily in order for US corporations and market forces to access a cheap
labor pool.[13] Of course, the relationship between Central American (and Latin
American) countries and the United States notoriously lacks transparency. I
argue that this invisibility of US political and economic interference in Central America and Latin America informs much of the conflict in the novel. In
parallel, migrant labor must embody varying states of invisibility, disposability, and social death in *The Ordinary Seaman*. Death becomes what stands for
the ethno-racial exploitations of a free-market economy that cares more about
cheap, flexible, containable labor than about the people doing that labor.

For Goldman's *The Ordinary Seaman*, necropolitics and social death come in the form of a disposable, racialized, and captive immigrant labor force. Inspired by a 1982 article in the *New York Daily News* titled "Sailors Abandoned," Goldman's novel tells the story of fifteen undocumented Central American men who work on a deteriorating freight ship called the *Urus* and who end up experiencing labor captivity. This is a story about Esteban, a young man who participated in the Nicaraguan civil war. Because of postwar instability, Esteban must leave for work. He leaves Nicaragua when a man solicits him and four other Nicaraguans, nine Hondurans, and one Guatemalan to work on the *Urus*. They are shipped to the Brooklyn docks, where they are left to do work with little to no direction from their employer. They are left without money and with very little food; they are told not to leave the ship or they will be deported or killed; and they are given little guidance or extra supplies to actually repair the *Urus*. The men are visited only fleetingly throughout the novel by the two entrepreneurs who own the ship, el Capitán Elias and el Primero (First Mate) Mark. They sometimes bring money and some food but eventually disappear entirely when the venture becomes more than they bargained for. Goldman calls them "phantom owners" throughout the novel. These migrant laborers become prisoners to the ship, some too afraid to leave and be deported, some slowly starving, some resorting to huffing paint, and some going crazy with their memories. The novel embodies varying levels of social death, from the state of the decayed *Urus*, the ghosts of Nicaraguan history, and a cat that haunts the crew.

The Ordinary Seaman demonstrates how the structures of death are inextricable from labor for these displaced Latinx migrants. Michael Templeton reads the novel as representing the tension between symbolic nationalism and "becoming transnational," analyzing how the men either embody this transnationality or succumb to the machinery of the ship. By looking at the men of the ship who resort to huffing paint, Templeton argues that the men become the "very machine that is their world": their bodies begin to match the same state of wreckage as the *Urus* itself.[14] Problematically, Templeton argues that primarily the men who are addicts or "those that collapse under this system" become machines, showing a weakness and inability to "become transnational."[15] But this reading elides the systemic processes that produce the addiction. On the contrary, the men abroad the *Urus*, addicts or not, are all reduced to a captive but mobile labor whose bodies and experiences are irrevocably tied to the machinations of the ship. As migrant laborers, their bodies are worth little more than, as Goldman describes, "wrenches as big as tennis rackets" or "a dead ship on its way to scrap."[16] The larger system of transnational enterprise, then, is not about becoming transnational but about how migrant bodies become confined to labor. Templeton's flip side to the so-called machines, however, is our protagonist, Esteban, who takes matters into his own hands, eventually going off the ship to steal and then earn supplies for the men. His role is important because he provides some relief to their labor captivity, but more, his off-ship excursions show the wider economies at play here. For instance, Kirsten Silva Gruesz notes that Esteban returns with frozen shrimp exported from Honduras at one point, which makes the Hondurans laugh about how they never ate such a thing when they were there. For Gruesz, this moment shows the inherent and irremediable unevenness of globalization.[17] His off-ship excursions also allow Esteban to meet many Latinx subjects who teach him how to survive in the global hub of New York City as an undocumented immigrant—they teach him to navigate the space of social death and use it to his advantage. Templeton wishes to see Esteban's movements as representative of a successful transnationality; however, Esteban's choices and actions are not necessarily indicative of his abilities to avoid subjugation or to evade being reduced to a machine. Instead, his storyline expands the already global and nationally fraught economic violence that they are all experiencing.

These readings, however, reenforce the significance of the *Urus*. The on-ship/off-ship plotlines never let us forget the centrality of the ship in the narrative. The ship is an indeterminate site globally and nationally because it is registered in Panama but the property of a private US owner, all while being docked in Brooklyn. Eventually, it is described as a "stateless vessel" after the Seafarers' Institute becomes involved in the situation.[18] The *Urus* connotes many of the global paradigms and interplays in the novel: it is both the space of violent enslavement and the symbol of global economic circulation. According to María DeGuzmán, the *Urus* is a "site for the crossing of paths of the living and the dead" and "for gradual transformation of the living into the dead," where death is both literal and a form of social death.[19] These workers are enslaved to this ship because if they leave, they have no legal existence, no rights, and must remain invisible. Unlike Ortiz Cofer's captive uncle, whose Puerto Rican status gives him legal citizenship in the United States (and thus a certain access to rights and protections), these men on the *Urus* are what Cacho would describe as "ineligible for personhood" because they are completely outside these rights and protections. I emphasize rights in this understanding of social death because, unlike Patterson's ideas of exclusive-inclusive slavery systems, rights under a contemporary neoliberal economy demonstrate an unresolvable paradox within the rule of law that migrant laborers and undocumented Latinx subjects must navigate. Cacho argues that US immigration law posits that if undocumented migrants can prove they are worthy and deserving of citizenship (via the "good moral character" clauses), then they may be able to gain rights and protections (or become documented); however, she points out that their undocumented status immediately places them as violating the rule of law and makes it impossible for them to be law-abiding and, thus, deserving of rights or protections.[20] This double bind further exacerbates the violent, ambivalent conditions for these men, wherein their legal state of nonbeing is mimetic of the stateless ship. The decaying and dead *Urus* equally mirrors the men's own bodies and legal status as dead labor.

The men arguably exist in this state of mobile but captive labor because of the United States' long history of involvement in Central American political unrest, which has driven them into this situation. The processes of social death and necropolitics evoke a historical entanglement of labor policy, foreign policy, and immigration policy between Central America and the United States. Much of Latinx scholarship and contemporary cultural production has interrogated the role of the North American Free Trade Agreement (NAFTA) between Canada, Mexico, and the United States. While the agreement is trilateral, it has largely operated unilaterally, propping up the United States' economic hegemony on the backs of Mexico and (to a lesser extent) Canada. From Guillermo Gómez-Peña's hypertexts in *New World Border* (1996) to Karen Tei Yamashita's character SuperNAFTA in *Tropic of Orange* (1997), NAFTA has culturally and historically shaped the understanding of free-trade agreements in the Americas as largely exploitative and uneven, the opposite of fair trade. The deployment of the Dominican Republic–Central American Free Trade Agreement (CAFTA–DR, 2004) appears only to have deepened the unevenness of the Americas, and it formally codifies the United States' long history of interference and hegemony in Central America. The agreement introduced more maquilas into Nicaragua and mandated certain imports and prices, which caused many industries to become unviable, from coffee to corn to handicrafts. Karina O. Alvarado, Alicia Ivonne Estrada, and Ester E. Hernández argue that CAFTA–DR intensified the exploitation of Central American economies and of natural resources, but these problems were not always directly economic, as the agreement also has intensified social unrest, gang violence, drug culture, and the disrepair of infrastructure.[21] Cacho also describes how the agreement radically restructured legal and social systems, resulting in more poverty and crime and accelerated undocumented migration.[22] The promises of so-called free trade and global integration were met with more insidious forms of governance, including intensified immigration control both in Central America and in the United States. In the Central American context, borders have been hardened in some instances, from the United States' use of Honduras for strategic military exercises since the 1960s to US-mandated policies such as Programa Frontera Sur in the early 2000s. Within the United States proper, the Immigration Reform and Control Act of 1986 (IRCA) establishes this intensified immigration control, followed by reforms and acts in 1990, 1996, and 2006. Immigration law has also notably become entangled with economic processes since 1986, with the IRCA's major reform making it illegal for businesses to *knowingly* hire undocumented immigrants. This mandate arguably handed over immigrant regulation to corporations and business owners.[23] Also, by entangling immigration law with economic processes, the US government assumed that labor, capital, and immigration were inextricably tied together, and this ideology liquidates the immigrant into the economic world. I momentarily turn to this history because it informs how the social death and necropolitics in *The Ordinary Seaman* grow out of this interplay between national regulations and economic deregulations, where the contradictory desires of cheap privatized labor and of a homogenous national population enact violence on Latinx bodies from all sides.

Significantly, the purpose of these migrants' dead labor is to resurrect, restore, and rebirth the ship. Their labor intends to bring a ship back to life so it can transport and circulate goods between the global south and the global north. For Ana Patricia Rodríguez, the *Urus* shows a "floating but immobile South produced by the economic forces of the North." Rodríguez argues that its decline represents a blockage in the "flow of capital."[24] However, the ship is also a figure for the endless drive to *re*produce capitalism, at the expense of the migrants' own bodies. I speak of reproduction here because the concept grafts intrinsic sexual and corporeal subtexts onto the ship and onto this necropolitical process. Mbembe describes necropolitics as "[t]echnologies of destruction" that are "more anatomical and sensorial," a point that Jasbir Puar claims makes necropolitics inherently sexual.[25] The heteronormative understanding of sexuality is almost always tied to the idea of reproduction and life-making. Parallel to Baudrillardian ideas of endless cultural reproductions that replace our sense of reality (simulacra) in chapter 3, "reproduction" here codes these processes with more corporeal features. The desire to reproduce, rebirth, and resurrect the *Urus*, then, shows how the life of the *Urus*, a material figure for global capitalism, matters more than the lives and bodies of workers. As a result, this life-giving is predicated on a destructive violence that socially and slowly kills these migrants. While reproductive imperatives appear to contradict these structures of death, they actually work in tandem with them. Furthermore, thinking about the inherent sexuality of necropolitics also evokes a line of thought that challenges the reproductive imperative within heterosexual norms. Queer theory especially rethinks sexuality through death, from Leo Bersani's "Is the Rectum a Grave?" (1987) to Lee Edelman's *No Future*

(2004). Edelman theorizes how reproduction operates as an absolute social value because it is fundamentally a drive for the future, for life, and for the figure of the child: reproduction regurgitates the pithy 1980s slogan "The Children Are the Future" and blankets it over all social life while ignoring its exclusionary and prescriptive imaginary.[26] To work against reproductive futurism, then, is to threaten these heteronormative structures and embody a more queer death drive. This anti-reproductive future would need to look radically different from what José Esteban Muñoz calls "straight time"—past to present to future—where the symbolic of reproduction reigns.[27] While I explore these ideas further at the end of this chapter, I briefly turn to them here because they return us to the primacy of the body in these constructions of violence, but the living dead body also becomes the catalyst for challenging these violences.

The novel presents different possibilities to resist and disrupt violence, although the role of the oldest lobo del mar, Bernardo, and his affinity for ghosts activate these politics of possibility. In some criticism, the disruption of this violence occurs when Esteban mobilizes his fellow workers who have not succumbed to huffing and they disappear into the shadows of New York at the end. For Gruesz, Esteban's role captures an ambivalence about America and Americanization in the novel: "*The Ordinary Seaman* is at once a rejection of Americanism as the utopian terminal port of every immigrant's dream, and an embrace of it—but an embrace in the prophetic mode of Martí, as a presentiment of a truer liberty yet to be."[28] Rodríguez, on the other hand, sees the novel as making visible America's mythical fiction, stating, "The inoperable, rust-smeared ship with neither electricity nor water—called by its crew a 'broken eggshell,' a 'ghost ship,'" and a 'disaster on water' (*OS*, 20, 107, 27)—will come to signify the men's broken dreams of coming to the United States for a better life."[29] I argue, however, that neither Esteban nor the myth of America is the figure of possibility and potentiality in the novel. Instead, the novel's politics of possibility at the end come from Bernardo. The men's disappearing into New York City for a new life (albeit not necessarily a better one) occurs because of Bernardo, endearingly called el viejo. Partly this is because Bernardo is the reason the crew is rescued from this labor captivity. He alerts an Argentine couple of their plight, even though he initially thinks they are ghosts since he has not seen other people in so long.[30] This couple in turn notify the Seafarers' Institute about the desolate *Urus* housing a group of migrant workers who are not getting paid or fed, and this notice results in the rescue. Bernardo with his visions of ghosts is a mechanism for possibility, and his role is further solidified when he challenges el Capitán Elias about what is happening at this site. After the captain gives a long speech explaining that the workers will not be paid until the ship is operating, Bernardo shouts: "Let's not hide the truth, Capitán, this ship is a swamp of safety and maritime labor violations, and now this, *un gran insulto*! . . . Instead, Capitán, you ask us to be slaves."[31] Bernardo is the prophetic, visionary speaker of truth throughout the novel, and his role in the novel motivates and preconditions the possibility of resistance.

Bernardo's significance comes from his spectral abilities: he is noted as having a "certain receptivity to ghosts."[32] While confined to and starved on the *Urus*, Bernardo befriends a stray cat, Desastres, whom he feeds, but when Desastres disappears, Bernardo is eventually visited by its ghost. At one point, the ghost cat rubs against his leg, a sort of warning for Bernardo that foreshadows his leg being severely burned with cooking oil, an accident that ironically occurs because of Desastres's hauntings. [33] These spectral visions within the story foretell his impending disappearance and presumed death. Bernardo gets no help for the burn until infection sets in and he develops a fever. When Mark finally makes an appearance, he sees how the situation on the *Urus* has devolved; he eventually agrees to take Bernardo to the hospital while the workers shout at him for their money and for help. Bernardo's disappearance is an uneasy, unreliable narrative. First, Mark tells of dropping Bernardo off at an overfilled hospital, and a very short chapter relates a doctor coming across an old man on a gurney with a necrotic wound who has died from the hospital's inadvertent neglect.[34] At the end, we discover that the Seafarers' Institute investigators cannot find Bernardo in any hospital in New York and that Mark has vanished and "absconded with all the money."[35] Instead, we are left to wonder if Mark dumped the injured, dying, undocumented laborer somewhere, the quick-and-dirty disposing of the dead when one flees legal repercussions and unsuccessful investment capitalism. When Esteban discovers that their employer may never have delivered Bernardo to any hospital in New York City, he ruminates: "And trying to comprehend or even imagine this mysterious abyss that had somehow swallowed Bernardo, he suddenly realizes that it isn't something that has been done to Bernardo. It's something that's been done to all of them, and that they never even knew or suspected the truth makes it all the more terrifying."[36] Bernardo's disappearance and death is a disappearance and death to all of them. Of course, Bernardo's oil-burn incident is one that might have been avoided, alluding to the absent boss, the absence of ethical labor conditions, and the absence of legal recourse. Bernardo, with his affinity for ghosts, embodies these processes of social death and necropolitics.

Nevertheless, Bernardo also instigates their rescue, gives Esteban a consciousness of his position in the world, and triggers the final revolutionary event in the novel. Gruesz reads Bernardo's symbolic and literal death as the catalyst for Esteban to have a revelation about how past violence, such as Nicaraguan political unrest, is never really in the past but signals a perpetually "unfolding present."[37] Bernardo's death, then, functions as that which breaks up what Muñoz calls "straight time." His death also precipitates the death of the *Urus*. For instance, the remaining migrants on the *Urus* who decide not to join Esteban in New York happily await the Seafarer's Institute to deport them. In one last act of resistance, they decide to steal the *Urus* and beautifully capsize the freighter onto the pier, making it unresurrectable scrap. While Bernardo's death stands in for all the violence of history and present-day globalization, the death of the *Urus* signals subversive possibility. Death is, thus, both celebratory and destructive, and it is one of the places where necropolitical structures—unseeable as the ghosts that haunt Bernardo, the invisible workers on the *Urus*, the violent specter of Central American history, or the phantom owners who desire cheap commodifiable labor—becomes visible.

The Consuming Zombie and Market Violence

Mbembe explores the contradictory potential in necropolitics by thinking about how these violent processes have created "new and unique forms of social existence in which vast populations are subjected to conditions of life conferring upon them the status of *living dead*."[38] The status of living dead evokes constructions of the zombie and asks us to consider how zombies may function as figures both of market violence and of subversive possibility. David McNally argues that zombies are always the victims of market violence, and he describes them as "those disfigured creatures [. . .] who have been turned into mere bodies, unthinking and exploitable collections of flesh, blood, muscle and tissue."[39] bell hooks, however, reminds us that the zombie is not simply anyone and everyone but is almost always racialized and largely hails from the histories of slavery, where black people had to learn "to appear before whites as though they were zombies, cultivating the habit of casting the gaze downward so as not to appear uppity. [. . .] Safety resided in the pretense of invisibility."[40] We can see here how the zombie embodies many features of necropolitics and social death: it is reduced to pure body; it must be invisible; it lives in a precarious and ambivalent state. It is from these ideological and discursive constructions of the zombie or the living dead that I approach Javier Hernandez's superhero comic book *El Muerto: The Aztec Zombie*.

Hernandez's comic *El Muerto* (and its film adaptation, *The Dead One*) tells the story of Diego de la Muerte, who is abducted and sacrificed by the god of death and the god of destiny in the Aztec land of the dead, Mictlan, on his way to a Día de muertos party. He is eventually sent back to the living a year later, with superpowers. Our Aztec zombie superhero is a sort of migrant who travels between times, dimensions, and borders. In the first issue, the narrative mostly focuses on twenty-one-year-old Diego getting ready and in costume for the Day of the Dead party, getting abducted on his way, sacrificed, and then coming back to the living only to discover a series of problems: he is permanently imprinted with his Día de muertos costume and makeup, all his family and friends have been mourning him for a year, and he has no idea why the Aztec gods did this to him. The issue ends with El Muerto heading to Mexico to find answers. While David William Foster reads the comic as an allegory for the "fraught" and "unresolved positions" of Chicano identity, I see it as presenting less an identity politics and more a cultural politics in which the superhero and zombie tropes complicate our understanding of Chicanx social power under global capitalism.[41]

Later issues, promotionals, and the film adaptation featuring Wilmer Valderrama present El Muerto in exceptional superhero situations.[42] Often these superhero elements follow formulaic comic book templates in which El Muerto fights a villain. Hernandez describes his protagonist as "the classic tragic and haunted hero, one whose powers and situation place him between being both gifted and cursed."[43] For the story "The Battle of Santa Muerte," for instance, Hernandez employs a mix of classic spaghetti Western and Batman. These popular tropes clash and diverge with the Mexican and Mexican American mythos of the folk saint Nuestra Señora de la Santa Muerte, who joins elements of pre-Columbian (primarily Aztec) cultural traditions with Catholic traditions. In this story, Diego must join with Weapon Tex-Mex to defeat an evil clairvoyant being who rises from hell and tries to possess Diego to gain his Aztec powers by inserting his heart into Diego. Weapon Tex-Mex saves Diego by ripping out the heart and killing himself, and Diego repays him by bringing him back to life with his powers. The two become friends with the promise of future buddy-hero narratives. Clichéd storylines and characterizations are mixed with the distinctly Mexicana/o and Chicanx content of Santa Muerte and Aztec mythology. Together, they produce a comic that both adheres to and upsets the norms of this literary graphic form. Mauricio Espinoza describes these narrative tensions through the character Diego himself: "he employs his powers [. . .] to help people in need and stop bad guys, contesting the traditional portrayal of the zombie as a mindless, ravenous creature."[44] Espinoza believes Diego's "humanity is stronger than his monstrosity," challenging the stereotypical image of Latinx "hordes" in mainstream media and popular culture.[45] However, Diego as a monster who fights and destroys other monsters demonstrates a more complex conception of the figure of the zombie because Diego's zombification grows out of a historically significant cultural politics, from Aztec mythology to colonial subjection to Chicanx reclamation. His monstrosity is both destructive and celebratory.

I wish to emphasize the Aztec roots of our superhero zombie here because it is crucial for thinking about whether the comic is constructing an empowering Chicanx cultural politics (that imagines community and mobilizes through the Aztec-inspired homeland Aztlán) or whether it is embodying a more systemic narrative on social death and necropolitics (wherein indigenous tropes provide histories of erasure and appropriation). In constructing an empowering cultural politics, the comic book series begins with a storyboard that leans more toward capturing Diego's introspections about his everyday life while formulating a mestizo consciousness in which Diego must negotiate his modern self and his precolonial indigeneity. This raises two questions: why must the superhero zombie come from a pre-Columbian and pre-capitalist mythos, and why must he be an *Aztec* zombie? In later manifestations of the comic series, we discover that El Muerto is imbued with all the power of the two Aztec gods, putting him in exceptional situations and allowing him to enact fantastic feats. In many ways, Diego's Aztec-induced power highlights the continued effects of Spanish and Catholic colonial appropriations of indigenous spiritism, as is underscored with his childhood obsession with Día de muertos. In pointed irony, his obsession with this cultural practice translates into his literal embodiment of that fascination in the narrative, calavera facial designs, mariachi suit, and all. However, this embodiment also highlights his border identity, in the Anzaldúan sense, where he is torn between the god of death and the god of destiny and between his indigenous-colonial past and his American present. In this sense, Diego's indigeneity imbues him with a fraught history that produces his *superhero* abilities.

Hernandez's use of Aztec mythology and indigenous power grows out of a complicated Chicanx and Mexican history that hinges on a pre-Columbian nostalgia to some extent. When unraveling the complex interchanges of a Chicanx indigenous consciousness, Sheila Marie Contreras largely elides the function of death in Chicanx culture. She only briefly calls out the exoticization and fetishization of Día de muertos imagery and celebrations by non-Mexicans, as exemplified by the United States' fascination with the holiday and by D. H. Lawrence's *The Plumed Serpent*.[46] For Contreras, the fascination with death comes from outside Chicanx culture and is not a fetish within Chicanx production and practice. Diego clearly disrupts this perspective with his own obsession with Día de muertos, and while Chicanx indigenous consciousness must negotiate multiple temporal and spatial settings and social dynamics, one of these dynamics is our own consumer culture. Furthermore, this is not only a US phenomenon but a transborder concern. Claudio Lomnitz historicizes and revises the ongoing significance of death as a Mexican national totem that embodies the mestizaje of Aztec and Catholic, capitalist and socialist, and festive and violent.[47] He argues that death and the dead—from the laughing skeleton image and La Catrina dolls to the enshrinement of the bones of ancestors—must be understood as central to the national structure itself, where in one instance it may produce a sense of imagined community and nationalism but in another instance a regressivity, anti-modernity, and anti-futurity in Mexico.[48] He sees this nationalization of death to also structure class and inequality in an increasingly neoliberalized Mexico. For instance, he ends on how the poor and working classes become synonymous with the skull imagery in popular political cartoons that ultimately show their dehumanization from the rich and the "depreciation of life" in Mexico with the onset of neoliberalism.[49] For Lomnitz, this imagery may originate from past indigenous practices that celebrated death, but through the histories of conquest, war and conflict, boom literature, and globalization, death now signals growing inequality (both within the nation and in the global sphere).[50] Of course, Mexican culture does not have a cultural monopoly on employing and celebrating the figure of death to make sense of the past, present, and future. Ghosts, spirits, angels, resurrected chieftains and saints dot the Latin American literature of Gabriel García Márquez, Julio Cortázar, and Isabel Allende, authors whose works were marketed as "magical realism," a genre whose First World consumers often and famously ignored the realism part of the genre in favor of its exotic, fantastic, "ethnic" phantasms.[51] The empowering figure of death and the dead in Latinx culture at the least looks back to the non-Columbian or indigenous past and at the most confronts the social and economic conditions of globalization. I say "non-Columbian" instead of "pre-Columbian" because African heritages that are not indigenous to these spaces imbue these cultural productions as well. While many critics focus on the Haitian zombie to talk about the African roots in Latin America and the Caribbean, Judith Ortiz Cofer immediately identifies the distinct but overlapping colonial histories at play around figures of death, where Santería and Mesa Blanca spiritism run as parallel, albeit racially demarcated, practices in Puerto Rico.[52] These contemporary formations of death wish to (re)value the things that colonialism and now capitalism have destroyed or appropriated.

The comic's film adaptation, *The Dead One*, capitalizes on these cultural politics, especially forms of Aztec and mestizo empowerment. Immediately, the film opens with an almost indistinguishable whispering voice, chanting in what is supposed to be Nahuatl. The black screen then presents the following text: "500 years ago, Spain invaded Mexico, unleashing a war on the Aztec religion. It's been said that with their faith destroyed, the indigenous people lost the will to live. Within 80 years, 28 to 32 million were dead. According to prophecy, the Aztecs and their religion will come to dominance in a time known as the Sixth Sun." This breaks to the first scene of the film, where we see a sleeping child—a young Diego—in a moving van lying in the dark with a sliver of sunlight falling across his face. The narrator, who is our protagonist, tells us, "In the old days, when our people died, they believed the soul made a long, hard journey across many deserts to reach the afterlife. The final crossing was a river, guarded by dogs, and on the other side, the land of the dead. The Aztecs called it Mictlan." On the word "Mictlan" the van stops, and our young protagonist opens his eyes; the van door opens, revealing about ten migrants. The coyotes force everyone out of the van into the desert; they will need to make the rest of the journey into the United States on their own. Two narratives arise here that seem to interplay with one another. The colonial history in the beginning implies that "the Aztecs will rise again" by ending on the legend of the Sixth Sun. We immediately see here a narrative about how the processes of colonialism were not enough to keep dead our indigenous being, in effect zombifying or resurrecting this state of being. The cinematic narrative also analogizes the crossing into the land of the dead to the crossing into the United States. The river dividing Mictlan and the living corresponds to the Rio Grande; the dogs guarding Mictlan are synonymous with both the Border Patrol and the coyotes who hold the keys to crossing the US-Mexico border. To drive the metaphor home and foreshadow its literalization, the film makes sure our protagonist's eyes open once the voiceover references the land of the dead; the word "Mictlan" resurrects him. Both colonial history and the modern manifestations of what we may call neocolonialism construct Diego's future as a zombie; both anticipate his fantastic transformation into an actual zombie. Once Diego becomes El Muerto, he is given the ability to bring others back from the dead who are innocent bystanders in the war of the gods, and in the end, he must destroy an evil abuelita to save his girl. Campy and sometimes painfully heteronormative and formulaic, the film makes sure to use Aztec indigeneity as what empowers Diego. The premodern mythos, Diego's new zombified self, and the resurrection of indigenous power establish a politics of possibility.

Alternatively, Hernandez's comics also introduce elements of the market that disrupt Diego's newfound power. Specifically, Hernandez's faux advertisements for the fictional company Tio Changos complicates the politics of possibility within the larger narrative frames. Hernandez, along with fellow cartoonists Michael Aushenker and Rafael Navarro, created Tio Changos and include the confectionary company and its fake products in their own work as well as their collaborative work, often accompanied with the slogans "¡Muy Bueno!" and "¡Que Rico!" These faux ads contribute to and parody a long history of comic book advertisements.[53] Hernandez's comic produces a hybridity between comic book formulas and Chicanx cultural politics that points to Chicanx power, but on the other side of this narrative of empowerment, his faux advertisements expose the subsuming power of the market. The ads, alongside the figure of the zombie, place us into the structures of social death once again, and in some ways, they hijack the potential of Aztec and/or mestizo (super)power. Social death in this sense is less about a structure of some *past* colonialism and slavery, as in Patterson's work, and more in the vein of Cacho's argument that current social and neoliberal structures of exclusion leave racialized peoples under constant scrutiny for their consumption patterns. If these consumption patterns prove less than successful or ideal, then these peoples become "beyond ethical obligation."[54] Social death describes a market process that always contains subaltern subjects within this market framework. If social death occurs because of unsuccessful consumption patterns, then the zombie that consumes mindlessly would appear to be the ideal consumer, in effect *not* socially dead. McNally argues, however, that this consumer-forward reading of the zombie comes from contemporary Hollywood: "Hollywood's zombies today are creatures of consumption, brazenly mobbing stores and malls and consuming human flesh, no living-dead producers of wealth for others."[55] George Romero's *Dawn of the Dead* (1978) with the battle over the mall perhaps captures this consumer-driven narrative best, although the social desire to contain and eradicate the zombie outbreak pushes and pulls against the economic desire for mindless consuming. McNally notes that zombies in the global south, especially in Haiti and sub-Saharan Africa, operate less as consumers and more as zombie-laborers or zombie-producers because these subaltern populations must make sense of their positions in the new world order.[56] Hollywood revises these larger global structures by eliding the zombifying process of labor in bourgeois society. In this sense, the zombie-consumer is a narrow view of the larger economic picture. For McNally, however, this lack of the laborer and of production practices is precisely what writes out any politics of possibility because it "de-radicalizes the zombie's potential for revolt."[57] Hernandez's fictional ads elucidate how the market contains the power of our Aztec zombie into consumption patterns and strangely forecloses the subversive potential of a superhero politics.

Market containment and foreclosure occur within Hernandez's Tio Chango ads through the primacy of the product, usually churros. Often the product being advertised upstages the superhero abilities of our Aztec zom-

bie, and in this case, the churros do the work for him. In one comic advertisement, El Muerto tries to defeat the monstrous El Cucuy from terrorizing a
multilingual classroom; this confrontation ends with one of the kids giving
the monster Tio Chango's churros and pacifying him with "tasty," "home-
made," "authentic" Mexican confections (fig. 4.1; plate 14). In the battle against
El Cucuy, a child's sharing of the product mollifies our monster, counteracting the possibility of an epic battle between good and evil. Alternatively, in
Hernandez and Aushenker's coauthored ad in which El Muerto encounters
Ghost Pirates, he stops them from pillaging a village by offering them churros
instead of using his Aztec-given superpowers (fig. 4.2; plate 15). Of course,
in both ads, everyone ends up happy, docile, and pacified, bodies contained
from dissent, from aggression, or from the dualities and multiplicities that
construct and arguably empower Diego. Unlike Romero's zombies in *Dawn of
the Dead*, who slowly and mindlessly roam a shopping mall in their endless
desire to consume living human flesh (just as they used to consume the latest
brands), the children's and Diego's quick and cunning use of churros allows
everyone—living or dead, monster or non-monster—in the ads to be happily
sated. In many ways, these fictional ads demonstrate how the market inevitably disrupts the historical and cultural complexities of Latinx narratives and
characters; consuming churros is all we need.

McNally tells us that, while zombies were figures of rebellion during World
War II (such as in Bela Lugosi's *White Zombie*), now they are creatures of imperialism.[58] Churros may not seem like the picture of imperialism we were all
expecting (notwithstanding the Caribbean sugarcane industry); nevertheless,
the comedic use of them in the faux ads makes them what contains, colonizes,
and pacifies through consumption. El Cucuy, one the scariest under-the-
bed monsters of Latinx folklore, is reduced to a docile body. Zombies beget
zombies. It is, then, with some irony that I quote Fredrick Luis Aldama's ambivalent praise for capitalism's target marketing that "benefits" Latinx comic
book artists: "The radically alternative and unconventional becomes a *meal
ticket* in the capitalist marketplace."[59] This meal ticket takes on new meaning
when read through the figure of the zombie in Hernandez's *El Muerto*, where
the faux ads disrupt our imagination about the radical potential to rise from
the dead and the empowerment of Aztec superpowers; instead, they eat our
brains and give us delicious churros.

While *The Ordinary Seaman* presents a picture of totalizing social death
for the migrant laborer, where necropolitics reigns, it ends with a glimpse at
the possibilities for subversion. *El Muerto* gives us the opposite in many ways:
the series and film begin with the premise of empowerment through Aztec
indigeneity, mestizo consciousness, and the negotiations of history, but the

Figure 4.1. "El Muerto versus El Cucuy." From *Comics!* by Javier Hernandez.
© 2013 Javier Hernandez; courtesy of Javier Hernandez.

Figure 4.2. "El Muerto in 'The Ghost Pirate!,'" written and illustrated by Michael Aushenker. From *El Muerto, the Aztec Zombie*, by Javier Hernandez. "The Ghost Pirate" © 2002 Michael Aushenker; courtesy of Javier Hernandez.

necromarketing of zombies inevitably presents ideal market subjects. Referencing Freud's uncanny and Marx's concept of labor as zombie-like, Annie McClanahan observes, "We imagine ghosts and zombies [. . .] because the premodern fear of corpses is itself a return of the historical past—from a collective prehistory—that we thought we had left behind." For contemporary exploitations of capital, such as labor production and consumer culture, these ghosts and zombies force us to confront what we thought we would overcome: our material limitations and the realities of labor and production.[60] These ghosts and zombies embody the ambivalent structures of political and social death and simultaneously nod to the possibilities of precapitalist mythos, of resurrection, and of resistance, even while these possibilities are recursively redistributed into the market. Goldman's novel makes this possibility a light at the end of a tunnel, whereas Hernandez's comic shows how the market can quickly subsume that light. Between these two Latinx genres and narratives, we see how the violence of the market causes the conditions for subversive potential and then eats that potential too.

The Dead Future

So far, this chapter has shown that the varying levels of death for migrant labor and Latinx subjects reveal and negotiate a contradictory and recursive politics where Latinx bodies are reduced to exploited laborers or consumers and where their social death potentially enables resistance and revolution against that exploitation. Nevertheless, my readings of Ortiz Cofer's "Talking to the Dead," Goldman's *The Ordinary Seaman*, and Hernandez's *El Muerto* comics and film adaptation also uncover a common thread across these narratives: questions of sexuality and gender imbue this ambivalent condition. As already discussed, Ortiz Cofer's story navigates the heteronormative and patriarchal gender roles of Papá and Mamá. Mamá's undercutting of Papá's patriarchy and masculinity is happily resolved in the end, when his "talking with the dead" saves their son from labor captivity. Elements of patriarchy, masculinity, and sexuality also saturate Goldman's novel and Hernandez's comic. *The Ordinary Seaman*'s figurations of the *Urus* illustrate the reproductive imperatives of global capitalism, encoding sexuality into the narrative. In distinction, the heterosexual and heteronormative relationship that drives the film adaptation *The Dead One* both parodies and reenforces the clichés of comic books and Chicanx culture. I want to end on these elements of sexuality and gender, which complicate these three narratives, because these elements bring me to questions of the future and what it means to embody a "dead future."

On one level, gender and sexuality evoke questions of futurity precisely because they force us to think about so-called normative understandings of biological sex, the body, and reproduction. Ideally, a queer analytic disrupts this normative worldview. As discussed earlier, Muñoz critiques the normative and problematic futurity housed in "straight time"—a form of reproductive futurism that, as Edelman argues, shows up in the figure of the child and excludes political hope for queer, anti-reproductive subjects.[61] Muñoz theorizes, instead, a queer futurity that must always account for race, sexuality, gender, and class, allowing for relational and dialectical performances and embodiments of the future.[62] I wish to end on how the figure of death in these narratives similarly upends reproductive futurism but also imagines interactive and paradoxical forms of futurity.

One form this takes in the narratives is through figures and characters that do not fit into normative constructs of gender and sexuality, especially the abuelita, the witch, and/or the genderless forms of the underworld. For instance, the evil abuelita in *The Dead One* is a destructive force in the film, and she/he is unnaturally skinny with very pale skin and long white hair, alluding to Santa Muerte. She/he first appears when the migrants are driven across the US-Mexico border and dropped off in the middle of the desert. She/he appears to be a man at this moment and a fellow migrant, watching the young Diego. After Diego transforms into the Aztec zombie, the witch or demon puts herself/himself into the position of the abuela of Diego's girlfriend. She/he is the source of conflict and unease throughout the narrative, which climaxes when she/he lures and attacks Diego. We learn that she/he is a spirit sent from Mictlan to perform three sacrifices (one being Diego's girlfriend) to bring about the Sixth Sun. Diego is supposed to bring this change as well, but his love for the living and his power to bring them back from the dead puts him in opposition to the spirit's task. During their epic battle in a graveyard, Diego goes through an internal war between his violent Aztec self, who must kill his girlfriend, and his modern ethical self, who must protect and resurrect the living. He ultimately realizes his true power comes from love, allowing him to stab the spirit in the heart and return him/her to Mictlan. Played by Billy Drago and referred to as "she" throughout most of the film, the evil abuelita/bruja/Aztec messenger both confuses and sharpens the tension between the violence and the possibilities of death.

The character's complicated gender politics produces a sort of queer imaginary, but this imaginary does not forget Latinx literary and cultural histories of gender and sexuality.[63] Instead, it arguably highlights them. Melissa W. Wright in her study of narcopolitics and feminicide in Mexico argues that gender politics are foundational to any reading of necropolitics in the borderlands, in the sense that gender creates a "mechanism of violence" that is fundamental to shaping the "violent status quo" of these spaces, ideologies, and politics.[64] While Wright directs our attention to the sexual violence on the US-Mexico border, this violence grows out of a long history of the corporeal regulation of women's bodies in particular. Russ Castronovo, for instance, unpacks how the somnambulist "linked women's gastrointestinal tract and genitals to a 'destructive' physicality" because women's bodies bind them to "a treadmill of contradictory impulses." Castronovo readily separates the medium or clairvoyant from the biological status of women because she "disconnects her organs, becoming an exemplary citizen precisely because she has estranged the materiality and historicity lived by her own body." For Castronovo, the medium or clairvoyant exemplifies a form of necro citizenship that celebrates the body without organs because her body transcends mundane social relations and "resists stratifications of the socius" by becoming lifeless, still, and dead.[65] McNally reminds us that in Western culture the evil bruja connotes the campaign to maintain and impose the social order and its "sharply patriarchal gender-relations," so women were demonized and accused of witchcraft when they were assertive or riotous.[66] Simultaneously, the witch, McNally argues, operates much like capitalism: "What capital does to workers, therefore, is exactly what witches are said to do when they create a zombie: 'to reduce a person to body, to reduce behavior to basic motor functions, to reduce social utility to raw labour.'"[67] These figurations, then, are not readily about gender binary or biological difference but are about reducing people to bodies. Thus, the spiritual woman and, in the case of Ortiz Cofer's Papá or Goldman's Bernardo, the spiritual man are devalued as inactive, hollow, impotent, docile, and dead. Castronovo argues, however, that the biological and gendered fixation with these representations produces a strategic misrecognition of late capitalism's workings, presenting ahistorical fantasy and evading the "traces of exploitation."[68] There is a literary and social history at play here that wishes to misplace the material exploitation of non-heteronormative and non-binary figures onto the idea of the (half-)living corpse who operates outside history and labor. Thus, a closeness with the dead, such as the clairvoyant and/or bruja/o, disembodies these figures, which is hyperbolically intimated with the evil abuelita in *The Dead One*, whose heart is an easily removable organ and whose chest literally explodes open with the light from Mictlan once Diego stabs it. But we should not forget that even the evil abuelita in *The Dead One* is an exploited tool of the pre-Columbian gods like Diego, encouraging us to recognize that she/he is but another pawn in the game.

Death, nevertheless, is precisely what propels these stories forward. For instance, Bernardo's affinity for ghosts in *The Ordinary Seaman* foreshadows future turning points or arguably starts the domino effect that saves all the men of the *Urus*. Diego's zombification in *El Muerto* becomes the very device to parody and reveal the way the market exploits Latinx/Chicanx cultural production, particularly in Hernandez's Tio Chango's ads. Papá's clairvoyance in "Talking to the Dead" leads to him envisioning his son's labor imprisonment, and the vision inspires his wife to remember significant familial connections that had been lost to daily life. The characters' seeing, communicating with, or colluding with ghosts, zombies, and the dead is a product of the economic violence they must navigate and negotiate, but these figures of death also create a narrative of futurity that unravels through various forms of resurrection.

The dead future, then, describes these valences and tensions. The neoliberal economy dictates and structures all aspects of life and death, normalizing this violence in everyday life and making any future appear to be more of the same—without progress, change, or difference—a sort of perpetual present.[69] Latinx narratives, however, are not simply reproducing a representation of this economic dead end. Instead, they show that the dead future is *both* a state of impotence and a mechanism for radical potentiality (even if that potentiality is without *telos*). The figures of resurrection, founded in ghosts and zombies, lay bare the structures of social death and necropolitics and make visible a violence at the heart of the political economy. Avery F. Gordon in *Ghostly Matters* muses on what ghosts really mean: "What kind of case is a case of a ghost? It is a case of haunting, a story about what happens when we admit the ghost—that special instance of the merging of the visible and the invisible, the dead and the living, the past and the present—into the making of worldly relations and into the making of our accounts of the world."[70] These figures of resurrection identify the slippery and paradoxical relations that structure the world, but they do not denote pure monstrosity or pure possibility of living again. Instead, they show how the deployments of market violence govern populations, making some more disposable than others and thereby enabling a revolutionary imagination against a political economy that is always trying to foreclose this futurity.

CHAPTER 5

Speculative Governances of the Dead: The Underclass, Underworld, and Undercommons

When Stefano Harney and Fred Moten theorize a "politics from below," they do not advocate for a bottom-up politics that describes human rights activism, grassroots organization, unionization, and other social mobilizations.[1] These bottom-up politics undeniably sound like a space of possibility, one in which those on the bottom rungs of the social ladder may take back some power, maybe even redistribute power. Harney and Moten, however, do not see a politics from below as promoting political idealism. Instead, their project locates forms of being within a larger, violent structure of governance, a structure that can never be fully upended.[2] In *The Undercommons*, they propose that "politics" in general is an "ongoing attack on the common" and is concerned only with producing (misplaced and unviable) ends.[3] A politics from below captures how we should no longer think of governance as a hierarchical deployment of power but as the dissemination and management of our own interests, from debt APR to financial investments to social media likes. We are governing ourselves (and each other) through the immaterial labor of interest-production: "solicited, offered up, and accumulated."[4] This understanding of politics describes the economies of exchange, misrecognition, and violence that inscribe all social relations. The necessary inverse to governance, for Harney and Moten, is criminalization, in which those who do not accumulate and proliferate interests are barred from the economy of becoming and are marked as "being without interests."[5] The politics from below, then, is always racialized, where governance is the "extension of whiteness," and criminality (or the ungovernable) is blackness.[6]

A politics painted only black and white makes sense within the historical contexts of the United States since Reconstruction, especially given Jim Crow and legal formulations of the one-drop rule. However, I read *The Undercommons* wondering what it may mean for other colonial subjects in the United

States, who do not easily fit within these black-and-white constructions, even while carrying the inheritances and hauntings of this history. What happens to politics from below when we think about the formation of Latinx subjects who carry the colonial histories of miscegenation and mestizaje or who come to the United States with various races, ethnicities, languages, nationalities, and stories? Furthermore, what happens if we complicate the politics from below with necropolitics or the politics of the dead? When Achille Mbembe theorizes necropolitics, he describes how Third World, mobile, racialized subjects are rendered into living dead status by a political economy that deploys "the creation of *death-worlds*, new and unique forms of social existence." These death-worlds describe the "repressed topographies of cruelty" which obscure "the lines between resistance and suicide, sacrifice and redemption, martyrdom and freedom."[7] I wish to lean into this idea of a death-world for this chapter. Harney and Moten's undercommons describe formations of "we" that require what Jack Halberstam describes as both "world-building" and "world-shattering encounters"[8] and that call for a coalition among those in states of exception, denied resources and rights, criminalized, racialized, and devalued, Mbembe's "living dead." In this chapter, I am interested in how Latinx literature participates in forms of world-building and world-shattering that both celebrate death and complicate black-and-white categorizations of power and social relations in the United States. On one level, this inquiry grows out of this book's bigger questions about whether Latinx cultures of death, as traced in Claudio Lomintz's *Death and the Idea of Mexico* or as seen in market appropriations of Día de muertos, disrupt or consolidate necropolitics. On another level, this chapter imagines how select Latinx speculative fiction, photography, and performance interrogate these violent structures by intersecting the underclass, the underworld, and the undercommons.

This chapter primarily looks at Daniel José Older's speculative fiction *Salsa Nocturna* to explore how its death-worlds cultivate both world-building and world-shattering processes. As a work that employs multiple storylines and intersections, *Salsa Nocturna* enacts world-building and world-shattering techniques that produce speculative imaginaries of dead governance and ways of living together. Older's *Salsa Nocturna* is part of his "Bone Street Rumba" series, which is a collection of books and stories that follow the underworld of New York City. Marketed as an urban fantasy series, the collection brings together elements of detective fiction, *Bildungsroman*, urban legend, buddy cop narrative, and ghost story. Reminiscent of Peter M. Lenkov's comic book series *R.I.P.D.* (*Rest In Peace Department*, 2001), the stories within *Salsa Nocturna* often focus on the half-dead, half-alive Carlos Delacruz, an agent for a shadowy governing body known as the Council of Dead (COD). The agents must do the Council's bidding and manage the ghosts and underworld monsters in the city. As the Council's corrupt and covert forms of state governance become increasingly problematic, Carlos, his partner Riley Washington, and an "unruly band of supernatural warriors, spies, magicians and griots" eventually rebel.[9] Carlos works from the inside, while Riley and friends build an underground resistance. Simultaneously, this collection is a short story cycle insofar as the stories can stand alone and do not always feed this primary storyline directly. Some stories relate the lives of those loosely connected to Carlos who are likeminded about the Council or who can see into and interact with the underworld: musicians, hired guns, ancient orders of story collectors, social workers, and paramedics, some who are Cuban, Ecuadoran, Afro-Latinx, former slaves, immigrants, queer, or descendants of Panamanian brujas. At times, these stories are tangents that do little for the story of resistance, but as a whole, the interwoven connections and arcs produce a world-making technique that creates an ever-expansive universe of living and dead that is not tied to a singular point of view or a narrative *telos*. The stories collectively upend top-down governances, imagining a politics from below.

Because *Salsa Nocturna* is an ever-expanding text, I also turn to the larger textual concerns that it invokes. For instance, the book parodies tropes of the superhero, so I consider the popular culture industry and imaginations of alternative governance by engaging Dulce Pinzón's photographic project *The Real Story of the Superheroes*. In other instances, the stories decry the way market forces worm into the Council's operations, especially in terms of maintaining racial and spatial inequalities. To further investigate these broader social and spatial problems embedded in the stories, I turn to Coya Paz's piece *Still/Here: Manifestos for Joy and Survival* in order to unravel the ties between performance, gentrification, and the histories of race. These departures in the chapter are generative tangents that elaborate on certain topics and/or arrive at different configurations of dead governance. In mimicry of Older's short story cycle, I compose critical composites through these departures and arrivals that build (and perhaps ideally shatter) the larger world of the living dead. These three texts complement one another, but they also draw out the different possibilities and different markets of world-building and world-shattering imaginaries.

On one level, my argument points to how world-shattering occurrences, embodied in a term like "death-worlds," give rise to and participate in world-making strategies, and vice versa. Latinx narratives produce significant forms of world-building from the ambivalent state of living dead. Mark C. Jerng understands world-making narratives to "form and organize our sense of the world" through and alongside their imaginary or possible worlds.[10] For Jerng, speculative genres reveal something about racial meaning in particular. When speculative fictions engage with racial capitalism, they complicate the notion of necropolitics. Jerng claims that, in select narratives, "racial capitalism does not lie in the exploitation or exclusion of racialized labor. Nor is it something that ended with the abolition of slavery, as the identification of contractual wage labor with freedom would suggest. Rather it lies in the embedding of racial meanings within economic functions of utility and uncertainty."[11] World-building narratives, as such, "point our attention" and shape our perception of a racial politics that is organized by "social transaction" and "economic exchange."[12] Narrative world-building unveils these perceptions, experiences, and knowledges of the world through racial and economic valences. Nevertheless, these social transactions and economic exchanges are also world-shattering processes under necropolitical governances. The tension between world-building and world-shattering within *Salsa Nocturna* exposes how governance works for the living, the dead, and those in-between.

Governances of the Dead

In *Salsa Nocturna*, the Council's central law is to prevent the living from seeing the dead and exposing the "mystery of the afterlife," which Carlos succinctly summarizes as "Stay the fuck away from the living."[13] Carlos regularly breaks this law, both unintentionally and intentionally. Two of his sidekicks in the resistance—Gordo Cortinas and Jimmy—are living, and he crashes on his living friend Victor's couch when things go badly. Part of his ability to get away with breaking this law is that he is the first and only half-dead, half-alive agent for the Council. His in-between status affords him a certain freedom to move between the worlds of the living and the dead, whether by choice or not. The Council is not presented as an omniscient eye, so they seemingly have no knowledge of what is happening on the streets of New York unless notified by ghost citizens and agents or alerted by news from the living. Their governance mimics the laws of nature for the living, stripped of any extra-ordinary imaginaries of what dead governance may be. Carlos criticizes the Council's structural banality as just another bureaucratic institution. At one point, he muses, "As I'm sure you've noticed, death is not the great equalizer it's made out to be. Layers of hierarchy remain, interlaced by the tangled webs of power and privilege. The dead, after all, are human, and what could be more human than an unnecessarily oppressive bureaucracy at the end all be all of existence?"[14] Their headquarters is a "towering, dull monstrosity" in the "industrial wastelands of Sunset Park, Brooklyn," where it "turns eternal circles like a cursed carnival ride."[15] Governances of the dead, in other words, are a series of middlemen, rotating doors, and runarounds. Locating these administrative bureaucracies in wastelands and having them operate like carnival rides emphasizes the discursive structures at play, but it also shows its recursive structure in that these administrations perpetually reproduce themselves.

Harney and Moten theorize governance first by what it is not: it is not "about government," not a "management neologism," and not a "retreat to liberalism from the market fundamentalism of neoliberalism."[16] Following the theories of Deleuze and Guattari, Harney and Moten explore how governance "becomes." It "generates" and "provokes."[17] It "collects" and "operates."[18] Harney and Moten's verbs require us to think about governance as an active, kinetic, and unfixed process. They eventually name what governance becomes: "the management of self-management." Self-governing persons generate interest that "appears as wealth, plentitude, potential," meaning they are already functioning well in a capitalist system of exchange.[19] Harney and Moten understand self-management to be a "politics from below," and they connect self-management to whiteness and forms of representation that criminalize blackness and those without interest.[20] While they warn us not to collapse governance into the term "management," management (or lack thereof) delineates these positionalities in contemporary political and economic institutions. Further, management names the very types of bureaucracy that now occupy most (all?) political and economic life. Lauren Berlant argues that "the question of politics becomes identical with the reinvention of infrastructures for managing the unevenness, ambivalence, violence, and ordinary contingency of contemporary existence," which is to say that political infrastructures and the management of existence, norms, and rules are indistinguishable.[21] Mbembe also argues that "management" outlines the order of things. He describes necropolitical governance—death-worlds—as *managing the multitude*," which arises when "we are increasingly faced with the question of what to do with those whose very existence does not seem to be necessary for our reproduction, those whose mere existence or proximity is deemed to represent a physical or biological threat to our own life."[22] Violence, war, camps, (re)Balkanization, and borders happen as a part of this management of "vulnerable, unwanted, surplus people."[23] While Harney and Moten and Mbembe use the term "management" to describe different (albeit equally violent) processes, they also identify how these forms of governance produce and need peripheral peoples, whether as surplus to be killed or as racialized others without interest. If the management of populations or multitudes depends on the economic reduction of peoples to surplus and interest, then these politics are in the service of capital. As I explored in chapter 1, the rule of law under neoliberal forms of governance often obscures and occludes the economic foundations to the contemporary state. One of the primary ways this occlusion happens is through contemporary bureaucracies that "manage" until it is nearly impossible to trace and unpack the entanglements of politics and economics.

Part of what makes necropolitical governance in *Salsa Nocturna* effective is how the management of the dead and the bureaucracy of the Council occur by keeping the Council largely invisible. They operate as a behind-the-scenes, shadowy set of rulers whose orders rarely have a transparent reason and whose plans mainly benefit themselves. For instance, the book begins with the story "Tenderfoot," in which Carlos's work for the Council reveals its problematic governance. Our Puerto Rican detective is "sure the ghostly dick-heads upstairs have selected [his] half-dead half-alive ass to do this job for some nefarious reason."[24] The vignette relates his investigation of a mysterious murder in Central Park, where a homeless man, Delton, is found trampled to death, smelling as if he had been "wrestling in a zoo and lost."[25] Later it is revealed that a "phantom pachyderm" is the cause. As the opening story to the collection, it introduces us to how the Council governs. Via one-way telepathy, the Council orders Carlos to capture the phantom pachyderm, but as his investigation proceeds, it becomes clear that the Council are behind it. They have trapped a ghost of a woolly mammoth during her dead herd's annual migration by enclosing her within the park with a force field crafted to keep all things dead in or out. When Carlos comes in contact with her, his knowledge that the Council covered Delton in baby "mammoth shit and sent him off to be trampled" and his sudden desire to give her freedom forces him to cut open the force field and release her, so she can rejoin her ghostly herd crossing what is now the Atlantic.[26] Carlos upends the Council's plan in building a top-secret zoo of "all things phantom" for "both study and entertainment."[27] A zoo of the dead is at once funny and troubling: it embodies a banal governmental project but also highlights the consumerism, conquest, and spectacle at the heart of this endeavor. This story shows us a regulatory body whose form of governance *appears* to organize or protect the world of the dead but actually maximizes its economic and imperialistic interests.

Like the opaque Council's schemes, Carlos's job in the stories is not always explicit either. At times, his work for the Council is mandated; at other times, it is impromptu. In some respects, he embodies what Harney and Moten call a "policy deputy," a person employed to fix, correct, and eventually break the planning of the undercommons, which is to say a form of governance that "is harvesting the means of social reproduction but [. . .] appears as the acts of will, and therefore as the death drive, of the harvested." In this sense, Carlos is a voluntary participant in the Council's work to "extract and abstract" labor.[28] While some mandates tell him to capture phantom pachyderms for planned spectacle, others present themselves without any orders. On one level, he is required above all else to follow the Council's "strict rule: Do not involve humans. Don't fuck with their lives, don't appear to them if you're a ghost, don't let on that you can see ghosts if you're not one. In short: Leave the greatest mystery of the afterlife a damn mystery."[29] However, his voluntary participation in this problematic governance of the dead is also disrupted regularly in the stories, especially when he breaks this rule or does not act on the Council's orders. In "Tenderfoot," for instance, early morning joggers see his "crazy laughing" body floating by when he rides the wooly mammoth to safety, and in the story "Skin Like Porcelain Death," he saves his friend Victor's living teenaged cousin, Jimmy, from a succubus-like entity who locks souls in porcelain American Girl dolls. Carlos, helped by his partner Riley, does this because Victor tells him something is wrong, not on the orders of the Council. While they are unable to detain the entity, they are able to release multiple souls from the American Girl dolls. Jimmy then becomes one of the main members of the resistance as Carlos's mentee.

The resistance is a collection of the ungovernable, all positioned as Latinx, black, and/or queer. Some work from the inside of the NYCOD, while others exist as civilians in the worlds of the living and the dead. Their goal is not necessarily to destroy the Council or to reimagine governance but to create a future of social collectivity. Cyrus, one of the unruly band who is the ghost of a former slave, calls for "a future where our destinies, in life and death, are not governed by some foul sprawling bureaucracy but rather by our own collective passions and morals. This is the future we fight for."[30] These insidious governances of bureaucracy, management, and obscurity are a direct affront to collective forms of existence, for both the dead and the living. Cyrus's teleological desire in his toast points toward what Harney and Moten call the undercommons—a "secret once called solidarity," a "secret about the conquest," and a "prophetic organization" for abolition[31]—but this futurism is constitutive of its preconditions: resistance.

Superhero Style

Salsa Nocturna imagines resistance through various genres of speculative fiction, employing slippages between and parodies of horror, fantasy, romance, magical realism, and noir. The generic parodies most obvious within the collection are its comic book representations of superheroes, antiheroes, and supervillains. "Parody" befittingly syncs with "comic" in this sense. The super-hero, of course, has always been a trope embedded in decidedly noncomic and nonfantasy genres, notably detective fiction and buddy cop narratives where extra-ordinary governance and regulation drive the narrative's purpose or plot. The clichéd trope of the superhero has been heavily commercialized in the past couple of decades as Hollywood has expanded the Marvel and DC universes through series upon series of films and reproductions. As I estab-lished in my reading of *El Muerto* in chapter 4, when the formulaic superhero and comic book storylines mix with distinctly Latinx cultural politics, the narrative complicates our understandings and imaginations of Latinx social power. On one level, superpower imbues the characters with power not often afforded in reality, allowing for new imaginaries; on another level, the popu-larity and Disneyfication of the superhero genre returns these narratives to a market imperative where identity and representation sell. *Salsa Nocturna* further challenges this tension by stripping away the extra-ordinary that is often housed in the comic book genre. The presence of bureaucratic gover-nance in this imaginary world disrupts the fantastic with the utterly ordinary. While considered the best agent in the NYCOD, Carlos is able to fight evil entities successfully not by some super ability per se but because he works well with his band of friends. Also, his heroism, such as freeing phantom pachy-derms from consumerist enclosures, is never meant to save the world(s) in *Avengers*-like grandiosity but instead establishes a common, everyday ethics. This ordinariness also has a problematic side, especially when the book leans into rather stereotypical norms, such as reproductive futurism, machismo, and interracial/interethnic conflict.

The properties within the collection tell us something about the common, the everyday, and the ordinary. To further develop this idea, I turn to Dulce Pinzón's photographic series *The Real Story of the Superheroes*. The photo-graphs present migrants as superheroes, largely as they perform their every-day jobs. By putting her subjects in Mexican and American superhero cos-tumes, she transforms their everyday labor into extra-ordinary acts. While the costumes produce striking images among the urban and workplace back-drops, they also create what Irene Mata describes as a rejection of the "tra-ditional immigrant narrative's schema of assimilation and resolution." For Mata, the superhero imagery combats the "invisibility of labor structures" and disrupts the seemingly common understandings and discourses around immigration.[32] It also broadens our definition of "heroism" to include the sac-rifices and importance of transnational labor in the United States.[33] The thir-teen photographs produce this definition both within the image through cos-tuming and space and in the captions that accompany each subject. Pinzón's captions include the subjects' names in boldfaced type, where they have migrated from, what labor they do, and how much they spend in remittances. These captions emphasize her subjects' identities and account for how capital flows, both in body and in international money transfers, while coupling migrant labor practices with heroic qualities.

The image that captures this coupling most strikingly is one depicting Sergio Garcia as Mister Fantastic (whom Pinzón labels "Mr. Elastic"; fig. 5.1; plate 16). Known for his superhuman elasticity and intelligence, Mister Fantastic is the leader of the Fantastic Four in the Marvel Universe. He is a character of invention and calculation whose elastic powers are gained when he tests a spaceship and is exposed to lethal doses of cosmic radiation. This image is captioned "Sergio Garcia from the state of Mexico works as a waiter in New York. He sends home 350 dollars a week."[34] The photograph shows Garcia/Mister Fantastic serving dinner to a customer in a sparsely populated small café. He stands out in this image in his electric-blue shirt padded with fake muscles, the brightest color in the entire shot. He is set against the front of the café windows with large golden-beige letters (reading BONITA backward)

Figure 5.1. *Mr. Elastic—Sergio Garcia,* by Dulce Pinzón (2012).

and the night's darkness, which help create this contrast. His arms stretch between an unseen spot behind the café counter and a basket of food that he is serving to a table. The Latina woman whom he serves equally draws our eye. Her hands are posed in graceful lines; her blond hair is professionally styled; and her face is in still repose as she stares at the newly arrived basket of food. She also appears as a secondary subject in an earlier photograph of taxi driver Frederico Martinez/Batman, so she has an air of familiarity. Garcia/ Mister Fantastic slightly smiles at her, a quiet expression that radiates dignity and kindness. Simultaneously, her lack of eye contact with him reminds us of the common mores of the service industry, in which servers smile kindly at customers and customers ignore the server to inspect their newly purchased goods. This image presents the service-industry worker whose labor is often disregarded, an expectation within our everyday lives. To make this labor extra-ordinary with a costume and elastic superpowers is to call out this now ordinary social relation.

In terms of her series' ethno-racial constructions, Pinzón's photographs consolidate and disrupt what is common among Latinx subjects in the United States. Primarily, she connects these subjects through the shared experience of migration and labor, a troubling and sometimes essentialized construction of Latinos. The series largely depicts workers who have migrated from Mexico and depicts only two Latinx subjects who are Other Than Mexican (OTM). The first is Bolivar Abril from Quito, Ecuador, who is dressed as Ice Man (notably one of the few openly gay comic book heroes in the Marvel Universe) as he serves ice cream to a line of waiting kids on 3rd Avenue and 104th Street, in East Harlem. The second is Roy Acosta, from Puerto Rico, a cop who is cosplaying as Captain America (fig. 5.2; plate 17). While Acosta may have migrated to the US mainland and sends money home, his position in this series is significantly different as a Puerto Rican, as he is a US citizen (even if the US government continues to deny Puerto Rico equal status as a state). Pinzón highlights this difference by dressing him in the Captain America costume. The photograph implores us to consider the commonwealth status of Puerto Rico, a colonial legacy that troubles concepts of the common. Frances Negrón-Muntaner describes Puerto Rico's status as a "colonial arrangement that has provided higher wages than most Latin American sovereign states, unhindered access to mainland ports, and cultural 'independence,' being incorporated to the United States as largely consensual colonial subjects has inevitably rendered Puerto Rican national identifications *constitutively* shameful."[35] Negrón-Muntaner identifies how the shame of colonial exploitation depends on an element of consent to that colonial status. There is an ambivalence and a state of exception here that imbues Puerto Rican identity

Figure 5.2. *Captain America—Roy Acosta,* by Dulce Pinzón (2012).

politics in the United States and distinguishes Puerto Ricans and Nuyoricans within larger Latinx collectives. As colonial subjects, they undergo a specific historical violence that renders them dead, but as US citizens, they partake in a certain privilege to national life. Markedly, Acosta is arresting another pos- sibly Latino man, an act that paints Acosta as assimilated and removed from other Latinx communities in poignant ways.

Significantly, not all these images show these migrant subjects performing manual or service labor. Jose Rosendo de Jesus/Harvey Birdman, a union or- ganizer, awaits the train in a beautifully tailored velvet coat, gray slacks, brown leather shoes, and a bright red tie, carrying a briefcase. He is one of the best- dressed primary subjects, and his costume (blue angel-like wings and a Bird- man mask) accessorizes his outfit rather than replacing it. The costume does not erase the subject but expands his already-established qualities, as is not always the case in the other photographs, especially when the costume con- ceals the hero's true identity. Another photograph that de-emphasizes labor is Alvaro Cruz/The Flash. It shows him partaking in his favorite pastime—

marathon running with the group *Los Compadres*—in the only image that is completely devoid of work economies, although the caption still notes that he is a cook and sends three hundred dollars a month home to Mexico. In some ways, these images disrupt the ideological collapse of migration with racialized manual labor in the United States, but the focus on labor and money sent home in the captions also normalizes an image of migration that is irrevocably connected to labor and global economy, even when in superhero costumes.

Pinzón, nevertheless, does not give us photographs of what we may consider ordinary labor or costumes of what we may consider a good fit (read: normative) for that labor. For instance, in the image captioned "Minerva Valencia from Puebla works as a nanny in New York. She sends home 400 dollars a week," Catwoman stands in the center of a den in a high-rise apartment holding and feeding children (fig. 5.3; plate 18). Valencia/Catwoman holds a child and a snack cup while another older child reaches up to her. Her costume is nonfunctional for the labor that she is performing: all black, a long-

Figure 5.3. *Catwoman—Minerva Valencia,* by Dulce Pinzón (2012).

sleeved Bardot top with straps, tight pants, vinyl sleeves, tall, shiny boots, an inflexible, uncomfortable-looking latex half-mask covering the top half of her head. Notably, her nails are manicured, silver, and rather long, making her appear more cat-like but also emphasizing the impracticality of this costume in this labor position. This raises the question: why Catwoman? Catwoman is a supervillain in the DC Universe who transforms into an antihero. She notably has a strong sexual chemistry with Batman, leading him to let her get away regularly. As a hypersexualized character, her superpowers include gymnastics and whipping people. This dominatrix-kitten image contrasts with the nanny image. However, both paint the female subject as largely corporeal and emotional, for sex or for caregiving. Mata considers this photograph to be an "ironic representation of Catwoman, the fierce and free-spirited woman who rejects convention and refuses to be 'housetrained.'"[36] While Catwoman may contradict the housewife, caregiver role, she is not necessarily a rejection of gendered convention. Instead, she represents a convention of the hypersexual woman whose superpowers are in seduction and cattiness. To make Valencia into this figure, then, is to call out the dual gendered and sexualized standards for women and to make us question these norms that have grown up around these expectations.

The setting itself also produces a significant class contrast at play. Valencia/Catwoman is positioned just in front of a picture window overlooking Central Park, with a single, phallic skyscraper rising above the trees. The lack of other skyscrapers and the haziness of the sky exaggerate the pictoriality of the scene. This window highlights the wealth of the space. This affluent, picture-perfect backdrop clashes with the room itself, which is strewn with toys; an old TV set sits in the upper left-hand part of the frame, while a monotone Mexican falsa blanket is folded on the couch to the right. The décor is mainly utilitarian, except for two small gold-framed paintings of the US southwest and a retro floor lamp. The walls are bright red, but a strangely unpainted strip in the far-right corner adds an unfinished quality to the setting. Our expectations of wealth, tied to location and view, are undercut by the *mise-en-scène*. Simultaneously, the materials and décor of the space fit the activities of the space: childcare. The photograph, thus, toys with our ideologies in multiple ways.

Another image that produces ideological entanglements around gender, sex, and work is captioned "Ernesto Mendez from Mexico City works as a gigolo in Times Square, New York. He sends home 200 dollars a week." Mendez is dressed as Robin, the Boy Wonder, and leans casually against a lamp post in Times Square in the middle of the night, an almost stereotypical pose of the prostitute who awaits his or her next trick, except now he is the boyish do-gooder Robin. As the consummate sidekick, Robin's boyish quality places him hierarchically beneath Batman, but their relationship also has histori-cally been sexualized as homosexual or ambiguous.[37] Thus, Pinzón's choice to dress Mendez as Robin to figure his sex work is pointed. Moreover, Robin is one of the few comic book characters who is not static but instead names five different people who cycle off as Batman's sidekick as they become older, join different superhero outfits, or undergo transformation. The numerous iterations of Robin also take on different aliases when they move on from this position. Displaying a green long-sleeved unitard overlaid with a red leotard, a bright yellow belt, and a black cape, eye mask, and boots, Mendez's/Robin's costume embodies an ambiguity and multiplicity in both what this superhero represents sexually and how many characters take on his persona.

Mendez's/Robin's costume, ironically, does not stand out in his setting; instead, it complements the lights of Times Square, especially with the photograph's shallow depth of field. The camera settings blur the background just enough to produce indistinct but colorful lights along the strip, and this shallow depth of field not only centralizes Mendez/Robin and his immediate surroundings but also paints him into the scene coherently. The photograph, nevertheless, frames Mendez/Robin in troubling ways. Half a police car takes up the left-hand side of the frame, and sex shops and adult bookstores over-whelm the right side. Mata argues that Mendez's placement between the police car and sex shops "functions as a reminder of the criminalization of Mendez's work" but also shows the "inability of city officials to fully control the activities of one of the city's most popular tourist destinations."[38] This jux-taposition of the policing of sex work and the consumption of adult pleasure places Mendez/Robin into a tension between state regulation and economies of pleasure, but the semblance of the photograph suggests this tension is a part of the ordinary. Mendez's/Robin's casual posture reinforces the unsettling coherence of this tension.

These questions of sexuality and gender in the photographs of Valencia and Mendez identify and challenge the ideological expectations of migrant la-bor and Latinx bodies in the United States. On one level, there is a slow death and social death permeating the shadow economy of undocumented migrant labor, which becomes exacerbated through the often criminalized labor of sex work. On another level, the sexuality and gender politics within these photo-graphs reinforce the figure of the living dead because they normalize these ex-ceptional conditions. *Salsa Nocturna* also interrogates the normal or common state of exception, especially in how it revolves around gender and sexuality. For instance, in the story "Love Is a Fucking River," the unnamed narrator is an almost comical parody of machismo and heteronormative masculinity "because what man, with all our strength and awesomeness, can really be *that* vulnerable?"[39] The collection also disrupts gendered and sexual conventions, such as in the story "Victory Music," which explores trans* politics and states of being "both and neither."[40]

Perhaps the most frequent sexual convention in the collection is reproductive futurism, which occurs in multiple storylines. In "Magdalena," for instance, two detectives named Krys and Big Cane, who eventually become part of Carlos's team, are sent to take care of parasitic entities who suck the memories and stories out of living people until they are left empty. The phantoms have descended on a kindergarten and are "draining these kids of their life force." Krys remarks that if she and Big Cane do not unleash their "warheads," then the "kids'll live but they'll just be shells, no vitality. Failure to thrive, it's called in medical textbooks." She enjoys killing the "tangled shadow web" of soul-sucking phantoms while rationalizing that "[c]hildren's lives are at stake."[41] This moment draws on many imaginaries that grow up around the symbolic child: Save the Children, The Children Are Our Future, and Fighting for the Children, to name a few. As explored in chapter 4, these imaginaries carry with them deep-seated ideologies of heteronormativity and reproduction that enclose our imaginations for the future. Another instance in which the child becomes a figure of reproductive futurism is the story "Red Feather and Bone," in which Carlos's crew defies the Council in one of their first acts. A ghost child, Damian, who is building a portal to release the enslaved ghosts of former slaves, carries an heirloom map of an old African burial ground, and when Carlos finds out that it is an heirloom, he ponders, "*That the children of our children's children may know from whence they came and uplift their spirits and our own.*" For Carlos, these "heirlooms" are not simply maps but "bloodlines."[42] Carlos understands that the resistance group's present possibilities depend on the passing on of heirlooms, a domino effect that can be possible only through both heterosexual and genotypic reproduction. Carlos contemplates this without question, making the figure of children normalize and naturalize these ideas of heterosexuality, race, and reproduction, what Lee Edelman describes as a "familial ideology [that] obsessively takes its own pulse."[43] The ordinary and normal housed in these ethno-racial and sexual figures problematically produce a common stake and a common cause.

The Real Story of the Superheroes and *Salsa Nocturna* show us how these conventions, expectations, and ideologies always trouble the notion of the common, or what Berlant would perhaps call the "lived ordinary."[44] When Harney and Moten conceptualize the undercommons, they ensure that we do not collapse it into understandings of the commons. To do this, they maintain a fine distinction between the commons and the common. The commons, for them, is a "false image of enclosure" and an "illusory right to what we do not have," a settler colonial myth that asks us to perform acts of revolution, freedom, and democracy as though these are achievable political ends in the ever-coming future.[45] Berlant calls this the "commons to come," an unbearable concept of the public that is "reinvented now, against, with, and from within the nation and capital."[46] For Harney and Moten, the politics of the commons threatens the common by thinking "we will be more than we are," when we "already are" and we are "good already."[47] Harney and Moten argue here that teleological and future-looking social politics mystify and correct our social presentness. Their point parallels Mbembe's claim that "in death the future is collapsed into the present."[48] The living dead either must navigate the present through futurity or their futurity is always in the service of the present. Edelman also understands futurity in a similar way. When it comes to reproductive futurism, Edelman argues that the symbolic child in constructions of political and social futurity ensures a future that can never reach maturity.[49] José Esteban Muñoz calls this reproductive futurism a "fantasmatic future," a fitting term for our ghost stories and superhero archetypes in chapters 4 and 5, which pinpoint the undead phantom and unreal fantastic of future-oriented ideology.[50] The figure of the child as the future is so common that we rarely question it, and we villainize those who do not celebrate the hope embodied in children. This is a future, though, that is never attainable, since it transfers ad infinitum to the next generation, much like the future Harney and Moten identify for those living and dying under the residues of settler colonialism.

But imaginations of the future are not always indicative of (n)ever-coming ends; instead, they also tell us about the present and about the nonlinear formations of history. Older's *Salsa Nocturna* may advance reproductive futurism at moments, but these moments also equally illuminate the colonial and racial histories of the United States that produce the living dead and that motivate present-day resistance to these states of exception. Furthermore, its structure does not mimic the chronological linearity common to ideas of futurity and progress. The stories do not always progress in linear ways, often deviating into tangents or breaking off and never resolving. As a result, the book creates a tension between the ordinary and the extra-ordinary that pushes and pulls against ideas of the common.

War Machines

The tension between a futurity that requires resistance and the (n)ever-coming future in *Salsa Nocturna* occurs within a supernatural war. While Older and Pinzón both draw on the tensions between exceptional/common and hero/

villain that superhero archetypes promote, they also utilize the superhero as a form of imagination for resistance and rebellion. I now turn more directly to these questions of resistance. In the case of *Salsa Nocturna*, resistance occurs against the Council. As an institution, the Council is undeniably corrupt and deceitful. Carlos has a general distrust and disgust especially for his immediate superior, Chairman Botus, who is the "only one of the seven Council Chairmen that anyone's ever seen; the rest lurk in some secret lair, supposedly for security purposes."[51] Although Carlos's and the other detectives' work depends on some structure of rules and justice, the Council never come across as having the public interest in mind, living or dead. Most notably, the Council's governance is thrown into question in the story "Protected Entity" when they order the protection of a dead plantation owner who is killing living black children on a middle-class block in Harlem. Carlos and his partner Riley investigate the murders, only to find the ghost of the owner of "the most heinous and successful slave plantation of the North," who is systematically cleansing his great grandson's neighborhood. Before dispatching the ghost into nonexistence, the Council orders the duo not to touch, harm, or insult Captain Jonathan Arthur Calhoun III because he is a protected entity. Riley, who is black and carries the colonial history of his own ancestors through the underworld, stabs the old racist anyway, defying the Council. His rebellion forces him to run to avoid his own termination into complete nonexistence. Carlos notes that word spreads of the disobedience, a threat much greater to the Council, because "[t]he gears of supernatural war are about to begin."[52]

The concept of nonexistence in *Salsa Nocturna* (and who is protected from it or not) parallels the concept of social and political death. Harney and Moten state, "The work of blackness is inseparable to the violence of blackness." Blackness is embedded with a "violent and cruel re-routing"—one that invokes the histories of slavery and diaspora but also describes the difficult rejection of the idea that something is wrong with the black subject. This cruelty encodes blackness with an ever-present "[m]ovement towards and against death," whether as the threat of premature death, from a willingness to break laws, or in always being ready to die.[53] This is a living-with-death. To disrupt this social order, as the story relates, means that Riley escapes the management of his own nonexistence. The story recognizes that this social and political break, a single act of disobedience that pushes toward and against death, can trigger the beginnings of war. Mbembe reminds us that the wars of the globalization era never favor the underclasses. Instead, these post–World War II politics aim to build a "patchwork" of rule through war machines that are part political organization and part "mercantile company."[54] These asymmetrical operations create "enclave economies" that extract resources and collapse social stability, ultimately breaking up populations into varying necropolitical subjects: terrorists, child soldiers, refugees, to be killed as enemies or to be confined to camps.[55] Social and political breaks feed these war machines and are always world-shattering processes.

Salsa Nocturna's supernatural war, however, is rarely the battle royale of Marvel or blockbuster movies. There are seldom large-scale, on-the-ground confrontations between good and evil, no strategic missile strikes on cities with obscene civilian casualties, and no clearly designated operations to produce as much death and destruction as possible. The vignettes largely offer no *event* of war. Often, this war is covert and process-driven, with small-scale steps to undermine the Council, as we see with "Protected Entity" and with the releasing of the ghosts of former slaves in "Red Feather and Bone." Plans are casually discussed in a pickup truck as Carlos and crew drive through Manhattan. Much of the war, in other words, is rather banal, as the grassroots politics and guerrilla tactics often occur in minutiae. The slow rise of resistance functions as an antithesis to forms of slow death. The only time we get a major battle is toward the end of the book, when Carlos is ordered to take care of a "Phantom Overload" in one of the Remote Districts (RD), which are autonomous zones outside the governance of the Council. A phantom overload has happened because a district bus driver stops moving the dead to the underworld, causing so-called overpopulation to the point that the souls "congeal and cause havoc."[56] "Overpopulation" returns us to the neo-Malthusian discourses that regularly saturate state and popular imaginaries of an "immigration problem."

When Carlos is getting his orders for the assignment, Councilman Botus instigates interethnic-interracial conflict between the district spokesman Silvan García, whom Botus identifies as Mexican (even though he's actually Ecuadoran), and Carlos, whom Botus identifies as doing "terrific work in the Hispanic communities" and whom Silvan assumes cannot speak Spanish and calls a Dominican (even though he's Puerto Rican).[57] Carlos sees Botus's description as making him "look like La Malinche."[58] One of Carlos's crew, a living Cuban musician, Gordo, critiques Botus's tactics that attempt to pit Latinos against one another: "It's always easier to blame one of our own."[59] Like Pinzón's pointed image of Roy Acosta as Captain America, a Puerto Rican who arrests other Latinx subjects, these interethnic-interracial conflicts may emphasize how ethnic and racial groups are heterogeneous, but these conflicts often produce chasms within the social fabric. Interethnic-interracial conflict produces social breaks. For Norma Chinchilla, Nora Hamilton, and James Loucky, the interracial and interethnic conflict occurring among Latino underclasses, specifically Central Americans and Mexicans in Los Angeles in the 1980s and 1990s, reflect "inegalitarian socioeconomic systems in which the opportunities of all are severely constricted."[60] These economically and politically produced wedges between peoples, then, manufacture imaginary power differentiations among groups as a way to keep them *all* down. These social breaks are the "hit-and-run affairs" of the war machines of globalization.[61] Harney and Moten argue that the "commitment to war" is about being "against the social," which simultaneously "disturbs" and "forms" the under-commons.[62] War names the actions that break and dismantle the social, a necropolitics that undoes ways of being together. Botus employs interethnic-interracial conflict to begin this process.

When Carlos arrives on the scene, he discovers a new phenomenon at play: the ghost world has deciphered a way to immigrate to new places. RD-17 is now full of ghosts who refuse to leave since they have traveled from different positions in the world to be near their families and friends, who currently live on the strip of East New York under the Fulton Street El. Carlos's Council-appointed partner for this assignment, Phoebus, brings all the reinforcements—Council soulcatchers—under the COD's power and forcibly attempts to remove the migrants. Gilberto Rosas reminds us that "ongoing wars" reinforce the "dominant representation of the border as a site of un-governability."[63] Significantly, the idea of ungovernability also returns us to Harney and Moten's ideas around governance and race, where blackness or those without interest (or both) are the ungovernable. The ongoing response to these states of living death, or what Rosas aligns with Agamben's state of exception, is war. Rosas argues that the public spectacle of state violence allows for the state to "marshal the technologies over life and death."[64] A war that holds power(s) over life and death has significant implications in the world of *Salsa Nocturna*, however. War, in effect, allows the Council to live above the law, negate their own protocols, and be both exception and rule. Embracing this law of exception, Phoebus escalates the battle by ordering new, militarized agents to take living hostages—the family members of the dead—and to kill them. The agents follow their orders but are also ethically torn by this turn of events. The state's extralegal position here is unsurprising, considering how many nation-states' regulatory offices (troops, police, political figures, donors) operate above the law. Nevertheless, war rationalizes and allows for these state-sponsored crimes, as long as these crimes manage or kill the living and dead multitudes.

Carlos realizes that only a Councilman could break the main protocol with such impunity, identifying Phoebus as one of the seven. Instead of sowing interdead conflict like his bosses, Carlos intervenes by getting Phoebus away from the Council soulcatchers and killing him behind the scenes, thereby ending the battle. This covert intervention is not the world-shattering act of war but is a world-building technique that keeps the new class of agents from having to attack Carlos and his crew and ultimately permits Carlos to remain in the NYCOD. Significantly, this last point allows for the never-ending possibility of future stories and books. When Carlos communes with the migrant ghosts who fought against Phoebus, he apologizes for the battle and states, "I know you just came here to be with your families, to carry on in an afterlife that's harmonious with the living. [. . .] But it's not time yet. There's more work to be done. Foundations to be laid." Carlos voices the goals of the resistance— for the living and the dead to find ways of living together—but he also occludes this future because it requires present work, preconditions that need to be organized. The dead migrants agree to "scatter" for the time being.[65] The world-shattering battle, thus, bares world-building that is taking place in the now and here, always pointing toward pasts and futures, toward there and everywhere. Social formations also take shape in these breaks.

Performative Reclamations of Space and Time

Salsa Nocturna's world-shattering elements give rise to various forms of coalition-building between the underworld and the living underclasses. The collection produces moments when the living, the half-dead, and the dead coexist, overlap, and messily blur into one another. Sometimes, this occurs through the shared experience of music making and musical performance, especially in stories that focus on Gordo. At other times, it happens in acts of reclamation over space and history. One of Carlos and his crew's first acts of resistance occurs when they release the enslaved ghosts of former slaves in the story "Red Feather and Bone." Carlos, Jimmy, Gordo, and Riley discover that the Council has locked these former slaves into an old African burial ground for contemporary gentrification purposes. They join forces with the ghost-child Damian and an ancient black ghost, Cyrus, who has figured out how to escape the enclosure momentarily in spurts of dance and other subversive acts. Carlos sees Cyrus busking in the Chambers Street train station, "doing an old fashioned jig to some scratchy canned music."[66] Cyrus's dance, what Carlos calls an "A train minstrel show," alludes to Saidiya Hartman's idea that performing blackness, such as juba, is on one hand a "reiteration and/or rearticulation of the conditions of enslavement" and, on another hand, an "unruliness" that is a "tactic of resistance."[67] He is "half visible, shiny," openly revolting against the Council's rule about "dead folks appearing to the living."[68] The "full raging force" of the COD soulcatchers, who Carlos thought were looking for

Riley, are from the Council trying to shut down Cyrus's disturbances in the force field, which may upset their real-estate deals by revealing the full size of the burial ground.[69] The crew decides to release the enslaved through an entrada, a part-mechanical, part-magical opening to release the entrapped.

While this story marks the moment when Carlos's crew comes together, especially with the addition of the powerful conjurer and dancer Cyrus, it is also a story that shows the Council's governance as directly tied to spatial economic concerns that reach across US history. Space and economy, as David Harvey theorizes, are in a perpetual dance as the historical geography of capitalism must form and re-form landscapes in its own image, often through war, death, and destruction.[70] In the case of Pinzón's photography, space organizes her subjects both politically and economically, especially when a cop car and a sex shop frame a queer Latinx superhero who does sex work for a living. The questions of gentrification in Older's speculative fiction equally ask us to consider the role of space. For Older, reclamation disrupts these geographies of capitalism and offers speculative forms of resistance. This resistance does not necessarily fix or solve the problems of capitalism, but it produces small communal acts and performances that ideally challenge these structures. To think more fully about this performance, I turn to Coya Paz's and Chicago's Free Street Theater's production *Still/Here* because it productively complicates gentrification's role in imagining pasts, presents, and futures and in forming/ breaking coalitions, communities, and solidarities.

Raised in Peru, Bolivia, Colombia, Ecuador, Brazil, and the United States, Paz is the founder of Chicago's Teatro Luna, cofounder of the Proyecto Latina Collective, and artistic director of Free Street Theater. She has developed a performance art style called "devised theater," which takes its content, material, and choreography from the stories and lives of the community. As such, her performance style pushes the boundaries of theater, where players and audience or theater company and neighborhood are no longer easily distinguishable. This form of theater creates performance art that wishes to "build community toward social change."[71] It significantly differs from Josefina López's style, cineatro, as discussed in chapter 3. Cineatro enacts social experience and bears witness to social conditions, blurring the line between testimonio and social realism and between film and theater. As a performance style, cineatro complicates our understandings of genre and form. In contrast, devised theater makes performances out of social relations. It requires a sense of community in the process of story-making and in constructs of enactment and embodiment. This performance, then, is a form of coalition-building and world-making.

The performance art piece *Still/Here* utilizes devised theater techniques to interrogate the politics and economics of space in Chicago. The Free Street Theater promo for the performance describes its setting as an apocalyptic Chicago, but this apocalypse is not a dystopia of a near or distant future. Rather, it describes the perpetual present of Chicago, a city that is constantly being "rebuilt again and again." "Part manifesto, part history lesson, part fever dream of the future," the performance asks for whom the city is being designed and how the city's past helps us to envision or disallows us from imagining a more equitable and joyful Chicago.[72] The theater company held workshops within the community to develop the questions, visions, monologues, choreographies, experiences, songs, and manifestos that make up *Still/Here*. As a company committed to racially and financially disenfranchised communities, the ensemble players represent these voices and perspectives as well. Some of the actors are clearly more experienced with timing and delivery than others, and most of the ensemble is made up of twenty-somethings, with only a few older members. The performance is in English, although some actors speak Spanish occasionally and others are ASL interpreters. The only live recording of *Still/Here* captures one of its four performances during the summer of 2019.[73] The ensemble set up in a park with minimal props (mainly black milk crates). The audience, both viewers and oral participants in the piece, sit on blankets. The performance begins suddenly and in vocal chaos as all the players shout what they want for Chicago. Some of the skits are symbolic of gentrification and erasures, while others are impassioned monologues that call out the material violences of late capitalism.

Following an interactive skit with the audience where people speak their visions for tomorrow, Char Lee, a young black player in the ensemble, performs a monologue about an encounter with a well-off white guy on the Metra. He complains about the needle-strewn streets of a neighborhood in Chicago, demanding that "they" need to clean it up, so people like him can enjoy the murals better. Lee relates,

> I didn't know what to say or what to do. What I wanted to say was *no*; what I needed to say was *stop*. But instead what I said was *Oh, that's very interesting. Um, what do you know about this neighborhood as a recent transplant from Michigan?* What did he know about tear down, remove, replace, rebuild? I wanted to say *no*, so I said *Stop! Stop taking and taking and taking land that isn't even yours, land that needs to be healed, not sold and sold and sold again.*[74]

The knowing a place, the gentrifying a place, and the healing of a place all center on the question of land ownership, a concept that depends on finance markets and real-estate markets that seek debt and credit. Harney and Moten's understanding of debt and credit grows from a racialized history of productivity, empire, and governance. Those who are accused of "bad debt" are "wrong" for "not working," for failing to "pay [their] debt to society," and for having "no credit." Bad debt, in this sense, is refusing to participate in forms of governance that ask us to invest and reinvest our interests, thereby saying no to building good debt that in turn builds good credit.[75] "Stop!" voices this refusal. Lee continues, "I shot blow darts of language I didn't even know I knew, but my verbal projectiles lie laying in the Metra seat next to me as he got up to leave. But before he left, he repeated his original demand. They should clean up so we can take up." Her voice falls short in the ever-pushing markets of ownership and entitlement. She ends on what this failure and death of voice means: "Failure is what gentrification looks like. Death is what erasure looks like. I got one last [joke] for you: how many gentrifiers does it take to make Chicago great again? I'll tell you. Three. One to embody fear, one to embrace hate, and one to distract us from even knowing that it's happening." These processes of gentrification remove and replace peoples. These forms of displacement create a community of the living dead, who must be hypermobile, who are often invisible, and who must work where they cannot live. Simultaneously, gentrification discourses also distract, elide, and hide what this dispossession and displacement does to a city.

A young Latina player, Marilyn Carteño, relates what has happened to the Pilsen neighborhood in Chicago. Originally a Polish migrant neighborhood in the early to mid-twentieth century, Pilsen grew to be the second-largest Mexican American community in the United States from the 1950s to the early 2000s. Gentrification in the last two decades has displaced many of these residents to Little Village. Carteño's monologue occurs as the final part of a "Remember Me" skit, in which the players describe how Chicago's disappearing past becomes visible in a pothole or haunts the architecture. Boogie McClarin beautifully choreographs the ensemble into a lyrical dance with the milk crates, and Tristan Zemtseff composes an effervescent background guitar sound for the skit. Carteño recalls, "Long ago at 18th and Blue Island stood two community serving institutions, Radio Arte and Yollocalli Arts Reach, the famed youth initiative of the National Museum of Mexican Art. Now in its place is a Wintrust Bank and a Giordanos." For those of us who remember, Yollocalli had huge, uncovered windows along the Blue Island side. The workspace was always visible and transparent from the street, so passersby could see works in progress and the debris of art projects. They would display the finished artwork in the windows along the corner. For it to be replaced with a bank and a Chicago pizza chain for tourists not only illustrates gentrification but also marks a particular brand of consumerism and commerce that eventually infiltrates all spaces. Nevertheless, with a hopeful lament, the performer relates how this disappeared past rises up and resurrects itself: "But when I pass the Pilsen site, I hear the ring of cash registers and the sting of boiled cheese, my eyes swear they see the youth artwork seeping through the tattered wallpaper, radiating resistance and bold visions for the future. They ask, they insist, remember me." Phantom governances that colonize spaces for the market give way to the ghosts of history that haunt these spaces indefinitely. The haunting is a result of and a momentary disruption to this political economy. When one is a part of these displaced communities, seeing our past seep through the veneer of the gentrified present reveals the structures of social death that gentrification creates across time and space.

Still/Here ends with the players asking the audience to shout out what they need and want to survive and to have joy. Ending on these questions of desire asks the community to confront and identify the kind of city Chicago should be. This is not an exercise in imagination; this is voicing a demand that does not create us/them dynamics or produce economies of violence. Furthermore, these questions are not about reproducing visions of the future or remembrances of the past. The performance regularly undercuts its futurisms and its nostalgias, returning to the objective of the monologues and skits: a present urgency. Nevertheless, the performance is devised from a community in constant states of spatial fluctuation, from Mayor Daley's beautification policies to economic demands for more consumer markets to intensifications in financial inequality. Gentrification delineates these slippages, tensions, and violences between and across the social, the political, and the economic.

Still/Here demonstrates the larger political and economic picture embedded in *Salsa Nocturna*'s narrative and *The Real Story of the Superheroes*' images. In the case of Older's fiction, the shady, phantom political bureaucracy satirizes a politics that never quite reveals the whats and whys of their orders and actions. They operate as empires that re-enslave peoples who have already historically been stripped of personhood, and they colonize spaces of rest as they participate in the market economies of gentrification. Set against this satiric governance, nevertheless, is community organization. Coalitions are built in response to and from the conditions of these market infrastructures. In the case of Pinzón's photographs, the migrant Latinx subjects whose labor is regularly consumed and exploited within the shadows of the city wear the extra-ordinary costumes of Marvel and DC archetypes to challenge this invisible and violent positionality. Pinzón draws on graphic novel and blockbuster film traditions to cast a light on a population who have been erased, threatened, and under constant siege because of the desire for exploitable, hypermobile, and displaced labor. *Still/Here* speculates on the possibilities of community-built performances and action in the now, even when failure and death seem inevitable. These narratives all imagine, in some way, incremental forms of resistance that shatter social orders, question the political economy, and build community.

Market Governance

The market, nevertheless, haunts the imaginations and imaginaries of the social within *Salsa Nocturna*, from the Council's plans to enslave ghost mammoths for profit-driven zoos to their land deals for gentrification. The market undercurrents in *Salsa Nocturna* ask us to consider the literary and cultural markets of *Salsa Nocturna* itself, returning me to the literary market for Older's "Bone Street Rumba" series. The "Bone Street Rumba" series has had an uneven publishing life, from independent to niche to mass-market publishers who have released the books in multiple media: JABberwocky ebooks, Ace paperbacks, and single digital stories released on Tor. *Salsa Nocturna* was the first written in the collection but was updated in 2016 to fit into the series more tightly as roughly number 2.5. Notably, each book in the series riffs on different Latinx and/or often racialized musical genres, *Half-Resurrection Blues*, *Midnight Taxi Tango*, and *Battle Hill Bolero*. While these titles refuse the clichés of fantasy novel titles, they establish music as a shared Latinx and black cultural politics structuring the stories. The series' emphasis on music also conveys how the market infiltrates culture. Frances Aparicio maps these discursive frameworks in the case of salsa music, arguing that salsa is both a "tool to imagine social identity" and a genre that is at the commercial whims of a music industry that "erase[s] the centrifugal, plural, and oppositional textures and voices" of salsa.[76] Aparicio describes the push and pull between shared cultural productions that build communities and the industry governances that appropriate these cultural performances. This tension is not lost in the stories of *Salsa Nocturna*, but those stories give a different framework for thinking about market governance. Instead of an appropriating industry, this market governance becomes a part of the common, everyday lives of the community.

The eponymous story of *Salsa Nocturna* represents this market governance most poignantly. The story introduces us to Gordo, a musician whose struggles for work land him on the night shift at a nonprofit children's care facility housed in an old opera house. Because of the building's past, ghosts come to hear music there. Gordo, who can commune with the dead, plays his keyboard every night to the ghosts of the dead, who visit and dance. They sometimes make music with him. Gordo describes,

> There's a jangle to the music of the dead . . . something that's so happy and so sad at the same time. The notes almost make a perfect harmony but don't. Then they do but crash into dissonance. They simmer in the sweet in-between, rhythm section rattling along all the while. Chords collapse chaotically into each other, and just when you think it's gonna spill into total nonsense, it stands back up. . . . That's the kind of music I make, and the dead do too. We make it together.[77]

The story demonstrates how music opens up a space for Gordo to intersect his music with the otherworldly and at times to appropriate the techniques of the underworld, a discursive violence that engenders both intercultural co- alition and varying forms of expropriation. In the same vein, the story ends on a troubled note: the dead's children—los muertecitos—force a young Ec- uadoran orphan, Marcos, who has "untold horrors" in his past and "rarely speaks," to play a mambo endlessly for their entertainment until Gordo saves him.[78] The succubus elements of *Salsa Nocturna* mimic a market that must consume culture, whether it is muertecitos demanding Marcos's music ad in- finitum or soulsuckers who feed on peoples' stories, memories, and histories until they are empty shells. Under this (il)logic of consumption, the music market unsettles any coalition-building, and an instance of intercultural ex- change becomes a venture in appropriation and forceful consumption within and across the community.

Music equally imbues Older's early attempts to market *Salsa Nocturna* before its publication. In 2012, Older made two short promotional films for the collection and posted them on his YouTube channel, one promoting the story "The Passing" and the other the story "Midnight Mambo" (which is ti- tled "Graveyard Waltz" in the 2016 edition of the book). Older's own musical compositions accompany the shorts, respectively entitled "Salsa Nocturna" and "Ghost Waltz." These being primarily piano progressions, neither com- position necessarily follows the conventions of a salsa or a waltz (or even a mambo), but they produce the spectral, discordant, and haunting sounds that the stories within the collection reference and imagine. These trailers market the book, but they do so in very different ways. One is live-action, presenting only suggestive elements of fantasy. The other is animated, depict- ing the whimsical, magical elements of the supernatural. They are beautifully produced shorts that provide a glimpse into the stories through a medium that can reach the masses quickly and effectively. They embody a tension between making art and economies of self-management.

The video for "The Passing" is taken in vertical mode on a cell phone, giving us a glimpse of the story of an old Afro-Cubana named Cici Cortázar, who is part of an ancient order known as the Story Collectors, and her young, white, hipster neighbor, Ben. The trailer opens with Ms. Cortázar in her New York City apartment having an internal dialogue taken directly from the book. Ben drives her to various destinations, while her internal monologues and memories occur in voiceover. The visual narrative and the voiceover do not always sync, producing a sense of two stories happening simultaneously. This narrative twoness, we learn in the book, is a part of being in the order of Story Collectors, who pass on their collected stories to new inductees at the time of their death. The story relates an intimate moment between living and dying for this transfer of stories, memories, and histories. When Ms. Cortázar feels something wrong among the order, Ben drives her to the apartment of her friend and fellow order member Hyacinth, where she discovers her being sucked dry by parasitic entities. In the book, she defeats the "takers" but cannot save her friend, so she has Ben lie down next to Hyacinth and performs the ancient rite of transfer, allowing the stories that remain in her friend to live on. Ben is the first white person inducted into the order, which is historically for women of color. In the short video, these supernatural elements or narrative details are never shown, although the voiceover and atmospheric qualities of Older's background music leave no question that something is amiss and unnatural. The promo puts into play a sense of the twoness and the uneasiness that Ms. Cortázar feels as she moves through her apartment and the streets of New York on Ben's moped. The short's suggestive elements play an important role in the marketing of the book, nevertheless, especially since they produce suspense and appeal to multiple narrative possibilities.

In the second promo for "Midnight Mambo"/"Graveyard Waltz," Older employs an animation artist and voiceover actor, producing an artistic black-and-white visual that captures the otherworldly and supernatural exchanges within the series. The promo begins with the voiceover: "It's a few hours from dawn and I'm lying in a fresh grave with two trash bags full of severed hipster parts." The voiceover reproduces verbatim Gordo's internal dialogue in the book as he works the night shift at a cemetery and watches souls rise into the night.[79] In the video, the voiceover relates that he sees his past, present, and future rise up into the sky, an image that makes him cry until morning. The voiceover ends with the line: "It's a beautiful morning, and something terrible is coming." This is a story that develops Gordo's character more intimately and gives him a dimension that resonates through the collection. Gordo's musical abilities become one of the ways the living and the dead can come into contact and build community, which culminates in the final story when everyone outside or against the Council goes to see his band play at a café. The story, both written and cinematic, captures his joys and burdens in this role. As an advertisement, nevertheless, Older again offers marketing hooks, such as suspense and an incompleteness, that only buying and reading the book can remedy. Perhaps ironically, the book does not necessarily give clear-cut, singular answers to the questions that the promos induce.

Older's DIY aesthetic here embodies a troubled Latinx literary market. In some ways, these promos employ a cultural politics of rasquache in that they utilize what is at hand to make art. By using cell phones, YouTube, and technology at hand, Older is actively promoting his own work in compelling ways. Rasquache is both an aesthetic and a sensibility, what Michelle Habell-Pallán describes as a "cultural practice of 'making do' with limited resources."[80] The history of rasquache in Latinx cultural production, according to Habell-Pallán, "acknowledged the struggles of everyday people," and these practices often "coincide with periods of social upheaval."[81] These acts of resourcefulness and the ability to create from disadvantaged positions push against the social and economic order. At one reading, Older calls out a publishing industry that keeps asking writers-of-color "where have you been?" while the writers echo this back. Parallel to the concerns of *Still/Here*, he states, "We are here; we've always been here; we will continue to be here and tell our stories."[82] Where *Still/Here* makes this claim that "we are here" through the performance of community-based concerns and experiences, Older makes this claim as a response to a market that desires a diversity of representation—but only when the numbers show it is profitable.

Nevertheless, the celebratory elements of what Older is doing also point back to Harney and Moten's idea of self-management. These promos, as such, serve an economy that wills and/or demands us to manage our own interests, and if we do not, then we are criminalized and rendered disposable. Pinzón's photographs perhaps elucidate this most pointedly because they present a clear tension between visibility and invisibility. These are "good" workers insofar as they are cheap, invisible, and performing the labor that few want to do, but by putting her subjects in superhero costumes, she reveals and complicates the normalizations of this market logic. The market logic here is a politics from below insomuch as it is a part of our everyday. Operating in a political economy that disallows anything alternative to the market means that the production of culture itself is at the mercy of the market's whims.

A Speculative Conclusion

When Harney and Moten describe how the undercommons allows us to "glimpse the hole in the fence where labor enters," they allude to Latinx/Latin American migrant labor and the US-Mexico border fence.[83] This metaphor implores us to consider the porous and taut interchanges between economic governances and the work of the undercommons. *Salsa Nocturna* and Older's position in the literary market also provide holes in the fence. While these stories may not upend the violent structures that they interrogate, they build the varying textures, voices, and dissonant harmonies of the underworld. By tracing the forms of world-shattering and world-building in this chapter, I have followed the slippages and antagonisms between race, governance, and speculative imaginaries of the social. Latinx studies has not always readily spoken about blackness within our social formations, which has created chasms within potential coalition-building in labor, in being, and in resistance. Furthermore, the colonial legacies that haunt this field also trouble our racial discourses as many of us descend from both oppressor and oppressed.[84] *Salsa Nocturna* refuses to elide the racial and colonial multiplicities and divisions of "us" and "we." In many ways, it challenges these historical and social divisions without denying their existence, and it points these social ruptures back at governances that are always (neo)colonial and necropolitical under market capitalism. The porous border fence symbolically reveals both these governances and undercommons.

The processes of world-shattering and world-building, nevertheless, shoulder a deeply speculative cultural politics. When Jerng theorizes the racial valences within the world-making narratives of speculative popular fiction, he understands these narratives to "challenge prominent historical explanations of the transformations of racial meaning," transformations including "the trajectory from biological racism to cultural racism" and "the transition from covert racism to overt racism." Simultaneously, these narratives, for better or worse, have a hand "in creating the conditions by which race gets embedded in the making of present and future world(s)."[85] Aimee Bahng understands world-building to have equally important migratory and spatial components: "Under the rubric of speculative fiction, various historical networks of affiliations (among Asian immigrants to the Caribbean and Mexico, Malaysian workers in Singapore, and Asian Brazilians who migrate for a second time to Southern California) are evoked that decenter the United States in the narrative of immigration in the Americas." For Bahng, these speculative narratives create transnational affiliations that move with the "intensified global flows" of finance capital.[86] These are a sort of undercommons in that a social relationality arises *under* the labor exploitations, community displacements, new forms of enclosure and enslavement, and creations of surplus peoples. A shared movement over space and for resistance grows from this state of being *under* capitalism, *under* laws or citizenship, and *under* war machines, while the purported elite exist above this so-called order of things.

When Older relates why he writes speculative fictions, he describes that writing about race across genres means writing stories where "all these different narratives crash into one another in a very complicated and ugly way" because that is the truth of our current social moment.[87] The speculative in this sense negotiates the future and the past insofar as it captures and reveals the social of the now. While in this chapter I have focused mainly on *Salsa Nocturna*, Pinzón's *The Real Story of the Superheroes* and Coya Paz's/Free Street Theater's *Still/Here* equally show these entanglements between the political, the economic, and the social. Together, these three narratives make clear that this type of work requires performance and performative dimensions. As Hartman argues, the interchangeability between performance and the performative accounts for a series of "cross-purposes": "displays of power, punitive and theatrical embodiment of racial norms, the discursive re-elaboration of blackness, and the affirmative deployment and negation of blackness in the focus on redress." [88] These fictions, images, and performances reveal and display a political economy that discursively organizes and negates these performances from below. They, however, neither leave us with a note of pessimism nor rehash the fatalism of necropolitics. Instead, they imagine ways of being in the ruptures, of existing in structural death, and of forming community under these displays and acts of power.

Dreaming of Deportation, or, When Everything "Goes South"

You understand. Abuelita, I can't go back and *return. There's no path to papers. I've got nothing left but dreams.*

JAVIER ZAMORA, "TO ABUELITA NELI," *UNACCOMPANIED* (2017)

Writing of his migration from El Salvador to the United States, Javier Zamora implores that we, like his abuelita, understand that being undocumented means return is not possible; going south again after migrating to the north is consigned to dreams, especially when one has "no path to papers."[1] The "no path to papers" embedded in this verse, however, carries a lot of illegible baggage, especially when considered through US immigration policy. At the end of every introduction to Latinx literature course that I teach, I spend a week or two walking my students through the major US government websites on immigration procedures and deportation policies to make it more legible.[2] These sites help them think about how the United States defines the terms of citizenship and borders for all to see. It is a relatively boring experience for my students, as we tread through legalese, long-winded documents, and unintuitive web design. I try to make the experience feel less tedious by calling out the hypervisible chat bot who scrolls through pages with you at times. The bot is represented as a racially ambiguous woman named Emma, welcoming visitors with a smile and letting them know they can ask her for help. I always note her absence on the websites that give the legal definitions for deportation, visas, and refugee/asylee processes or the pages that deal with tariffs and customs. While working our way through these sites and documents, we also discuss the current events that shape our understanding of these processes.

In the past decade, deportation practices in the United States have been exceptionally terrifying. In 2014, thousands of unaccompanied minors from Central America were detained, causing uproar about the imprisonment of children in overburdened detention centers, as discussed in chapter 2. Then in 2018, the US government began to detain large numbers of families seeking asylum at ports of entry, implementing a separation policy that split children from their parents and guardians. To deal with the surplus bodies, the US government created camps and tent cities to detain these children. These detainment practices are unquestionably cruel and inhumane. They imprison people simply for arriving at a border. They are predicated on families being ripped apart. And they strip racialized bodies of basic rights and personhood. At one time, the US administrations and congresses knew the system was broken and offered policy band-aids that attempted reform, such as the 2012 Deferred Action for Childhood Arrivals (DACA). DACA allowed for undocumented subjects to defer any government action to deport them for two years (renewable) while they acquired work permits or education visas. Eligibility requirements include(d) those who came to the United States as children before age sixteen, have no criminal charges in the United States, and have completed high school/GED/military service, to name a few. It was a small step toward shaping the laws and practices into more humane forms, even if it was far from actually fixing broken legislation. On September 5, 2017, the Trump administration announced they were rescinding DACA, further demonstrating that their policies were xenophobic and that they had no interest in reform. Notably, from 2018 to 2020, it became more difficult to find DACA information to show my students on the government websites, with the information relegated to the archived section.[3] In 2021, under a new US administration, constituents hoped the closing of the child border camps would be achieved in the first hundred days, but the camps remain open as I write this. The current violence on immigration and migration is sharpening, materializing in both the criminalizing of bodies and the increasing lack of access to information.

I end *Visible Borders, Invisible Economies* on the practices and discourses around deportation not because they tell us something about Latinx identity. Many Latinx subjects may not have directly experienced immigration or deportation under these terms and/or may be distant from the processes by way of generational differences, citizenship status, or histories in which the border crossed them. Instead, I end on deportation because it reveals something about the kind of world we are living and dying in. When Sara Ahmed states, "Bodies that do not follow the line of whiteness, for instance, might be 'stopped' in their tracks, which does not simply stop one from getting somewhere, but changes one's relation to what is 'here,'" she asks us to think about how the things that "stop" bodies—borders, deportation, death—may unveil our relationship to this current time and space.[4] As a global population, we charge ever deeper into the Anthropocene (or more aptly the Capitalocene, if we want to point toward the primary catalyst for man-made climate change and extinction events), and this has very real ramifications. What we are seeing here and now are the reactions, or what Ahmed calls the "stress points," of these economic conclusions: atrocities that must occur at the expense of those of us deemed disposable and unworthy of life. As the idiom goes, everything seems to be "going south." Nevertheless, I turn at the end to provocative and suggestive cultural productions about deportation as a way to hopefully reposition our norte-oriented perspectives and see the so-called global south differently.

Latinx literature has historically seen deportation as a negative because of these broken policies and human rights violations, from Ana Castillo's *The Guardians* to Diane Guerrero's *In the Country We Love*, and rightly so, in view of the systemic and economic practices that encourage migration in the first place. Tanya Maria Golash-Boza's recent ethnographic study *Deported* bolsters this perspective, as she traces the lived impacts of US government practices on the US-Mexico border. She argues that deportation is complementary and crucial to the sustainability of neoliberal economies: "mass deportation reflects global capitalism's demand for the free flow of goods across borders and the controlled flow of labor."[5] For Golash-Boza, both border control and capital mobility want the repression, exploitation, and dehumanization of racialized bodies.[6] This singular aim grows out of strategic policymaking that closely aligns local police with ICE, such as the 287(g) Program, Secure Communities, the Criminal Alien Program (CAP), and the National Fugitive Operations Program (NFOP).[7] In all four cases, police officers are deputized as ICE agents and arrest suspects for their undocumented status, creating new ways to control labor and bodies. In some ways, these policies demonstrate the way immigration policy and incarceration practices have collapsed and blurred, creating "crimmigration." This political maneuver is carefully constructed because it sets the stage for the popular imaginary, our ideologies and norms, and cultural imaginations to be unable to fully distinguish between migration and crime. Golash-Boza reminds us that these contemporary practices of detainment and deportation ensure a weak labor force, provide fodder for the cutting of social benefits, and further increase inequality.[8] This is economic in that it manages and maintains the interests of global capitalism.

The rising violence around deportation and border fortification across the Western world is a part of a larger economic phenomenon. As discussed in chapters 1 and 2, walls and fences are just as much about keeping people in as they are about keeping people out, but they are also porous in that holes are intentionally created for the passing of goods or for the controlled funneling of bodies. Wendy Brown identifies the four fantasies of walled democracy that imbue these border fortifications: the fantasy of the dangerous alien in an increasingly borderless world, the fantasy of containment, the fantasy of impermeability, and the fantasy of purity, innocence, and goodness.[9] While I have focused largely on the first three of these popular and problematic imaginaries in *Visible Borders, Invisible Economies*, the last is a significant part of border violence because this is where imaginations about national exceptionalism occur. For Brown, "Walling expresses and gratifies this desire for a national imago of goodness, one that wholly externalizes the nation's ills and disavows its unlovely effects on others, its aggressions, needs, and dependencies."[10] These fantasies feed the idea that el norte, particularly the United States and increasingly Canada, is a space of hope and possibility, one predicated on the disparagement of the global south. These questions of walls and fences differ from the discussion of enslavement and enclosure that vexes the readings in chapters 3, 4, and 5, where market violence produces more specialized forms of corporeal and labor control. Nevertheless, walls and fences also function similarly to enslavement and enclosure insofar as they are both grounded in what Saskia Sassen calls "expulsion." Sassen argues that imprisonment, mass incarceration, deportation, and other exclusions and erasures are all forms of social expulsion that possess a great capacity for labor and profit generation.[11] According to Sassen, expulsion describes the current stage of advanced capitalism ordering the global north and the global south, where the global north maintains its power through economic asymmetries, especially through structural adjustment programs.[12] To call this a form of expulsion is to understand that these economic and political violences require the forcible removal of marginalized and racialized bodies and peoples.

Nevertheless, a very small selection of Latinx fiction does not completely accommodate a narrative of cruelty and violence around deportation or state-enforced expulsions, specifically Malín Alegría's *Sofi Mendoza's Guide to Getting Lost in Mexico* and Maceo Montoya's *The Deportation of Wopper Barraza*. Instead, these novels, first, pointedly refuse to denigrate Mexico or other Latin American countries and, second, present forcible returns as a catalyst for personal and social change. In some ways, these deportation narratives share an affinity with celebratory (or at least transformative) narratives of return, such as Pilar's journey to Cuba in Cristina García's *Dreaming in Cuban* (1992) or Felita's Puerto Rican summer in Nicholasa Mohr's *Going Home* (1990). But return narratives often employ nostalgia as something that causes the going home, and this nostalgia often discursively reinforces the United States as a better place by the end. Because deportation is not nostalgic return but state-mandated violence, these deportation narratives neither vilify the home of their ancestors nor buy into the exceptionalism of el norte. Moreover, they challenge the widespread imaginaries about the global south as perpetually in development, in corruption, or in collapse.

In the case of *The Deportation of Wopper Barraza*, the story shows how deportation becomes a way for our protagonist to imagine otherwise. In his piece "The Anxiety of Influence," Maceo Montoya relates:

> I hear about the kids at Donnelly Circle who set fire to the sandbox and I can't help but think of the tragedy of their misdirected imaginations. Or I pass by Beamer Elementary and I see the playground full of happy children, [. . .] smiles everywhere, and I wonder how long it will take before those brown faces harden and those smiles disappear. [. . .] Sometimes I get so tired of it all . . . what it means to be Chicano, what it means to be a Chicano artist. I just am and my only responsibility is to create, and that is the truth. But I know it's not. Nobody just is, no artist creates in a vacuum. But still, I want to escape this inheritance, to be left alone in the realm of my imagination, [. . .] I believe in my solitude but I also know that the great pain in my heart, the aching store of my creativity, has never been mine alone.[13]

Montoya conveys the varying tensions between a solitary imagination and a social imagination. This anxiety shapes his authorial choices, describes his existential relationship to the world, and imbues his consciousness with the ever-present histories and the almost inevitable futures for Chicanx and Latinx subjects. These anxieties around imagination also take shape in Montoya's *The Deportation of Wopper Barraza*.

While the novel recognizes the political and economic violence of deportation, it finds a flicker of hope in a legally mandated divorce from the United States. The novel is about Roberto "Wopper" Barraza, who has spent his whole conscious life in Woodland, California, as an undocumented migrant. At first glance, he embodies the situation of many DACA recipients, who have known only the United States and whose parents' ties to home—Mexico, in this case—do not necessarily extend to them, even if they are technically still citizens of that home. DACA was one response to this position of precarity. Even more promising, the Development, Relief, and Education for Alien Minors (DREAM) Act proposed to give DACA recipients a path toward citizenship, and their attainment of permanent residency would largely depend on their success at being good citizens, determined by enrolling in college, joining the military, and showing good moral character. While the DREAM Act continues to be but a dream, it envisioned new policy under great violence. Wopper, however, initially represents the opposite of a DREAMer/dreamer. He attends a junior college at one point, but otherwise he has spent most of his life as a slacker with few prospects and multiple DUIs. He lives with his parents, cannot hold a job, and spends most of his time on the couch watching TV with his girlfriend, Lara. He lacks imagination or "dreams," choosing instead to while away his present and foreclose any futurity or possibility.

When he finds himself with his fourth DUI, a court date, and an expedited deportation ruling, the people in his life change their perception of who he is.[14] For instance, his only friend, Raul Leon, drunkenly foreshadows, "I kept looking at the white wall and it was spinning, but not what you think. It was spinning and spinning, and I swear to God I thought I saw Wopper's future. And instead of punching the wall I started laughing. I said, 'Motherfucker, you lucky son of a bitch!' I couldn't stop laughing."[15] Wopper ends up in the town of La Morada, Mexico, stays on his father's former farmland that has been taken over by Don Cirilo, and falls in love with Don Cirilo's daughter, unimaginatively named Mija. Her name demarcates her gendered status in La Morada, perceived as a perpetual child and never taken seriously. She becomes an equal force in the novel, a protagonist who lifts up Wopper and gives him purpose, although her gender-normative world allows her to operate only through men. With Mija, Wopper becomes a major figure within the community, a man of few words who is respected. Simultaneously, Mija finds power through Wopper's new positionality and begins transforming her community through his influence. The symbiotic relationship between Wopper and Mija gives them each a future, even though it is troublingly and rigidly gendered. However, their future possibilities are fleeting, as corrupt officials eventually chase Wopper out of town. Wopper ends up back in Woodland, working at a Walgreens and seemingly returned to his former, banal American life. Despite this conclusion, the novel ambivalently celebrates Wopper Barraza's deportation as a positive and transformative experience. It puts into question the blind love of the United States for those making the United States home and attempts to imagine otherwise a subjectivity that can break free from a US ideological imperialism that demonizes the global south, even while being beholden to those ideologies.

In a very different mode, Alegría's young adult fiction *Sofi Mendoza's Guide* employs *Bildungsroman* and romantic idealism to demonstrate Sofi's slow but necessary detachment from the United States as a seemingly better place. Sofi does not even know she is undocumented until she goes on a spring break trip to Mexico against her parents' wishes and then cannot reenter the United States. Her discovery that her papers are fake is world-shattering, but experiencing everyday life in Mexico transforms our protagonist in profound ways, and miraculously, she is eventually able to return to the United States, a changed woman who understands the world and realizes her place in it. While *Sofi Mendoza's Guide* provides more saccharine forms of transformation than *The Deportation of Wopper Barraza*, both utilize this transformation to empower these characters after undergoing a system that easily criminalizes and disposes of them. Furthermore, *Sofi Mendoza's Guide* and *The Deportation of Wopper Barraza* refuse to fully show how "return" to the United States happens. In the case of *Sofi Mendoza's Guide*, her parents write that they are working with immigration lawyers to ensure her return, but their actions occur on the peripheries of the narrative.[16] Eventually, she discovers her abuela was born at a farm in the United States during the Bracero Program, and if they find the midwife or documentation of her delivery, Sofi may be able to return to el norte. Her abuela eventually finds a birth statement from the midwife, and the lawyer explains the process for her return from there, but the legal steps and proceedings for this conclusion are largely missing.[17] The choice to elide the bureaucratic political structures in favor of transformation repositions our perspective. Our eyes do not look at the political system that demands the social death of disposable subjects but gaze toward the global south as a space of possibility.

Both novels were written before the atrocities defining the US-Mexico border under the Trump administration and, thus, are coming from a moment when deportation politics are not necessarily synonymous with increasingly fascist policies in the United States. Their publication dates, in particular, afford them a certain privilege in questioning the exceptionalism of US citizenship, but these are not necessarily celebratory narratives, and they problematically uphold individual transformation over social and political transformation. For example, in *The Deportation of Wopper Barraza*, Wopper finally sends a letter home to his ex, Lara. In humble surprise, he explains that he is now a municipal representative, a licenciado who is trusted and respected by the community, but the letter relates that his success as a politico has gotten him in trouble with his more corrupt counterparts. His Woodland Community College counselor Mr. Beas (also Lara's cousin) reads the letter, exclaiming, "A year had already passed since he left, and from the sound of it, Wopper was my most successful student. Associates degree or not, he was a citizen of influence."[18] At this moment, Mr. Beas easily replaces the state citizenship denied to Wopper with a subjecthood of success as a "citizen of influence." But this new citizenship also intones elements of neoliberalism, where Wopper's success is synonymous with his abilities to maximize his own value as someone who can influence local politics and threaten corruption. So, on one hand, this newfound subjecthood in Mexico *reimagines* normative migrant narratives about deportation, where deportation is a form of social death and sometimes a literal death sentence, a narrative that makes US citizenship a desirable and necessary conclusion. But on the other hand, Wopper's newfound subjecthood in Mexico does not subvert these norms at all, instead conforming to the economic narrative of Western modernity, where success and value (pointedly marked by Wopper being seen as an American rather than a mexicano in La Morada) are the only ways to attain a "successful" subjecthood.

Montoya describes his novel as an exploration of the way Latinx subjects are constructed on both sides of the border and "why so many bright minds, on both ends of the diaspora, fail to reach their full potential."[19] He ends on a wistful note: "For me, the border is inconsequential here. The roots go deeper than 1848, and it's probably a much longer conversation to be had, but I think a lot about the legacy of colonialism, the damage that's been done to us, but also what we do to one another, as a community, where instead of focusing our energies on helping each other flourish, we succumb to negativity. Yes, a community is represented in this novel, but each character is very much alone. I know I wrote the story, but I still wish it were different."[20] Montoya's wish echoes the double bind of his creative positionality on imagination. While he desires a solitary imagination unbeholden to the social, he knows that his work is always a part of a social imaginary. Of course, imagination and community building are different projects, but Montoya identifies a community that has collectively lost its social imagination and its social consciousness here.

To briefly explore what this means, I turn to Kandice Chuh's groundbreaking work *Imagining Otherwise*, which perhaps offers a different angle for considering this social bind. While Chuh's work is an investigation of specifically Asian-American experience, it considers how literatures and histories from below threaten US exceptionalisms and ideological imperialisms. To imagine otherwise is to understand that citizenship (and the question of subjectivity imbuing it) is not enough to "remedy injustice," even while it remains the only way to access certain material resources.[21] These deportation narratives also grapple with both a desire for forms of citizenship that may inspire change and a recognition of the strangely empty promises of citizenship. Aimee Bahng, in her recent work *Migrant Futures*, takes up Chuh's call to imagine otherwise. She explores the cultural politics of refusal in speculative fiction, or narratives that refuse the "relentlessly anticipatory trajectory of time" that defines citizenship and modernity under neoliberal pluralism.[22] While this refusal is a laudable literary goal, *The Deportation of Wopper Barraza* and *Sofi Mendoza's Guide* instead more truthfully reproduce the sense of anxiety under neoliberal modernity, especially for peoples living a border politics. For Montoya's novel, the *out* to Wopper's stagnation and powerlessness in the United States (deportation) leads back only to the ideological trajectories that originally expelled him (whether a Western and neoliberal notion of success in Mexico or literally back to Woodland and menial labor), and his attempts to find an *in* socially seem futile in some instances and seem to continue unraveling in surprising ways in others. Wopper is both a representative and a refusal of neoliberal modernity. The novels struggle between their desire to reject the ideology that US citizenship is the end goal and to celebrate citizenship's very economic and political promises of belonging and success.

In *Visible Borders, Invisible Economies*, we have seen many stories that arrive at this ambivalence around deportation and "going south." The old lobos del mar in Francisco Goldman's *The Ordinary Seaman* decide to capsize the freighter while they await the officials to come detain and deport them. They *want* to be deported—not because they desire the violence of these practices but because they never planned to stay in the United States: they came to work on a ship and return once the work was done. When that work ends up being a hellacious landscape of global capitalism where being paid is the least of their worries, they need the United States (or in this case the Seafarers' Institute) to deport them simply to afford the return home. With this ending, *The Ordinary Seaman* disrupts the United States as the only end point for many migrants because it refuses to present all migrants from Latin America as perpetually fleeing the global south for something better. Instead, el norte is a space that offers work and needed money, momentarily; nothing more or less. And in the case of Goldman's novel, this space is not even necessarily the United States but the politically ambiguous and stateless ship docked in Brooklyn, further disrupting US national exceptionalism under global capitalism.

Other narratives in *Visible Borders, Invisible Borders* have evoked this desire or need to leave the United States for the global south. Cornejo Villavicencio begins *The Undocumented Americans* by saying that one cannot write the story of undocumented immigrants if "enamored by America."[23] US exceptionalism "disqualifies" a writer from being able to tell this story, and she ensures that the stories she relates keep el norte ambivalent. Few of her subjects "go south" within the parameters of the narrative, but many relay why and how they may have to "go south." The trend across the stories is that "going south" is a necessary response to their foreclosed futures in the United States and a place to finally rest in peace. In one instance, the narrative of Paloma, a Ground Zero cleanup worker, recounts how she returns to Colombia after being diagnosed with breast cancer and receiving compensation money from the September 11th Victim Compensation fund. Cornejo Villavicencio emphasizes that she returns only to die.[24] In another instance, the story of Octavio Márquez, an older day laborer from Guatemala who has been the victim of wage theft, shares his sentiments about staying in the United States. He discloses to Cornejo Villavicencio that he does not feel at home in the United States and tells her, "Even immigrants in extreme poverty find a way to send their deceased loved ones back home to be buried." For Octavio, the dead need a place to rest, and the United States does not offer that for first-generation, undocumented, Latinx immigrants.[25] These narratives demonstrate how the imminence of literal death catalyzes return, even while these subjects undergo various forms of social and slow death in el norte. The book even ends on a note that all undocumented Latinx immigrants will eventually return, whether "by choice, force, or casket."[26] By "going south," they in effect prevent their erasures in the United States.

In a different vein, Alex Rivera's *Sleep Dealer* also gestures to the need to "go south." Rudy's choice to help Memo and Luz blow up the Del Rio dam marks him as a terrorist and means he can never return to the United States. As an exile, Rudy's future cannot be el norte. At the end of the film, we see him get on a southbound bus, flipping up his hoodie as he boards. The hoodie is a gesture of anonymity but also reminds us that the US surveillance state reaches everywhere. Heading south for Rudy becomes his only option as he must flee the border zones, but this act also carries other possibilities. One possibility is that south from Tijuana means Chiapas, suggesting that he will join the Zapatista-like "aqua-terrorists." Another possibility is that he will rediscover his Mexican heritage or will finally escape the parental expectations of a military career. The film offers his future as an open ending, not written yet but still a space for interpretative imagination.

This idea of the global south as a space of possibility for the dispossessed and/or for enemies of the state brings to mind Claudia Milian's definition: "the global south is an undefined but active terrain that is in-the-making."[27] This "in-the-making" initially seems to be a part of the problematic discourses about the global order, where the world is divided into developed/developing. Under these terms of development, the south is always living in the shadow of the north: its future is either (1) already written by those states and empires (the so-called First World) that have progressed to some imaginary modern endpoint or (2) already foreclosed by the neoliberal logic of uneven development, where the Third World must perpetually shoulder the exploitation of the First World.[28] In response to these discourses of development that effectually naturalize and normalize Western modernity, María Josefina Saldaña-Portillo calls on us to not think about revolutionary moments as anti-developmentalism or anti-progressive. She argues that the revolutionary potential is never fully against or outside these discourses and ideologies but operates "within a racialized and gendered developmentalism."[29] While Milian's idea of a global south that is "in-the-making" evokes this structure of development discourses, she discursively problematizes this world-making. The global south is "undefined" insofar as it is not beholden to northern exceptionalism, and it is "active" in that it offers states of change that do not oblige the teleological fantasies or violent markets of the developed. Nevertheless, it is also undefined in that it remains unmade. Latinx narratives of "going south," then, present this tension that only the figure of the south can provide.

I end on these suggestive possibilities and tensions around deportation because they ask us to see differently. They also further show us the ambivalent push and pull within the conditions of the living dead that I have regularly considered in *Visible Borders, Invisible Economies*. The Latinx narratives in this book rarely embrace simple black-and-white binaries that present the social order as divided into citizen/criminal, native/foreign, in/out, global south/global north, expelled/enclosed, or dead/living. Instead, these narratives navigate what it means to move through the world as both and neither. These ambivalent conditions of being expose the violence at the heart of the political economy. Necropolitics offers one lens for reading this violence and for considering how Latinx subjects become pawns in the game. Processes of global capitalism focus our eyes in one direction while setting the stage for misrecognition, zones of indistinction, and states of exception, all while profiting from distributions of cruelty, siege, and inequality. The living dead, however, are building underworlds.

Notes

Introduction

1. Virginia Grise, *Your Healing Is Killing Me* (Pittsburg, PA: Plays Inverse, 2017), 17, 12.

2. Ibid., 56–57.

3. See Wendy Brown, *Undoing the Demos: Neoliberalism's Stealth Revolution* (New York: Zone, 2015), 33–34.

4. Suzanne Oboler, *Ethnic Labels, Latino Lives: Identity and the Politics of (Re) Presentation in the United States* (Minneapolis: University of Minnesota Press, 1995), xii–xiv.

5. Ibid., xiv–xv. These ideas of pan-latinidad have a lot of potential and power when organized among community, but within larger US imaginaries, they can also lead to problematic understandings of Latinos/Hispanics in that they impart a political and demographic homogeneity. Cristina Beltrán sees the discourses on pan-latinidad in the 1990s to misrepresent Latino politics, especially since studies have shown this demographic "lack[s] a shared sense of the common good." Ricardo Ortiz extends Beltrán's deconstruction of Latino unity by arguing that latinidad as performance, practice, and process allows for a "fuller consideration of actual political ontologies" and of Latinx literature. In this book I hope to answer Ortiz's call to think together performance/practice, the political, and the literary. See Beltrán, *The Trouble with Unity: Latino Politics and the Creation of Identity* (Oxford: Oxford University Press, 2010), 114–115; Ortiz, *Latinx Literature Now: Between Evanescence and Event* (Cham, Switzerland: Palgrave Macmillan, 2016), 7–8.

6. Oboler, *Ethnic Labels*, xv.

7. For Alicia Schmidt Camacho, "migrant" is a term that connotes peoples who cross national borders, whose movements have "changed the character of both US and Mexican national life," but it also marks a condition of exclusion and subordination to national institutions and rights. Significantly, these movements produce narratives that imagine different social orders, different relationships to space, and different definitions of justice. I also use the term "migrant" to speak to these political and economic global circuits that subjugate certain groups of people but also generate potential, powerful imaginaries. Schmidt Camacho, *Migrant Imaginaries: Latino*

Cultural Politics in the U.S.-Mexico Borderlands (New York: New York University Press, 2008), 5.

8. Lorgia García-Peña, *The Borders of Dominicanidad: Race, Nation, and the Archives of Contradiction* (Durham, NC: Duke University Press, 2016), 11.

9. Personally, I prefer the use of "Latina/e/o/x" as an inclusive term, and I recognize the language incongruities of using "Latinx." I do not think of "Latinx" as a replacement term within larger Spanish language usage. My use of "Latinx" throughout this book does not ask readers to reimagine and reconstruct an entire language structured through lexical gender. However, I find it is a term that works well in the written form, where the -x draws the eye and implores readers to note the gendered elements of language, the power dynamics wrought through language, the erasures of language, and the written crossing out of these social orders.

10. Michel Foucault, *The Birth of Biopolitics: Lectures at the Collège de France, 1978–1979* (New York: Palgrave Macmillan, 2008), 116; David Harvey, *A Brief History of Neoliberalism* (Oxford: Oxford University Press, 2005), 66.

11. Foucault, *History of Sexuality*, vol. 1: *An Introduction* (New York: Vintage, 1990), 21, 138, 141–145; Brown, *Undoing the Demos*, 20, 33. Jodi Dean reminds us, however, that democracy has always been infused with violence against various demographics, and market capitalists use the ideals of democracy to make neoliberalism appear less violent than it actually is. See Dean, *Democracy and Other Neoliberal Fantasies: Communicative Capitalism and Left Politics* (Durham, NC: Duke University Press, 2009), 17–18.

12. Foucault argues that *homo oeconomicus* disciplines the social order through entrepreneurship, where we are all entrepreneurs of our own lives. Wendy Brown rewrites Foucault's understanding of *homo oeconomicus* and argues that this self-care and self-interest seeps into every sphere of our lives, so that our humanity and subjectivity is now measured by our "capacity for 'self-care.'" Foucault, *Birth of Biopolitics*, 226; Brown, *Undoing the Demos*, 42.

13. Foucault calls this management a "phenomenal republic of interests." For Foucault, these new administrations of governance ultimately put into question the "utility of a government" in a society "where exchange determines the true value of all things." *Birth of Biopolitics*, 46, 47.

14. Ibid., 65. In this shift from classical liberalism to neoliberalism, the idea that economic processes are within governmental and legal control and reason (such as Rousseau's social contract) is replaced with markets that now govern the discourses and actions of nation-states and their respective populations. According to Harvey, this interplay between the nation-state and market is a problem because neoliberalism's desires for a "well-being for all" and neoliberalism's aims to restore class power produce an "unstable political form." Foucault, *Birth of Biopolitics*, 22, 116, 131–132; Harvey, *Brief History of Neoliberalism*, 79.

15. Roberto Esposito, *Bios: Biopolitics and Philosophy* (Minneapolis: University of Minnesota Press, 2008), 36; Alexander G. Weheliye, *Habeas Viscus: Racializing Assemblages, Biopolitics, and Black Feminist Theories of the Human* (Durham, NC: Duke University Press, 2014), 13.

16. Foucault, *Birth of Biopolitics*, 63–65.

17. Ibid., 67.

18. Ibid., 67–68.

19. Friedrich A. Hayek, *The Constitution of Liberty* (Chicago: The University of Chicago Press, 2011), 165. He follows this claim by warning against equal distribution and arguing that the poor should not feel "entitled to a share of the wealth" simply because they occupy the same community with those who are richer and more comfortable. His argument against giving the poor any benefits is the same argument made against social welfare now.

20. Inderpal Grewal, *Saving the Security State: Exceptional Citizens in Twenty-First-Century America* (Durham, NC: Duke University Press, 2017), 15–16.

21. Hayek, *Constitution of Liberty*, 165. See also Michael W. Clune's reading of Hayek's early work, where he argues this work is an exercise in analyzing "what would happen in a world where market prices are left to organize things without the interference of other kinds of order." Clune draws out the literary imagination and speculative nature of Hayek's work. Clune, *American Literature and the Free Market, 1945–2000* (Cambridge: Cambridge University Press, 2010), 92.

22. Saskia Sassen, *Losing Control? Sovereignty in an Age of Globalization* (New York: Columbia University Press, 1996), 42–43. For a more comprehensive engagement with the many histories, forms, and modalities of citizenship, see Étienne Balibar, *Citizenship* (Cambridge, UK: Polity, 2015).

23. Friedrich A. Hayek, *The Political Order of a Free People: Law, Legislation, and Liberty*, vol. 3 (Chicago: University of Chicago Press, 1979), 56.

24. See Harvey, *Brief History of Neoliberalism*, 39–40, 71–73; Dean, *Democracy and Other Neoliberal Fantasies*, 51–55, 67–68.

25. Grewal, *Saving the Security State*, 14.

26. For "brown peril," see Mike Davis, *Magical Urbanism: Latinos Reinvent the U.S. City* (New York: Verso, 2001), 83–92.

27. Hayek, *Constitution of Liberty*, 99. For more on First World–Third World development discourse, see also Arturo Escobar, *Encountering Development: The Making and Unmaking of the Third World* (Princeton, NJ: Princeton University Press, 1995), and María Josefina Saldaña-Portillo, *The Revolutionary Imagination in the Americas and the Age of Development* (Durham, NC: Duke University Press, 2003).

28. Hayek arguably abstracts the material realities of the economy throughout *The Constitution of Liberty*. For instance, Hayek seems to care little about actual resource waste or poverty. Even when he directly interrogates taxation, his objective engagement with data exists only to demonstrate the imaginary and potential devastation to wealth production. There is also an argument to be made about how this need to abstract is part of our new cognitive normal, à la the Flynn effect. James R. Flynn explores the human proclivity for abstract problem solving that is removed from any concrete reality. Flynn at one point indicates that this new cognitive normal grows out of the 1930s preoccupation with the "business of life" when more and more jobs required abstract problem-solving. Hayek, *Constitution of Liberty*, 129, 366–367, 312–313; James R. Flynn, *What Is Intelligence?* (Cambridge: Cambridge University Press, 2007), 26–27, 42–43, 108.

29. Javier Duran, "Virtual Borders, Data Aliens, and Bare Bodies: Culture, Securitization, and the Biometric State," *Journal of Borderlands Studies* 25, nos. 3–4 (2010): 226.

30. For instance, Saskia Sassen argues that the United States' foreign investment in export resources has moved corporate agriculture into the southern hemisphere, displacing subsistence farmers into commercial work. Sassen also explores why the

United States, where corporate ventures have been the cause of this displacement, often becomes the endpoint for worker migrations so often: US interference in Latin American economies has been accompanied with a "rapid expansion of the supply of low-wage jobs in the United States and the casualization of the labor market associated with new growth industries, particularly in the major cities." Néstor García Canclini and Aihwa Ong also argue that these forms of displacement, primarily from agricultural economies to urban industrialization, motivate much of the migratory movements from Latin America to the United States. Sassen, *Globalization and Its Discontents: Essays on the New Mobility of People and Money* (New York: New Press, 1998), 41, 45. García Canclini, *Consumers and Citizens: Globalization and Multicultural Conflicts*, trans. George Yúdice (Minneapolis: University of Minnesota Press, 2001), 53, 57–58, 124, 126; Ong, "The Gender and Labor Politics of Postmodernity," in *The Politics of Culture in the Shadow of Capital*, ed. Lisa Lowe and David Lloyd (Durham, NC: Duke University Press, 1997), 62–66.

31. Kitty Calavita, *Inside the State: The Bracero Program, Immigration, and the I.N.S.* (New York: Routledge, 2010), 80–83.

32. Esposito, especially, sees the relationship between biopolitics and thanatopolitics (a term equivalent to necropolitics) as contradictory. David Harvey also explores foundational and moving contradictions created by the economic engine of capitalism, specifically capital accumulation, and he argues that the contradictions of capital allow for both innovation and crisis. When it generates crisis is when it can reinvent and transform into something else, for better or worse. These moments of transformation are also moments when disruptive work can happen. Nevertheless, Harvey describes how many of these contradictions "interlock in a variety of ways to provide a basic architecture for capital accumulation." My uneasiness with the term "contradiction" stems from the way these paradoxes, defects, and inconsistencies are not necessarily resolvable or even rooted in a logic that may correct them. They are, rather, a part of the architecture of the social order, and they often play off one another as they enact more and more specialized forms of violence. See Esposito, *Bios*, 39; Harvey, *Seventeen Contradictions and the End of Capitalism* (Oxford: Oxford University Press, 2014), 4, 14, 88.

33. Achille Mbembe, *Necropolitics* (Durham, NC: Duke University Press, 2019), 68, 70. Sovereignty continuously troubles this book but largely remains a background apparatus to my analyses because its definition(s) seem to feed the abstractions that allow for capitalist violence, as discussed with Hayek above. Sovereignty describes slippery and varying organizing politics, from monarchies to juridical law to nation-building practices to classic liberalism's autonomous individual to corporate personhood. Mbembe specifically characterizes sovereignty as what enacts and determines (and ultimately transgresses all limits of) human existence and human rights through "*the material destruction of human bodies and populations.*" Mbembe calls this its "capacity to define," but this understanding of sovereignty paints it as an extra-human, extra-material, omnipotent actor that puts into play very real and material institutional violence. For Giorgio Agamben, "sovereignty" describes the state of exception or the threshold of indistinction that controls the life and death of populations. With similar concerns, Grewal considers exceptionalism as a form of sovereignty, especially in how American exceptionalism ideologically forwards the United States as a sovereign actor on the world stage. Lauren Berlant sees Agamben's and Mbembe's ap-

proaches to sovereignty as about "events of decision making" that emphasize "individual autonomy" and encourage a "militaristic and melodramatic view of agency." Instead of this approach, they argue that we must think about mediating labor, governmentalities, and unconscious desires that have little to do with the fantasy of an effective and intentional agency and that make up a "truly lived life." This space of unconsciousness becomes visible in the idea of slow death, where sovereignty is an endemic disease and "structural inequalities are dispersed." Like Berlant, I am wary of viewing sovereignty as a form of intentional and absolute power of specific subjects, laws, or institutions. Instead, this book would rather consider how Latinx literature reveals the structural inequalities that produce violence and varying forms of death on subaltern populations and racialized bodies. This violence is not necessarily about an omniscient, omnipotent sovereign agent but about how the line between exploitation and justice, between captivity and empowerment, between docility and revolution are in flux. Agamben, *Homo Sacer: Sovereign Power and Bare Life*, 27; Berlant, "Slow Death," *Critical Inquiry* 33, no. 4 (2007), 755, 757, 759; Grewal, *Saving the Security State*, 8–9; Mbembe, *Necropolitics*, 68, 80. See also Gilberto Rosas, "The Fragile Ends of War: Forging the United States-Mexico Border and Borderlands Consciousness," *Social Text* 25, no. 2 (2007): 81–102, and Jasbir Puar's *Terrorist Assemblages: Homonationalism in Queer Times* (Durham, NC: Duke University Press, 2007).

34. Foucault, *History of Sexuality*, 138.

35. Mbembe, *Necropolitics*, 92.

36. Ibid., 75, 86.

37. Ibid., 80.

38. Ibid., 74.

39. Orlando Patterson, *Slavery and Social Death: A Comparative Study* (Cambridge, MA: Harvard University Press, 1982), 38, 42.

40. Mbembe, *Necropolitics*, 75. Of course, the figure of the slave also has deeply racial and racialized valences. For Saidiya Hartman, the performative utterance of "blackness" is encoded with a corporeality and resides in the shadows of slavery. The black body, as such, undergoes a "discursive constitution," where its meaning is "inescapable" and "inseparable" from the violence of slavery. Hartman, *Scenes of Subjection* (Oxford: Oxford University Press, 1997), 57–58.

41. Patterson, *Slavery and Social Death*, 39.

42. Ibid., 39–40, 42.

43. Sharon P. Holland, *Raising the Dead: Readings of Death and (Black) Subjectivity* (Durham, NC: Duke University Press, 2000), 38.

44. Ibid., 23–24.

45. Frances Negrón-Muntaner, *Boricua Pop: Puerto Ricans and the Latinization of American Culture* (New York: New York University Press, 2004), 51.

46. Russ Castronovo, *Necro Citizenship: Death, Eroticism, and the Public Sphere in the Nineteenth-Century United States* (Durham, NC: Duke University Press, 2001), 4.

47. Ibid., 13.

48. Ibid., 17.

49. Avery Gordon, *Ghostly Matters: Hauntings and the Sociological Imagination* (Minneapolis: University of Minnesota Press, 1997), 208.

50. Agamben, *Homo Sacer*, 21, 24–25. Mbembe, Grewal, and Agamben all conceive of the state of exception through the work of Carl Schmitt. Grewal specifically

considers this juridical state through exceptional citizens in US history, such as the white militias and expansionist settlers, arguing that their exceptionalism normalized and sanctioned violence to make the nation. For Grewal, this exceptionalism coincides with Schmitt's idea of "the state having the sovereign right of violence through suspension of law." Schmitt's political theories describe the rule of law as having two distinct elements: norm and decision. He argues that norm dictates certain forms of self-governance and helps make sense of legal order, but the belief in law means "the legal order rests on a decision not a norm," a decision rendered by a sovereign-like judge. The "exception" in Schmitt's understanding describes a "situation of peril," an emergency, or a "danger to the existence to the state," and pre-formed laws and norms can never fully account for these exceptions. Because of this inability to codify these exceptions, the sovereign decision becomes more powerful and totalizing because it must be made anew each time. Exception here seems to be less about subjects who occupy zones of political indistinction or violent states who suspend law to start/quell revolution and/or consolidate subalternity; it is more about how the rule of law allows for sovereign forms of power under liberalism that easily grow into dictatorships, showing "curious contradictions" to the foundations of liberalism. Grewal, *Saving the Security State*, 194; Carl Schmitt, *Political Theology: Four Chapters on the Concept of Sovereignty* (Chicago: University of Chicago Press, 1985), 6, 9–13, 36, 60–66.

51. Agamben, *Homo Sacer*, 25.

52. Ibid., 123–125, 164.

53. Puar, *Terrorist Assemblages*, 3.

54. Patterson, *Slavery and Social Death*, 48.

55. Mbembe, *Necropolitics*, 75.

56. Lisa Marie Cacho, *Social Death: Racialized Rightlessness and the Criminalization of the Unprotected* (New York: New York University Press, 2012), 99.

57. Ibid., 145.

58. Ibid., 22–23.

59. Patterson, *Slavery and Social Death*, 45. Weheliye argues that "viscous deviances" under liberal democracies sanction violence and lie "dormant" in the concepts of bare life and social death, whether "found in current practices of torture in U.S. domestic and foreign prisons, or the hauntological histories of the Holocaust, slavery, and colonialism." Weheliye, *Habeas Viscus*, 112.

60. Ibid., 101.

61. Puar, *Terrorist Assemblages*, 35.

62. Frank B. Wilderson III calls on us to actively work against what he calls a "parasitism" in the discourse that collapses necropolitics and social death. He calls on a greater attention to "the difference between Humans who suffer through an 'economy of disposability' and Blacks who suffer through 'social death.'" Wilderson draws on the work of Jared Sexton, who argues that current racist fantasy does not "render blacks, like much of the planet's inhabitants, subject to death in an economy of disposability" but rather renders black lives *and* death meaningless. For Sexton, this important critical difference forces us to acknowledge that this violence is occurring epistemologically and is able to put on "endless disguises" that "adapt and mutate to meet the exigencies of the now." Both Wilderson and Sexton are hailing Patterson's ideas that we must think about the social process of slavery as a "relation of parasitism" because it emphasizes the "asymmetry of unequal relations." This historical framework of domi-

nation continues to structure racialized social relations. I must add, however, that the critical slippages between necropolitical distributions of disposability and the histories of social death are indicative of a social order that homogenizes racialized subjects, normalizes inequality, and determines who gets to matter and who gets meaning. It is parasitic insofar as it lives and feeds within the body of the political economy itself. Wilderson, *Afropessimism* (New York, Liveright, 2020), 16; Sexton, "Unbearable Blackness," *Cultural Critique* 90 (2015): 167–168; Patterson, *Slavery and Social Death*, 335.

63. Berlant, "Slow Death," 759.

64. Ibid., 754.

65. Ibid., 761. In parallel, Rob Nixon wishes to replace the "static connotations of structural violence" with his concept of slow violence because it "foregrounds questions of time, movement, and change." For Nixon, slow violence captures imperceptible changes that allow for violence to be "decoupled from its original causes." Nixon, *Slow Violence and the Environmentalism of the Poor* (Cambridge, MA: Harvard University Press, 2013), 11.

66. Mbembe, *Necropolitics*, 200n36, 75.

67. Sexton, "Unbearable Blackness," 163.

68. Jason De León, *The Land of Open Graves: Living and Dying on the Migrant Trail* (Oakland: University of California Press, 2015), 5.

69. Ibid., 16–17, 68.

70. Eduardo Mendieta, "The U.S. Border and the Political Ontology of 'Assassination Nation': Thanatological *Dispotifs*," *Journal of Speculative Philosophy*," *Journal of Speculative Philosophy* 31, no. 1 (2017): 85.

71. John D. Márquez, "Latinos as the 'Living Dead': Raciality, Expendability, and Border Militarization," *Latino Studies* 10, no. 4 (2012): 475.

72. Ibid., 476.

73. Ibid., 480.

74. Cacho, *Social Death*, 99.

75. John Alba Cutler, "The New Border," *College Literature* 44, no. 4 (2017): 499, 503.

76. Sassen, *Globalization and Its Discontents*, 14–18.

77. "Dusty foot" status is also used to pit Cubans against other Latinx migratory communities and to create interethnic-interracial conflict. See Patricia Zengerle and David Adams, "U.S. Turns Back Central Americans, Welcomes 'Dusty Foot' Cubans," *Reuters*, July 23, 2016, https://www.reuters.com/article/us-usa-immigration-cuba/u-s-turns-back-central-americans-welcomes-dusty-foot-cubans-idUSKBN0FZ2E420140730.

78. García-Peña, *Borders of Dominicanidad*, 7.

79. Gloría Anzaldúa, *Borderlands/La Frontera: The New Mestiza* (San Francisco: Aunt Lute Books, 1999), 24.

80. Rosa Linda Fregoso, "We Want Them Alive!," *Social Identities* 12, no. 2 (2006): 110.

81. Ibid., 111.

82. Ibid., 112.

83. Ibid., 110.

84. Nicole Guidotti-Hernández, *Unspeakable Violence: Remapping the U.S. and Mexican National Imaginaries* (Durham, NC: Duke University Press, 2011), 2–3.

85. Ibid., 4.

86. Ibid., 8, 6.

87. Arlene Dávila, *Latinos, Inc: The Marketing and Making of a People.* (Berkeley: University of California Press, 2001), 11.

88. Raphael Dalleo and Elena Machado Sáez specifically distinguish between the literary tropes that characterize these two types of Latinx subjects: "The immigrant, who is mobile by definition, must travel into the United States and be transformed by that crossing, while the resident Latino/a ironically has a more secure oppositional stance because s/he is always already within the borders of the United States." Dalleo and Machado Sáez, *The Latino/a Canon and the Emergence of Post-Sixties Literature* (New York: Palgrave Macmillan, 2007), 74.

89. Dávila, *Latinos, Inc.*, 95.

90. Dalleo and Machado Sáez, *The Latino/a Canon*, 41.

91. Fregoso, "We Want Them Alive!" 127.

92. Anzaldúa, *Borderlands/La Frontera*, 100–101.

93. Schmidt Camacho, *Migrant Imaginaries*, 265.

94. We see distinctly literary terms cropping up in decidedly nonliterary scholarship. For instance, Mbembe labels neoliberal ideology and colonial power "fictions" throughout *Necropolitics*. Deirdre McCloskey also describes an intersection between the literary and the political economy, and she argues that economics "is a collection of literary forms." Most recently, Thomas Picketty considers the resonance between economics and literary study because literature uniquely offers insights and windows into how "inequalities are experienced." See Mbembe, *Necropolitics*, 78, 97, 183; McCloskey, *The Rhetoric of Economics* (Madison: University of Wisconsin Press, 1998), 21; Picketty, *Capital and Ideology* (Cambridge, MA: Belknap, 2020), 15.

95. Ramón Saldívar, *Chicano Narrative: The Dialectics of Difference* (Madison: University of Wisconsin Press, 1990), 5.

96. Ibid., 6–7.

97. Marcial González, *Chicano Novels and the Politics of Form: Race, Class, and Reification* (Ann Arbor: University of Michigan Press, 2008), 30–32.

98. Ellen McCracken, *New Latina Narrative: The Feminine Space of Postmodern Ethnicity: The New Memory of Latinidad* (Tucson: University of Arizona Press, 1999), 3

99. Ibid., 66, 71, 94.

100. Ylce Irizarry, *Chicana/o and Latina/o Fiction* (Urbana: University of Illinois Press, 2016), 8–10.

101. Ibid., 9.

102. See Holger Marcks and Janina Pawelz, "From Myths of Victimhood to Fantasies of Violence: How Far-Right Narratives of Imperilment Work," *Terrorism and Political Violence* (2020), https://doi-org.du.idm.oclc.org/10.1080/09546553.2020.1788544. For a consideration of so-called liberal narrative, see Amitai Etzioni, "The Liberal Narrative Is Broken, and Only Populism Can Fix It," *The Atlantic*, May 8, 2013, https://www.theatlantic.com/politics/archive/2013/05/the-liberal-narrative-is-broken-and-only-populism-can-fix-it/275600/.

103. Puar, *Terrorist Assemblages*, 119, 146.

104. Arturo Escobar, *Encountering Development: The Making and Unmaking of the Third World* (Princeton, NJ: Princeton University Press, 1995), 56.

105. Puar, *Terrorist Assemblages*, xxvii, 222; Escobar, *Encountering Development*, 155.

106. José Esteban Muñoz, *Cruising Utopia: The Then and There of Queer Futurity* (New York: New York University Press, 2019), 41.

107. Ibid., 12.

108. Agamben, *Homo Sacer*, 169–171; Cacho, *Social Death*, 82–83.

109. Stated at a rally; quoted in Amy Davidson Sorkin, "Countering Trump at the Border," *New Yorker*, December 10, 2018, https://www.newyorker.com/magazine/2018/12/10/countering-trump-at-the-border.

110. Grise, *Your Healing Is Killing Me*, 67.

Chapter 1: Games of Enterprise and Security in Luis Alberto Urrea, Valeria Luiselli, and Karla Cornejo Villavicencio

1. Luis Alberto Urrea, *The Devil's Highway* (New York: Back Bay Books, 2004), 28.

2. Ibid., 173.

3. Michel Foucault, *Birth of Biopolitics: Lectures at the Collège de France*, 1978–1979 (New York: Palgrave Macmillan, 2008), 174.

4. Mike Davis originally coins "brown peril" in *Magical Urbanism*. Justin Akers Chacón and Davis later outline its significant parallels to the "yellow peril." Luis H. Zayas also draws significant parallels between the brown peril and the yellow peril in US politics, arguing that the "brown peril" signifies end of the world sentiments and racisms not only about undocumented immigrants but also about citizen children and documented ("legal") migrants. As a result, there is a collapse between documented/undocumented, legal/illegal, citizen/foreigner within anti-immigrant discourse, and this phenomenon has a long history. Natalia Molina investigates Depression-era policies in Los Angeles that disassembled these distinctions. When looking at public health records of the Department of Charities' general hospital, she notes, "*Race* and *alien* both came to be synonymous with *Mexican*, to the exclusion of all other racialized groups" and the reports "depicted Mexicans as a dual threat—a population at once large and unhealthy." Mexicans and Mexican Americans are being conflated with "pathogen," as well here. This moment in US history is significant for many reasons, as the Johnson-Reed Act (Immigration Act of 1924) was reinforcing "yellow peril" sentiments and policies. These collapses in political and social distinctions feed anti-immigrant sentiments all the more. Davis, *Magical Urbanism: Latinos Reinvent the US City* (New York: Verso, 2001), 67–76; Chacón and Davis, *No One Is Illegal: Fighting Violence and State Repression on the U.S.-Mexico Border* (Chicago: Haymarket Books, 2006), 84, 102, 202, 208, 217; Zayas, *Forgotten Citizens: Deportation, Children, and the Making of American Exiles* (Oxford: Oxford University Press, 2015), 49–50; Molina, *Fit to Be Citizens? Public Health and Race in Los Angeles, 1879–1939* (Berkeley: University of California Press, 2006), 129.

René Galindo and Jami Vigil argue that many anti-immigrant statements come from a complex interplay between racism and nativism that grow out of US policies like Operation Wetback in the 1950s and English Only initiatives in the 1990s. They consider the case of country musician Chad Brock, who made anti-immigrant statements while performing in my hometown's Colorado Independence Stampede in Greeley, Colorado, in 2002. Brock condemned immigrants for not speaking English during his performance, and when responding to accusations of racism, he said, "I am not racist. I wasn't directing the comments toward any particular group. I was speaking my mind as an American during the 4th of July holiday. But I had no idea that there were so many Hispanics in Greeley." Also, in 2002, Juan Flores succinctly sums up these critical concerns about brown peril sentiments:

> Typically, awe and fascination mingle with a sense of foreboding, an alarmism over the imminent threat Latinos are perceived to present to the presumed unity of American culture and to an unhampered control over the country's destiny. An integral component of this nervous prognosis, repeated with mantra-like predictability when public discussion turns to the "browning of America," is the identification of Latinos as the country's "fastest growing minority," the group whose numbers are on pace to exceed that of African Americans as early as the end of the first decade of this new millennium. The fear of an "alien nation"—the title of a xenophobic book on immigration—veils but thinly an even deeper phobia, the fear of a non-white majority. And this without mention of the next sleeping giant: The "brown peril" is soon to be eclipsed by another "yellow peril," as Asian Americans are poised to outnumber both blacks and Hispanics by mid-century.

Galindo and Vigil, "Are Anti-immigrant Statements Racist or Nativist? What Difference Does It Make?," in *Immigration and the Border*, ed. David Leal and José Limón (Notre Dame, IN: University of Notre Dame Press, 2013), 372–381; Flores, "Nuevo York—Diaspora City: U.S. Latinos Between and Beyond," *NACLA Report on the Americas* 35, no. 6 (2002): 47.

5. By "neo-Malthusian," I draw on the work of Mohan Rao, who argues that neo-Malthusianism is a doomsday discourse that frames many policies for nation-states, particularly policies on immigration and the environment. This doom comes from the belief that all a nation-state's social and economic problems "stem primarily, if not only, from population growth," a neo-Malthusian logic that Rao describes as "truly protean, they are like Vishnu avatars, taking myriad forms: that poverty in our country primarily persists due to population growth; that the poor do not know what is good for them and for society as a whole, behave irrationally, and thus need to be educated; . . . that population growth in Third World countries can act as a security threat to the interests of freedom and democracy in the world, and so on." These fears and anxieties, for Rao, operate in a neoliberal mode, with fear being not only a growth industry but also a way to depoliticize and naturalize social inequality, resource exploitation, and the dispossession of the poor. According to Daniel Daou, neo-Malthusianism highlights the false dichotomy between doomsters and boomsters, whereby discourses of doom were historically reserved for environmental activists and boom was for economists; now these worldviews complement one another. Rao, "An Entangled Skein: Neo-Malthusianism in Neo-liberal Times," in *Markets and Malthus: Population, Gender, and Health in Neo-liberal Times*, ed Mohan Rao and Sarah Sexton (Los Angeles: Sage, 2010), 103, 105, 106, 121; Daou, "The End of Civilization," *Thresholds* 40 (2012): 252.

6. I draw on Balibar's idea of misrecognition as a function of the "racist complex." For Balibar, misrecognition allows people to tolerate the violence that they are engaging in when defining and naturalizing social relations through race. Furthermore, the racist complex "inextricably combines" the "function of *misrecognition*" with "a 'will to know,' a violent *desire* for immediate *knowledge* of social relations." By this statement, Balibar points to a contradiction within academic racism here: the need to scientifically understand social relations through race (with visible evidence and visible facts) while simultaneously ignoring that this scientific desire only bolsters and

consolidates racism and racist theories. While this specifically academic phenomenon for Balibar is outside the purview of this book, I am still interested in how misrecognition works within popular and political discourse as a structure for these violences against the subaltern and foreign Other. Balibar, "Is There a Neo-Racism," in Étienne Balibar and Immanuel Wallerstein, *Race, Nation, Class: Ambiguous Identities* (London: Verso, 1991), 19.

7. See also Jason De León, *The Land of Open Graves: Living and Dying on the Migrant Trail* (Oakland: University of California Press, 2015); Alexander D. Barder, "Power, Violence, and Torture," in *The Geopolitics of American Insecurity: Making Sense of Insurgency and Legitimacy Crises in Past and Present Wars of Attrition*, ed. François Debrix and Mark J. Lacy (London: Routledge, 2009), 54–70; Partha Chatterjee, "Sovereign Violence and the Domain of the Political," in *Sovereign Bodies: Citizens, Migrants, and States in the Postcolonial World*, ed. Thomas Blom Hansen and Finn Sepputat (Princeton, NJ: Princeton University Press, 2005), 82–100.

8. For example, under free-trade agreements, the multinational commercial factories and farms will close and move in favor of cheaper (and less organized) outsourced labor, which devastates local economies and encourages migration by those newly unemployed; disposable labor becomes synonymous with displaced labor under free-trade economics. Miriam Ching Yoon Louie notes that this labor history begins in the 1960s and 1970s, when US companies such as the Gap and Levi-Strauss closed down factories in San Antonio and El Paso, moving their production to supposed subcontractors and sweatshops in Mexico, Central America, the Caribbean, and Asia, upending the economies of the US borderlands. NAFTA, according to Louie, consolidates these corporate maneuvers, a governmental nod of approval for more specialized forms of exploitation. See Saskia Sassen, *Globalization and Its Discontents: Essays on the New Mobility of People and Money* (New York: New Press, 1998); Nestor García Canclini, *Consumers and Citizens: Globalization and Multicultural Conflicts*. Trans. George Yúdice (Minneapolis: University of Minnesota Press, 2001); Tanya Maria Golash-Boza, *Deported: Immigrant Policing, Disposable Labor, and Global Capitalism* (New York: New York University Press, 2015); Louie, *Sweatshop Warriors: Immigrant Women Workers Take on the Global Factory* (Cambridge, MA: South End, 2001), 83–87. See also Rachel Louise Snyder, *Fugitive Denim: A Moving Story of People and Pants in the Borderless World of Global Trade* (New York: Norton, 2009), for a look at the lived experience of these global factory workers as they navigate this economic history and their rights.

9. See Julianne Burton, "Don (Juanito) Duck and the Imperial-Patriarchal Unconscious: Disney Studios, the Good Neighbor Policy, and the Packaging of Latin America," in *Nationalisms and Sexualities*, ed. Andrew Parker, Mary J. Russo, Doris Sommer, and Patricia Yaeger (New York: Routledge, 1992), 21–41.

10. Valeria Luiselli, *Tell Me How It Ends: An Essay in Forty Questions* (Minneapolis: Coffee House, 2017), 78.

11. The term "security state" to describe US homeland and foreign policy comes up often after 9/11. However, it is important to note that the Department of Homeland Security—which now houses the Immigration and Customs Enforcement (ICE), the Customs and Border Protection (CBP), and the United States Citizen and Immigration Services (USCIS)—comes half a century after the creation of the National Security Agency (NSA) (instituted by Truman in 1952), which meant to protect the nation through the cryptology of foreign signals. While the DHS and the NSA were created

as separate institutional entities at very different historical moments, they have formed various intelligence partnerships since 2002. For historical discussions of the United States as a security state, see Martin Sicker, *The Geopolitics of Security in the Americas* (Westport, CT: Praeger, 2002). For a consideration of how the security state operates through (and profits from) "anticipatory governance" and "disaster management," see Claudia Aradau and Rens van Munster, *Politics of Catastrophe: Genealogies of the Unknown* (London: Routledge, 2013).

Grewal also emphasizes that there is a difference between the "security state" and the "national security state," where the former lays bare the expanding and uneven hegemonies of empire and (neo)colonialism and the latter speaks to the governmentalization of security, often ignoring nonstate actors and making the nation and the law exceptional. For the latter, Belinda Linn Rincón offers a reading of the national security state, arguing that it relies on gendered, patriarchal, and ideological spatializations of home and homeland to militarize subjectivity and maintain the social order. Inderpal Grewal, *Saving the Security State: Exceptional Citizens in Twenty-First-Century America* (Durham, NC: Duke University Press, 2017), 20; Rincón, "Home/Land Insecurity, or, *Un Desmadre en Aztlán:* Virginia Grise's *blu,*" *MFS: Modern Fiction Studies* 63, no. 2 (2017): 248.

12. Grewal, *Saving the Security State*, 21.

13. Peter Andreas, *Border Games: Policing the U.S.-Mexico Divide*, 2nd ed. (Ithaca, NY: Cornell University Press, 2009), 91.

14. Urrea, *Devil's Highway*, 16 (my emphasis).

15. Ibid., 17.

16. Ibid.

17. Mike Davis argues that our current border troubles grow out of the War on Drugs. This war has morphed in the past three decades into a strangely abstract and uncontainable process that seems to have more to do with US interference in Latin American economies than with a desire to stop drug smuggling into the United States. Davis sees the War on Drugs as becoming just as much a War on Immigrants, stating, "In practice, the distinctions between immigration control and narcotics interdiction, or between policing and low-intensity warfare, have become so blurred that border-dwellers speak routinely of the 'war against drugs *and* immigrants.'" This conflation between drugs and immigrants reduces the immigrant to just another black-market commodity and makes the civil offense of the immigrant into a perpetually criminal offense. For Davis, the War on Drugs was a program designed without any real results. The United States' program against smuggling (whether drugs or immigrants) "contrasts with its famous inability to arrest notorious border drug barons, supposedly the most wanted men in the hemisphere, as they brazenly lounge at Caliente racetrack and boogie the night away in trendy discos." Peter Andreas ends his comprehensive history on smuggling and trade in the United States with how the War on Drugs legitimized the militarization of the border, while "the illicit drug trade not only survived, but thrived." Andreas reveals the contradictory tension between governments that want more results (an increase in drug seizures) and simultaneously should be seeing a decrease if there were actual results, or perhaps this contradiction is better described as a symbiotic relationship between global trade and border regulation. Davis, *Magical Urbanism*, 35, 37; Andreas, *Smuggler Nation: How Illicit Trade Made America* (Oxford: Oxford University Press, 2013), 289, 319.

18. Nicholas De Genova, *Working the Boundaries: Race, Space, and "Illegality" in Mexican Chicago* (Durham, NC: Duke University Press, 2005), 242–249.

19. Urrea, *Devil's Highway*, 28.

20. Chacón and Davis, *No One Is Illegal*, 16.

21. Grewal, *Saving the Security State*, 194–195.

22. Andreas, *Border Games*, 36.

23. Within much of the subtext of this critical conversation is the field of game theory, founded by mathematician John von Neumann and economist Oskar Morgenstern (1947). Extending these theories into the twenty-first century, Mark Seltzer breaks games down to multiple types: parlor games, war games, crime games, and form games. Seltzer's work considers how games structure reflexive and "recursive social systems and their media," through strategists and rational actors, as a society's way of "recognizing itself." As a result, games self-condition, monitor, and "make visible all the paradoxes of that self-implication" and, thus, reveal a "self-modeling modern world." The question of rational actors and rational choices is a notable problem in the history of game theory, which Seltzer grapples with, but there is also an assumption of agency within game theory that presupposes a level of privilege and hegemony of the gamers. I would argue that game theory does not readily account for populations who are pawns in the political and economic game on the US-Mexico border or the recipients of its consequences. Grewal, when considering the culture of gamers and first-person shooter games, notes that online gaming culture allows for a sense of distance from the world: "War is in distant places, against brown and black people, and thus these games share some key American ideologies of empire." She argues that, simultaneously, online gaming allows players a greater ability to enact social violence, such as white supremacy, misogyny, and heteronormative masculinity. Seltzer, *The Official World* (Durham, NC: Duke University Press, 2016), 90–95; Grewal, *Saving the Security State*, 201–202. For an example of how digital gaming culture complicates some of the traditional premises of modern game theory, especially the online game *Border Patrol*, see also Leo Chavez, *Latino Threat: Constructing Immigrants, Citizens, and the Nation* (Stanford, CA: Stanford University Press, 2008), 77–78.

24. Urrea, *Devil's Highway*, 35.

25. While there may be increases in im/migrant populations in certain areas that are hypervisible, the United States since 2007 has seen a decline in Mexican immigration and an overall decline in undocumented immigration. See Ana Gonzalez-Barrera and Jens Manual Krogstad, "What We Know about Illegal Immigration from Mexico," Pew Research Center, Dec. 3, 2018, http://www.pewresearch.org/fact-tank/2018/12/03/what-we-know-about-illegal-immigration-from-mexico/; Jeffrey S. Passel and D'vera Cohn, "U.S. Unauthorized Immigration Flows Are Down Sharply since Mid-Decade," *Pew Research Center*, September 1, 2010, http://www.pewhispanic.org/2010/09/01/us-unauthorized-immigration-flows-are-down-sharply-since-mid-decade/.

26. Chacón and Davis, *No One Is Illegal*, 84.

27. Ibid., 84–85.

28. Chavez discusses the Minutemen Project, following claims similar to those of Justin Akers Chacón and Mike Davis. He argues that the Minutemen are not only "delineating simple dichotomies" (such as us/them, illegal/legal, and invaders/invaded) but are enacting a historical desire: "there must have been the appeal to performing a contemporary version of an Old West narrative of cowboys versus the Mexicans,

or Texas Rangers versus the Mexicans, or simply border vigilantes" that comes from the historical period after the Treaty of Guadalupe Hidalgo, when the United States wanted to "pacify the Mexican-origin population in the border states." But this desire was particularly performative, according to Chavez, in which the Minutemen Project becomes another form of border theater or a "symbolic ritual of surveillance." I wish to extend Chavez's claim about this being a spectacle for fearful citizens to consume, since it seems to be in the service of larger economic phenomena. The need for cheap labor in the United States and the need for immigrants to provide this cheap labor must be mystified through these spectacles in order to keep citizens tolerant of exploitation and docile to neoliberal practices, and these performances are key to this mystification. Chavez, *Latino Threat*, 138, 144. For a reading of how vigilantism, specifically the Minutemen Project, directly influenced political and economic policies, see also Alicia Schmidt Camacho, *Migrant Imaginaries: Latino Cultural Politics in the U.S.-Mexico Borderlands*, 294–296.

29. Urrea, *Devil's Highway*, 71.

30. Ibid., 72, 73.

31. Ibid., 79, 80.

32. Luiselli, *Tell Me How It Ends*, 7.

33. Ibid., 13.

34. Ibid., 21–22.

35. Ibid., 15.

36. Ibid., 62.

37. Ibid., 74–75.

38. Ibid., 75.

39. U.S. DHS and DOJ Form I-598, rev. 5/16/17.

40. Luiselli, *Tell Me How It Ends*, 73.

41. Ibid., 80–81. (my emphasis).

42. Foucault, *Birth of Biopolitics*, 169–173.

43. Ibid., 174–175.

44. Schmidt Camacho, *Migrant Imaginaries*, 302–303.

45. Luiselli, *Tell Me How It Ends*, 71–72.

46. Karla Cornejo Villavicencio, *The Undocumented Americans* (One World: New York, 2019), xv–xvi.

47. Stacey Alex also considers how *The Undocumented Americans* interpellates readers, although she understands this as a way for readers to recognize their own role in the social order rather than an experiential process. Alex, "Undocumented Latinx Life-Writing: Refusing Worth and Meritocracy," *Prose Studies* 41, no. 2 (2020): 121.

48. Cornejo Villavicencio, *The Undocumented Americans*, 114.

49. Ibid., 116, 119.

50. Ibid., 5–6.

51. Ibid., 114–115.

52. Ibid., xv.

53. Ibid., 28–29.

54. Ibid., 30.

55. Ibid., 31–32.

56. Ibid., 9.

57. Ibid., xv.

58. Ibid., 13.

59. Ibid., 11,78.

60. Ibid., 96.

61. Ibid., 99.

62. Ibid., 101.

63. Urrea, *Devil's Highway*, 119, 5.

64. Ibid., 115.

65. Ibid., 120.

66. Cornejo Villavicencio, *The Undocumented Americans*, 149.

67. Ibid., 148.

68. Schmidt Camacho reminds us that the Bracero Program (and the imaginaries it inspired once it ended) marks this conflation between labor resources fears and a desire for increased national security. Schmidt Camacho, *Migrant Imaginaries*, 68, 109, 200.

69. Maritza E. Cárdenas, *Constituting Central American-Americans: Transnational Identities and the Politics of Dislocation* (New Brunswick, NJ: Rutgers University Press, 2019), 84.

70. Cornejo Villavicencio, *The Undocumented Americans*, 40–41.

71. Ibid., 56.

72. Ibid., 62.

73. Davis gives the example of California talking heads "stoking white anger" to help pass the 1994 Proposition 187 (an initiative to establish immigrant screening and deny the undocumented from public education, nonemergency health services, and other social infrastructure). The main talking point was that there was an "invasion of California" with the "hordes" coming to murder young white men. Thomas Robertson argues that neo-Malthusianism reveals a discursive slippage between quality-of-life and quantity-of-life. Neo-Malthusian sentiments, such as those found in Paul Ehrlich's *Population Bomb* (1968), promote the faulty presumption that there is a direct causation between the abundance of population and a drop in the standards of living. Often, overpopulation fears pushed by neo-Malthusian environmentalists are misplaced: they instead protect class privilege, revive eugenics movements, ignore how material and toxic waste of wealthy neighborhoods are sent downstream/downwind to poorer communities, and support varying forms of NIMBYism ("not in my backyard"). Davis, *Magical Urbanism*, 83–84; Robertson, *The Malthusian Moment* (New Brunswick, NJ: Rutgers University Press, 2012), 61–84.

74. David Harvey, *Spaces of Capital* (New York: Routledge, 2001), 65.

75. Ibid., 63.

76. Thomas Robert Malthus, *An Essay on the Principle of Population* (New York: Norton, 2018), 58–60.

77. Cornejo Villavicencio, *The Undocumented Americans*, 92.

78. Harvey, *Spaces of Capital*, 42–43.

79. Malthus, *Principle of Population*, 63.

80. Harvey, *Spaces of Capital*, 65.

81. Sassen, *Globalization and Its Discontents*, 41, 45. Canclini, *Consumers and Citizens*, 53, 57–58, 124.

82. Cornejo Villavicencio, *The Undocumented Americans*, 20

83. Ibid., 84.

84. Ibid., 153–154.

85. Ibid., xvi.

86. Ibid., 169.

87. Schmidt Camacho, *Migrant Imaginaries*, 8.

88. Urrea, *Devil's Highway*, 220.

89. Cacho, in discussing flaws in post-9/11 US immigration law, argues that this violence has been legalized: "Generally, the state does not necessarily have to comply with laws presumably meant to protect people from blatant abuses of state power, especially if such persons are illegible to personhood." By this, Cacho is describing how the 9/11 Commission and subsequent Patriot Act allowed the state to revoke immigration benefits, such as naturalization and visas, if migrants were suspect of terrorism or other crimes. The noncitizen's already precarious status in the nation-state was now legally erasable and punishable. The migrant, documented or not, could be easily stripped of rights under "suspicion," an act that Cacho argues is a form of racial profiling and means "explicitly to deprive noncitizens of legal personhood." For Cacho, these policies and strategies built into the legal system "underscores that legal recognition is not and cannot be a viable solution for racialized exploitation, violence, and poverty." The narratives respond to this systemic violence, but they also problematize Cacho's claim that the "politics of misrecognition" are ineffective. Lisa Marie Cacho, *Social Death: Racialized Rightlessness and the Criminalization of the Unprotected* (New York: New York University Press, 2012), 103, 8.

90. James Sterngold, "Devasting Picture of Immigrants Dead in Arizona Desert," *New York Times*, May 25, 2001, https://www.nytimes.com/2001/05/25/us/devastating -picture-of-immigrants-dead-in-arizona-desert.html.

91. Urrea, *Devil's Highway*, 35.

92. In a similar vein, Guidotti-Hernández argues that the lynching of Josefa/Juanita in 1851 demonstrates how the "body is turned against itself" in the spectacle of the killing, but the reproduction of texts and narratives of her dead body "makes her visible in the historical record," giving her subjectivity. This phenomenon of subjects-after-death is problematic because it only allows for racialized and sexualized bodies to have subjectivity because of state-sanctioned violence. Nicole Guidotti-Hernández, *Unspeakable Violence: Remapping the U.S. and Mexican National Imaginaries* (Durham, NC: Duke University Press, 2011), 78–79.

93. Mark Maguire, "The Birth of Biometric Security," *Anthropology Today* 25, no. 2 (April 2009): 13. For a larger discussion on how biometric security practices readily lend themselves to false consciousness, state ideology, and the subsumption of imagination, see Benjamin J. Muller, *Security, Risk, and the Biometric State* (London: Routledge, 2010).

94. Javier Duran, "Virtual Borders, Data Aliens, and Bare Bodies: Culture, Securitization, and the Biometric State," *Journal of Borderlands Studies* 25, nos. 3–4 (2010): 221.

95. Similar to Urrea's narrative, the documentary *Who Is Dayani Cristal?* (2013) also considers what it means to document dead bodies discovered by tourists and USCIS in the desert. The film furthers this idea of the forensic photograph as occupying an ambivalent position between a state bureaucracy that wants social control and a state bureaucracy that must document the fatal consequences of its violence. See *Who Is Dayani Cristal?*, directed by Marc Silver (London: Pulse Films, 2014).

96. Urrea, *Devil's Highway*, 145.

97. Ibid., 146.

98. Ibid., 147.

99. Marta Caminero-Santangelo argues that this embedded humanism in *The Devil's Highway* often operates as an empathy-building device, thereby asking "readers to close the distance between the migrants and themselves," but it also fails to differentiate the structures of "privilege and circumstance." Caminero-Santangelo, *Documenting the Undocumented* (Gainesville: University Press of Florida, 2017), 53.

100. José Esteban Muñoz, *Disidentifications: Queers of Color and the Performance of Politics* (Minneapolis: University of Minnesota Press, 1999), 65.

101. Ibid., 66–67.

102. Ibid., 68, 72–73.

103. Puar, *Terrorist Assemblages*, 101.

104. Ibid., 104.

105. Ibid., 107.

106. Ibid., 110–111.

107. Ibid., 113.

108. Luiselli, *Tell Me How It Ends*, 14.

109. Duran, "Virtual Borders," 221. Duran's analysis draws on Nicholas De Genova's study of "border spectacle." De Genova argues that "the true social role of much U.S. immigration law enforcement (and the Border Patrol, in particular) has historically been to maintain and superintend the operations of the border as a revolving door, simultaneously implicated in importation as much as (in fact, far more than) deportation." Security theater, then, is an "enforcement ritual" that "fetishizes migrant 'illegality'" to "filter the unequal transfer of value." Jonathan Xavier Inda also describes the "visual devices" employed by INS and other government entities to construct "illegality" and an "immigration problem." For Inda, these practices show that border security is "dramatizing the problem of illegal immigration using the U.S.-Mexico border as a stage." See De Genova, *Working the Boundaries*, 248; Inda, *Targeting Immigrants* (Malden, MA: Blackwell, 2006), 79–93, 139.

110. Duran, "Virtual Borders," 221.

111. Cornejo Villavicencio, *The Undocumented Americans*, 77.

112. Ibid., 134.

113. Ibid., 152.

114. Cacho, *Social Death*, 8.

115. Urrea, *Devil's Highway*, 97.

116. Ibid., 5.

117. Cornejo Villavicencio, *The Undocumented Americans*, 153.

118. Thomas J. Ferraro's seminal work on American literature and immigration is one of the first to construct the cooperations between blood and money, arguing that the codes of "blood," such as ethnic solidarity and family, structure the codes of business (and vice versa), most notably in his reading of Mario Puzo's *The Godfather*. Blood money defines how the marketplace requires a construct of "blood" and how "blood" rationalizes and aids market enterprises. More recently, Michael Clune reads "blood money" as the literary "process of transforming nature into currency" where the "fusion of blood and money encloses all human relations within a natural market without history, ideology, or code." His interest in the intersections of blood and money grows out of his reading of Kathy Acker and Friedrich Hayek, yet at one point in Clune's

analysis, it becomes clear that Acker is not simply writing about blood in its many racial, biological, and national terms; she is writing about bleeding. Clune writes, "The wound pierces the epidermis and opens the body, the locus of authentic and natural experience prior to language and the accretion of the social. The body, and particular the body that has been opened, wounded in intense, unsettling experiences, stains and distorts the subject's discourse, which spills into public spaces with the defiant, vivid, and disturbingly intimate quality of blood." Clune echoes Walter Benn Michaels's reading of Acker here in that Michaels understands Acker's "writing as bleeding" to disarticulate writing as representation and make writing much more material. For Michaels, writing is ontologized through blood in Acker, much like politics now corporealizes ideas, both of which transform literary and political critique into "a commitment to new subject positions instead of to more just societies." These scholars, nevertheless, gloss over the distinction between blood and bleeding; none explicitly recognize that "blood" connotes life(lines), while "bleeding" describes structural forms of death. Ferraro, *Ethnic Passages* (Chicago: University of Chicago Press, 1993), 24–25; Michael Clune, *American Literature and the Free Market, 1945–2000* (Cambridge: Cambridge University Press, 2010), 125, 123; Michaels, "Empires of the Senseless: (The Response to) Terror and (the End of) History," *Radical History Review* 85 (2003): 109.

119. Luiselli, *Tell Me How It Ends*, 50–51.

120. Cornejo Villavicencio, *The Undocumented Americans*, 155.

121. Although outside the purview of this book, Alejandro Morales's *The Rag Doll Plagues* (1992) productively complicates these literary questions of blood and money with its speculative imaginaries of labor and race.

122. Hayek, *Constitution of Liberty*, 63, 71–72, 330–331.

123. Ibid., 71.

124. Ibid., 141, 147.

Chapter 2: Documenting the US-Mexico Border

1. Don Bartletti, "Don Bartletti: Spotlight on Immigration," interview by Dean Brierly, *Photographers Speak*, February 19, 2010,http://photographyinterviews.blogspot .com/2010/02/don-bartletti-spotlight-on-immigration.html.

2. Justin Akers Chacón and Mike Davis, *No One Is Illegal: Fighting Violence and State Repression on the U.S.-Mexico Border* (Chicago: Haymarket Books, 2006), 83–85.

3. Leo Chavez, *Covering Immigration: Popular Images and the Politics of Nation* (Berkeley: University of California Press 2001), 220.

4. Peter Andreas, *Border Games: Policing the U.S.-Mexico Divide* (Ithaca, NY: Cornell University Press, 2000), 29.

5. Leo Chavez, *Covering Immigration: Popular Images and the Politics of Nation*, 38.

6. Rebecca M. Schreiber, *The Undocumented Everyday: Migrant Lives and the Politics of Visibility* (Minneapolis: University of Minnesota Press, 2018), 122, 124.

7. The desire to extend the wall on the US-Mexico border was politically recharged with the election of Donald Trump, who was unaware that major portions of a wall had been built. See Amnesty International, *In Hostile Terrain: Human Rights Violations in Immigration Enforcement in the US Southwest* (New York: Amnesty International Publications, 2012), http://www.amnestyusa.org/files/ai_inhostileterrain_final031412

.pdf. His political rhetoric about out-of-control crimmigration largely has ignored the Pew Research Center's findings that the United States has seen a reversal in Mexican immigration since 2009. See Ana Gonzalez-Barrera, "More Mexicans Leaving than Coming into U.S.," *Pew Research Center*, November 19, 2015. http://www.pewhispanic .org/2015/11/19/more-mexicans-leaving-than-coming-to-the-u-s/.

8. For an investigation of photographic truth, see Richard Bolton, "Introduction," in *The Contest of Meaning: Critical Histories of Photography*, ed. Richard Bolton (Cambridge, MA: MIT Press, 1992), xvi. See also Allan Sekula, *Photography against the Grain: Essays and Photo Works, 1973–1983* (Halifax: Press of the Nova Scotia College of Art and Design, 1984), 53–56.

9. On photography and the question of visibility, see Jayne Wilkinson, "Art Documents: The Politics of Visibility in Contemporary Photography," *InVisible Culture* 22 (Spring 2015): https://du.idm.oclc.org/login?url=https://www-proquest-com.du .idm.oclc.org/scholarly-journals/art-documents-politics-visibility-contemporary /docview/1771029175/se-2?accountid=14608.

10. Roland Barthes, *Camera Lucida: Reflections on Photography* (New York: Hill and Wang, 1981), 6.

11. I am loosely referencing Octavio Paz's idea of *un poesia en movimiento*, the poetic impulse to construct the future that always results in a reinvention of the past. Paz, *Poesia en movimiento: México, 1915–1966* (Mexico, D.F.: Siglo Veintiuno Editores, 1991), 5. "Photography in (frozen) movement" wishes to evoke this cyclical and oscillating concept. See also Mary Pat Brady, "The Fungibility of Borders," *Nepantla: Views from the South* 1, no. 1 (2000): 185.

12. Claire F. Fox, "The Fence and the River: Representation of the U.S.-Mexico Border in Art and Video," *Discourse* 18, nos. 1–2 (1995–1996): 58. I will mainly be referencing this article, along with Fox's monograph *The Fence and the River: Culture and Politics at the U.S.-Mexico Border* (Minneapolis: University of Minnesota Press, 1999), which includes an updated version of the original article. "Establishing Shots of the Border" was republished in *Border Culture*, ed. Ilan Stavans (Santa Barbara, CA: Greenwood, 2010), 30–49.

13. See also Bartletti, "Between Two Worlds," *Don Bartletti Photography*, https:// donbartlettiphotography.com/between-two-worlds.

14. Bartletti, in "Don Bartletti: Spotlight on Immigration."

15. Fox, "The Fence and the River," 56.

16. Chavez, *Covering Immigration*, 100–152.

17. Saskia Sassen, "Black and White Photography as Theorizing: Seeing What the Eye Cannot See," *Sociological Forum* 26, no. 2 (2011): 438, 439.

18. Ibid., 442 (my emphasis).

19. Bartletti notes, "*The Los Angeles Times* was my primary medium of expression. I was never asked or expected to fulfill an editorial impulse, especially for hypernationalist discourse. I'm only one of many authors of my photographs. Besides the camera, the printing press, the internet, additional authors of my work are the viewers. They have the constitutional right to pen or voice their own sympathies or xenophobic opinions." Bartletti, personal communication, November 1, 2017.

20. Some of these photographs originally were published alongside Sonia Nazario's reporting in the *Los Angeles Times* series "Enrique's Journey" (September 29– October 12, 2002), while others were published on the "Framework" page of the pa-

per's website. See also Bartletti, "Enrique's Journey," *Don Bartletti Photography*, https://donbartlettiphotography.com/enriques-journey/. For the literary companion, see Sonia Nazario, *Enrique's Journey* (New York: Random House, 2006).

21. Bartletti, "Framework: Enrique's Journey; #25," *Los Angeles Times*, posted June 29, 2010, https://web.archive.org/web/20161116210447/http://framework.latimes.com/2010/06/29/enrique%E2%80%99s-journey/#/24.

22. Arturo Arias famously coined the term "Central American Americans" to recognize this segment of the US population, which has remained invisible within US Latino multiethnic, multiracial representations. Arias, "Central American-Americans: Invisibility, Power and Representation in the U.S. Latino World," *Latino Studies* 1, no. 1 (March 2003): 170, 171, 179.

23. Andreas, *Border Games*, 35.

24. Chacón and Davis, *No One Is Illegal*, 238. See also Thomas G. Tancredo, *In Mortal Danger: The Battle for America's Border and Security* (Nashville, TN: Cumberland House, 2006). Securing the border began in 1990 with the San Diego portion of the fence; the Real ID Act of 2005 and the Secure Fence Act of 2006 sped up fortification. See Wendy Brown, *Walled States, Waning Sovereignty* (New York: Zone Books, 2010), 35–37.

25. David Taylor, qtd. in "David J. Taylor 1994," *100 Stories Archives, 1990s*, posted May 16, 2012, https://design.uoregon.edu/david-j-taylor-1994.

26. Astrid Böger foundationally argues that the "medium of truth-recording" always has a public dimension. Böger, *People's Lives, Public Images: The New Deal Documentary Aesthetic* (Tübingen, Germany: Gunter Narr, 2001), 11–12.

27. Hannah Frieser, "Surcando el margen/Navigating the Margin," in David Taylor, *Working the Line* (Santa Fe, NM: Radius Books, 2010), 21.

28. .

29. Luis Alberto Urrea, "Saluda a los malos/Say Hello to the Bad Guy," in Taylor, *Working the Line* (Santa Fe, NM: Radius Books, 2010), 85.

30. Andreas, *Border Games*, xiv.

31. Ibid., 111.

32. Ibid., 91–92. Roger D. Hodge argues that the military technology on the border shows how the "U.S.-Mexico border is now a state unto itself: borderworld." See Hodge, "Borderworld: How the U.S. Is Reengineering Homeland Security," *Popular Science*, posted January 17, 2012, http://www.popsci.com/technology/article/2011-12/how-us-reengineering-homeland-security-borders.

33. Jason De León, *The Land of Open Graves: Living and Dying on the Migrant Trail* (Oakland: University of California Press, 2015), 154, 160.

34. Brown, *Walled States, Waning Sovereignty*, 38.

35. Ibid., 42.

36. Claire F. Fox, *The Fence and the River: Culture and Politics at the U.S.-Mexico Border* (Minneapolis: University of Minnesota Press, 1999), 2, 100.

37. Saskia Sassen, *Globalization and Its Discontents: Essays on the New Mobility of People and Money* (New York: New Press, 1998), 34, 48.

38. Fox, *The Fence and the River*, 136.

39. Chacón and Davis, *No One Is Illegal*, 251.

40. For a conversation on lowbrow, middlebrow, and highbrow culture, see Pierre Bourdieu, *Photography: A Middle-Brow Art* (Stanford, CA: Stanford University Press,

1990), and Joseph B. Entin, *Sensational Modernism: Experimental Fiction and Photography in Thirties America* (Chapel Hill: University of North Carolina Press, 2007).

41. For an analysis of the frozen nature of a snapshot in which the subject is obviously in motion, see Thierry de Duve, "Time Exposure and Snapshot: The Photograph as Paradox," in *Photography Theory*, ed. James Elkins (New York: Routledge, 2007), 109–123.

42. Rudy Adler, Victoria Criado, and Brett Huneycutt, *Border Film Project: Photos by Migrants and Minutemen on the U.S.-Mexico Border* (New York: Harry N. Abrams, 2007), unpaginated.

43. See *Border Film Project*, https://web.archive.org/web/20190322164854/http://www.borderfilmproject.com/en/photo-gallery/.

44. Schreiber, *The Undocumented Everyday*, 152.

45. Ibid., 153–154. On the problematic paradigm of documentary photography, see also Rosalind Krauss, "Photography's Discursive Spaces," in *The Contest of Meaning*, ed. Richard Bolton (Cambridge, MA: MIT Press, 1992), 287–301; and Allan Sekula, ibid., 343–388.

46. Paula Rabinowitz, *They Must Be Represented: The Politics of Documentary* (London: Verso, 1994), 36.

47. Schreiber, *The Undocumented Everyday*, 154–155; Rabinowitz, *They Must Be Represented*, 51.

48. For a discussion of the paradox between knowing the image is in movement and seeing it frozen in time, see de Duve, "Time Exposure and Snapshot," 109–114.

49. Bourdieu, *Photography*, 9.

50. Ibid., 80.

51. Ibid., 84.

52. Susan Sontag, *On Photography* (New York: Farrar, Straus and Giroux, 1977), 174–176. See also Ariella Azoulay, *The Civil Contract of Photography* (New York: Zone Books, 2008).

53. Sontag, *On Photography*, 176–177.

54. Ibid., 6.

55. Bourdieu, *Photography*, 80–81.

56. Susan Sontag and Jonathan Cott, *Susan Sontag: The Complete Rolling Stone Interview* (New Haven, CT: Yale University Press, 2013), 52–53.

57. Bourdieu, *Photography*, 80–81.

58. Judith Butler, *Notes toward a Performative Theory of Assembly* (Cambridge, MA: Harvard University Press, 2015), 36.

59. Ibid., 36. See also Charles Taylor, "The Politics of Recognition," in *Multiculturalism: Examining the Politics of Recognition*, ed. Amy Gutmann (Princeton, NJ: Princeton University Press, 1994), 45.

60. Butler, *Notes toward a Performative Theory of Assembly*, 37.

61. Bartletti notes, "Ironically, even though the last remaining yellow and black warning sign has been removed from every San Diego County freeway, it has become a worldwide popular culture icon used by pizza delivery outfits, surfers, editorial cartoonists and even by immigrant advocates to emphasize the need to run from hunger, traffic, politics, poverty, corruption and war." Don Bartletti, personal communication, November 1, 2017.

62. Sontag, *On Photography*, 55.

63. See also Böger, *People's Lives, Public Images*, 76–82.

64. Entin, *Sensational Modernism*, 259.

65. Parvati Nair, "The Razor's Edge," in *Photography and Migration*, ed. Tanya Sheehan (London: Routledge, 2018), 97. There's also the question of other sensorial elements evoking this problematic humanism. Tina M. Campt complicates the viewer's relationship to images through the photograph's haptics. According to Campt, the act of touching photographs, turning pages of albums, and feeling the materiality of images forces viewers to "engage through embodied encounters" that produce intimacy (sometimes fetishistically) and multiple understandings of temporality and history. This haptic element also shows up in the *Doc/Undoc* exhibit of Guillermo Gómez-Peña et al. The collaborative and experimental artwork-in-a-box show questions the parameters of borders, regulation, migration, and citizenship, but the medium also requires the audience to touch and participate in these questions/this art. In this sense, the haptic closes the traditional distance between artist, subject, and audience. See Campt, *Listening to Images* (Durham, NC: Duke University Press, 2017), 75, 90, 96; Jennifer A. González, "A Critical Commentary," in Guillermo Gómez-Peña et al., *Doc/Undoc: Documentado/Undocumented; Ars Shamánica Performática* (San Francisco: City Lights, 2017), 14–16.

66. Andreas, *Border Games*, 144.

67. Brown, *Walled States, Waning Sovereignty*, 92.

68. Tanya Sheehan draws out how globalization disrupts traditional histories of photography and requires different methodologies and organizing principles in the study of photography. The "global turn" requires scholars to detach historically othered or underrepresented photography from "normative narrative." Sheehan, "Introduction: Questions of Difference," in *Photography, History, Difference*, ed. Tanya Sheehan (Lebanon, NH: Dartmouth College Press, 2015), 5–6.

69. Sontag, *On Photography*, 178.

70. Ibid., 179.

71. Walter Benjamin, *Illuminations* (New York: Schocken Books, 1968), 224, 228, 239, 241.

Chapter 3: Latinx Realisms

1. Rebecca M. Schreiber argues that documentary photography is an aesthetic form that depends on the principles of social realism, thereby making these two narrative conventions share historical genealogies, formal techniques, and structures of power. This idea of documentary realism also comes under investigation in cinema studies. Bill Nichols reminds us that "documentary as a concept and practice occupies no fixed territory," and must be defined from the perspectives of the filmmaker, the text, and the viewer. He sees the conventions of documentary to be associated with realism, although he also posits a category of documentary realism, which describes a form of visual historiography: "We live in histories but we also read histories. We see documentaries but we also see past them. We engage with their structures but we also recognize a realist representation of the world as it is." Brian Winston, engaging with the established documentary theorists Michael Renov and John Grierson, sees realism to be the fundamental component of traditional documentary. Both scholars understand real-

ism as a form or convention that inflects our understanding of documentary (and its offspring mockumentary, docudrama, or reality television, among others) in particular ways. I spend this chapter thinking more pointedly about this question of reality, truth, and history imbuing so-called documentary. Schreiber, *The Undocumented Everyday: Migrant Lives and the Politics of Visibility* (Minneapolis: University of Minnesota Press, 2018), 4; Nichols, *Representing Reality: Issues and Concepts in Documentary* (Bloomington: Indiana University Press, 1991), 12–31, 177; Winston, *Claiming the Real: Documentary; Grierson and Beyond* (Hampshire, UK: Palgrave Macmillan, 2008), 10.

2. Ramón Saldívar, *Chicano Narrative: The Dialectics of Difference* (Madison: University of Wisconsin Press, 1990), 5.

3. Marcial González, *Chicano Novels and the Politics of Form: Race, Class, and Reification* (Ann Arbor: University of Michigan Press, 2009), 33.

4. Elena Machado Sáez, *Market Aesthetics: The Purchase of the Past in Caribbean Diasporic Fiction* (Charlottesville: University of Virginia Press, 2015), 20.

5. Ibid., 167.

6. Gary D. Rhodes and John Parris Springer call this "docufiction." See "Introduction," in *Docufictions: Essays on the Intersection of Documentary and Fictional Filmmaking,* ed. Gary D. Rhodes and John Parrish Springer (Jefferson, NC: McFarland, 2006), 1–10.

7. Josefina López, *Detained in the Desert and Other Plays* (Carlsbad, CA: WPR Books, 2011), 19.

8. David Riker, "David Riker and the People of 'La Ciudad,'" *Revolutionary Worker,* March, 26, 2000, https://revcom.us/a/v21/1040-049/1048/riker.htm.

9. While these entities appear to be multinational corporations (MNCs) based in the United States, they may also operate as transnational corporations (TNCs), whose foreign offices have more autonomy. For a consideration of the differences and similarities between MNCs and TNCs, see Masao Miyoshi, "A Borderless World? From Colonialism to Transnationalism and the Decline of the Nation-State," *Critical Inquiry* 19, no. 4 (1993): 735–742.

10. "Interview with Director Alex Rivera," Latino Film Festival and Conference, Bloomington, IN, 2012, https://www.youtube.com/watch?v=dtbBG48m_Eo.

11. Alicia Arrizón, *Latina Performances* (Bloomington: Indiana University Press, 1999), xvi.

12. Leticia Alvarado, *Abject Performance: Aesthetic Strategies in Latino Cultural Production* (Durham, NC: Duke University Press, 2019), 162.

13. Ibid., 165.

14. Gad Guterman, *Performance, Identity, and Immigration Law: A Theater of Undocumentedness* (New York: Palgrave Macmillan, 2014), 59.

15. Frances R. Aparicio, "Jennifer as Selena: Rethinking Latinidad in Media and Popular Culture," *Latino Studies* 1, no. 1 (2003): 94. García-Peña also argues that the racialized and sexualized Latinx body carries the "burden of coloniality." For García-Peña, when in modes of performance such as dancing and singing, the body becomes a "site of historical contestation" that reveals the colonial and heteronormative hegemony but also disrupts, revises, and contradicts these "historical and rhetorical narratives." As such, performance makes visible the embodiment of these tensions and contradictions. See García-Peña, *Borders of Dominicanidad,* 6, 194.

16. Jean Baudrillard, *Symbolic Exchange and Death* (London: Sage, 1993), 75.

17. Frederick Luis Aldama, *A User's Guide to Postcolonial and Latino Borderlands Fiction* (Austin: University of Texas Press, 2009), 29, 64, 115, 124; Ralph Rodríguez, *Latinx Literature Unbound: Undoing Ethnic Expectation* (New York: Fordham University Press, 2018), 54.

18. M. González, *Chicano Novels*, 30.

19. R. Rodríguez, *Latinx Literature Unbound*, 59, 54. Rodríguez also calls on Latinx criticism to pay attention to the narratives that "surpass" the mimetic conventions of (naïve) realism and "unbind" us from our traditional understandings of Latinx literature and Latinx realities. For Rodríguez, these transcendent narratives are metafiction, which he argues "employs strategies and conventions that exceed the boundaries of the real" and "thereby makes the real more perceptible and more knowable by defamiliarizing it" (ibid., 54).

20. Aldama, *A User's Guide*, 50. Aldama has a rather traditional understanding of realism as a genre of fiction that is opposed to magic, myth, and romance. Nevertheless, he also identifies many types of realism, disallowing a stable definition or set of conventions: straightforward realism, commonsense realism, magical realism, stolid realism, suprarealism, behavioralistic realism, social realism, hysterical realism, extravagant realism, rural realism, and dreamlike subjective realism. He also navigates the slippages in convention and technique around "realism and antirealism" in select postcolonial writing, ultimately thinking through how these writers produce "wholly imagined worlds or quite real life circumstances" on their pages. Dalleo and Machado Sáez maintain a similar distinction, arguing that in some Latinx literature, realism critiques the anticolonial romance that "promises a better world" or counters the political idealism of the Sixties. Aldama, *A User's Guide*, 64–65, 158n13; Raphael Dalleo and Elena Machado Sáez, *The Latino/a Canon and the Emergence of Post-Sixties Literature* (New York: Palgrave Macmillan, 2007), 42, 46, 63.

21. Ibid., 77. Nancy Glazener offers a version of uppercase realism in what she calls "high realism," in which realist texts produce and enforce social hierarchy and consolidate the authority of the bourgeoisie. Glazener, *Reading for Realism: The History of a U.S. Literary Institution, 1850–1910* (Durham, NC: Duke University Press, 1997), 14.

22. There are elisions about what constitutes realness in naïve realism. Marcos Becquer and Alisa Lebow call out this concept of realness directly and propose the idea of "docudrag," in which realness becomes imbued with questions of performance and authenticity. For Becquer and Lebow, "docudrag" describes a documentary fiction in which filmmakers "cast a fictive shadow" on documentary forms "while still partaking of the truth claims of an authenticated positionality." This paradox translates for Becquer and Lebow into a critical reckoning: the documentary film constructs the reality that it means to record and, thus, brings to light that "such reality is itself only available in ways mediated by representation." Documentary, then, does not reflect reality but constructs it. Becquer and Lebow ultimately argue that docudrag, especially in the black and Latinx LGBTQ+ tradition of *Paris Is Burning*, allows for "transdoc" practices that transcend these constructs of realness through "cuts and augmentations." These ideas also evoke Karen Christian's work on identity, performance, and the "drag motif" in Latina/o/x literary production. Becquer and Lebow, "Docudrag, or 'Realness' as a Documentary Strategy," in *The Ethnic Eye*, ed. Chon Noriega and Ana M. López (Minneapolis: University of Minnesota Press, 1996), 145, 150, 154; Christian, *Show and*

Tell: Identity as Performance in U.S. Latina/o Fiction (Albuquerque: University of New Mexico Press, 1997), 16–17, 79.

23. J. López, *Detained in the Desert and Other Plays*, 20.

24. Ibid., 48–49; *Detained in the Desert* (DVD), dir. Iliana Sosa (Los Angeles: Real Women Have Curves Studio, 2013).

25. J. López, *Detained in the Desert and Other Plays*, 41; *Detained in the Desert* (DVD), directed by Iliana Sosa.

26. M. González, *Chicano Novels*, 30.

27. Ibid., 33–34. For González, the logic of contradiction in Chicanx realism neither reproduces the totality of social class inequality required by strict Lukácsian realism nor attacks the concept of totality, as some interpretations of postmodern narratives advance; instead, realisms are imperfect because they imply totality through its absence (ibid., 32–33).

28. J. López, *Detained in the Desert and Other Plays*, 53.

29. Ibid., 59.

30. Saldívar, *Chicano Narrative*, 108.

31. Ibid., 103–104.

32. Elizabeth Jacobs argues that we cannot read López's use of the imaginary and mythical as magical realism, since López has denounced this narrative form. Nevertheless, Dalleo and Machado Sáez remind us that magical realism is a "potential avenue for depicting a specifically Latino/a historical baggage" in some Latinx fiction, especially when it "represents a historical past still relevant to the Latino/a present." Of course, for Dalleo and Machado Sáez, this is not without a "market valuation." Jacobs, "Undocumented Acts: Migration, Community and Audience in Two Chicana Plays," *Comparative American Studies: An International Journal* 14, nos. 3–4 (2016): 286; Dalleo and Machado Sáez, *The Latino/a Canon*, 95.

33. Jacobs, "Undocumented Acts," 286. Peggy Phelan also emphasizes that all representations of the real are about producing "believable images" that negotiate "an unverifiable real," but these images are "always, partially, phantasmatic" and contain elements of things "not 'really' there." This slippage between real and apparition also is significant to Harvey's Marxist reading of the contradiction of capital, in which he argues that the most important contradiction structuring the economic engine is the contradiction "between reality and appearance in the world in which we live," where "surface appearances disguise underlying realities." See Phelan, *Unmarked: The Politics of Performance* (London: Routledge, 1993), 1; David Harvey, *Seventeen Contradictions and the End of Capitalism* (Oxford: Oxford University Press, 2014), 4–5.

34. R. Rodríguez, *Latinx Literature Unbound*, 18.

35. Tiffany A. López, "Introduction," in J. López, *Detained in the Desert and Other Plays*, 17. Jacobs also argues that "cineteatro" [*sic*] is allegorical for the trauma experienced on the border because the "action of the play that moves quickly"—its jump cuts—"effectively contextualises migration within a broader framework of violence and border control." Jacobs warns that this style of trauma-driven performance does not construct Latinx and migrant subjects as perpetual victims, but, rather, it means to "promote action and agency." Jacobs, "Undocumented Acts," 283, 285.

36. M. González, *Chicano Novels*, 30.

37. Marta Caminero-Santangelo, *Documenting the Undocumented: Latino/a Narratives and Social Justice in the Era of Operation Gatekeeper* (Gainesville: University Press

of Florida, 2017), 24, 130. See also C. Christina Lam, "Bearing Witness: Alternate Archives of Latinx Identity in Raquel Cepeda's *Bird of Paradise: How I Became a Latina*," *Studies in American Culture* 43, no. 1 (June 2020): 26–40.

38. Whereas González understands Chicano realism to reveal the social significance of things that cannot be represented or exposed, Saldívar argues that Chicano narratives challenge the realities constructed by those with authority and legitimacy. M. González, *Chicano Novels*, 144, 145; Saldívar, *Chicano Narrative*, 76, 88.

39. Caminero-Santangelo, *Documenting the Undocumented*, 58.

40. Nichols, *Representing Reality*, 170.

41. Nichols unpacks how neorealism seeks and represents reality through aesthetics rather than logic (ibid., 167).

42. José Esteban Muñoz, *Disidentifications: Queers of Color and the Performance of Politics* (Minneapolis: University of Minnesota Press, 1999), 82.

43. Leticia Alvarado, *Abject Performances: Aesthetic Strategies in Latino Cultural Production* (Durham, NC: Duke University Press, 2019), 138, 44.

44. Daniel Bell argues that the "post-modern temper" (which he sees largely embodied in Michel Foucault's work) understands the "ruined" city (a metaphor for soul and being) as "no longer the decline of the West, but the end of civilization." For Bell, this "modish" doctrine on the postmodern and post-industrial pushes the limits of rationality into the absurd and surreal. Nevertheless, this understanding also establishes the industrial and modernist moment as a space of civilization (or at least the belief in the possibilities of civilization) that the postindustrial and postmodernist moment upends. The trope of urban ruin signals a *telos* to so-called civilization that carries the baggage of colonialism, whiteness, the West, and heterosexual patriarchy. *La Ciudad* complicates this reading of the postindustrial since the ruined space is not really upending these violent historical terms of civilization; instead, the film seems to be showing more specialized and insidious forms of control and colonial impulse. Bell, *The Cultural Contradictions of Capitalism* (New York: Basic Books, 1976), 52.

45. Saskia Sassen, *The Global City: New York, London, Tokyo* (Princeton, NJ: Princeton University Press, 2001), 322. I should note that these questions of incorporation and exclusion are integral to the space of the city for Sassen. This raises the question whether these are the same processes for rural spaces or not. In parallel to these concerns, scholars present a spatial and temporal distinction in categorizing forms of realism. Dalleo and Machado Sáez primarily unpack contemporary urban or "ghetto realism" which largely emerges from "resident Latina/o fiction" and tells us something about the resident versus immigrant. In contrast, Aldama also identifies "rural realism," which concerns itself with character fate and is a genre of the late nineteenth-century writer Thomas Hardy. See Dalleo and Machado Sáez, *The Latino/o Canon*, 47, and Aldama, *A User's Guide*, 59.

46. Saskia Sassen, *Expulsions: Brutality and Complexity in the Global Economy* (Cambridge, MA: Belknap, 2014), 15–16.

47. "David Riker and the People of 'La Ciudad,'" *Revolutionary Worker*, March, 26, 2000, https://revcom.us/a/v21/1040-049/1048/riker.htm. It is no coincidence that Riker marks these new enclosures as beginning in the mid-1970s, the exact time period David Harvey considers to be the birth of US neoliberalism (and what I characterize as a launching in localized libertarian policies and discourses of privatization). Harvey

looks at the 1974 New York stock market crash as a catalyst for revamping the social programs of welfare and education in favor of a more privatized organization of the economy and the people. See David Harvey, *Brief History of Neoliberalism* (Oxford: Oxford University Press, 2005), 23–27, 45.

48. The committee was initially made up of the INS, the departments of justice, labor, state, and agriculture, and the War Manpower Commission. Calavita traces the history of the Bracero Program and uncovers the fluid relationship between the government and the economy that this intergovernmental contract created. Kitty Calavita, *Inside the State: The Bracero Program, Immigration, and the I.N.S.* (New York: Routledge, 2010), 19.

49. Ibid., 30–31, 60–62, 80–89.

50. Seth M. Holmes, *Fresh Fruit, Broken Bodies: Migrant Farmworkers in the United States* (Berkeley: University of California Press, 2013), 50. Not all scholars see the Bracero Program or its contemporary manifestations as a system of exploitation. Deborah Cohen argues that painting the program as exploitation "leaves little room to recognize the multiple ways that migrants acted on their own behalf and the many-sided repercussions of such actions." I mean not to strip Latinx migrant braceros of their power but to show the structures in play that attempt to make these workers powerless. Cohen, *Braceros: Migrant Citizens and Transnational Subjects in the Postwar United States and Mexico* (Chapel Hill: University of North Carolina Press, 2011), 221.

51. This contractual change is not met with docility. The day laborers immediately start shouting in Spanish, a language the boss/contractor obviously does not understand, about how unfair this change is after being driven out into the middle of nowhere. A single black day laborer helps with translations but to no effect; the altered contract remains the same, and the boss/contractor leaves the site. While a contract shapes this business transaction, this moment shows how contracts are symbolic. Carole Pateman defines contract through "property of person," wherein people own within their own bodies, property that they can contract out in exchange for money. For Pateman, this concept of having property of person creates relationships of subordination. Charles Mills examines how this relationship of subordination is intoned with white supremacy, where the racial contract may look like a moral and normalizing hierarchy but is "calculatedly aimed at economic exploitation" in which the black underclass undergoes continuous "labor market discrimination" as "payoff for its white beneficiaries." Both Pateman and Mills show how contracts create a myth about the worker's status as individual "free" labor, while often contracts exploit workers and strip them of anything except a body. Laborers under contract are contracting out not themselves but instead the corporeal part of themselves. Contracts, thus, allow the worker to believe that he is a free agent in the employer-employee relationship, but it instead consolidates the workers' oppression in various ways. When we see this scene in *La Ciudad*, it is no surprise that the fight over the contractual change is short-lived. The workers, starved for pennies, agree to the dubious change in contract; the communication does nothing. It is a symbolic formality for employers to legitimize exploitation and for workers to *appear to agree*. But when looking at the utter need for money when they were begging for work on the street, the space they have been driven to, and the racial and lingual barriers, the workers obviously have no choice in the matter—choice is an appearance. Pateman, *The Sexual Contract* (Stanford, CA:

Stanford University Press, 1988), 5, 65; Mills, *The Racial Contract* (Ithaca, NY: Cornell University Press, 1999), 32, 39. See also David Harvey, *Spaces of Hope* (Berkeley: University of California Press, 2000), 107–108.

52. Jean Baudrillard, *Symbolic Exchange and Death* (London: Sage Publications, 1993), 39.

53. Ibid., 39, 42.

54. Lauren Berlant, "Slow Death (Sovereignty, Obesity, Lateral Agency)," *Critical Inquiry* 33, no. 4 (2007): 759.

55. Ibid., 759, 761.

56. Baudrillard, *Symbolic Exchange and Death*, 39.

57. Jean Baudrillard, *Simulations* (New York: Semiotext(e), 1983), 141–142. I should also note that Baudrillard does not readily distinguish between hyperrealism and the hyperreal, although the former seems to denote the reproductive medium or cultural text and the latter seems to connote the greater cultural phenomenon.

58. Nichols, *Representing Reality*, 28, 184.

59. Calavita, *Inside the State*, 60–66.

60. Ibid., 80.

61. Puar explores this interplay between the nation and neoliberalism, arguing that what is central to necropolitics is that there is "a privatization of death." Puar claims that death is kept private (and taboo) because it must be kept invisible so that the national and quotidian norm may persevere, or metaphorically *live on*. This privatization is essential to the "distribution and redistribution" of biopolitics or to "optimize life." Jasbir Puar, *Terrorist Assemblages: Homonationalism in Queer Times* (Durham, NC: Duke University Press, 2007), 33, 38–39.

62. M. González, *Chicano Novels*, 192.

63. Guterman, *Performance, Identity, and Immigration Law*, 4.

64. Cacho, *Social Death*, 22–23.

65. Berlant, "Slow Death," 758.

66. Ibid., 760.

67. Garrett Stewart, *Transmedium* (Chicago: University of Chicago Press, 2018), 62.

68. Baudrillard, *Simulations*, 141–142; Baudrillard, *Symbolic Exchange and Death*, 71–72.

69. Amy Sara Carroll, "From *Papapapá* to *Sleep Dealer*: Alex Rivera's Undocumentary Poetics," *Social Identities* 19, nos. 3–4 (2013): 495. In parallel to this reading, Mark Fisher also discusses Baudrillard's ideas about how cybernetic feedback systems have become the primary "mode of control" under capitalism: the audience of a film is no longer "subjected to power from the outside" but is "integrated into a control circuit." See Fisher, *Capitalist Realism: Is There No Alternative?* (Winchester, UK: Zero Books, 2009), 47–49.

70. Baudrillard, *Symbolic Exchange and Death*, 71–72.

71. For a more exhaustive discussion of this structural distance, see my article Agua, Inc.: Water Wars, Aqua-Terrorism, and Speculative Economy in Latinx and Transborder Cinema," *ASAP/Journal* 6, no. 2 (2021): 431–458.

72. Duran, "Virtual Borders," 225.

73. Ibid., 225.

74. Sarah Ann Wells, "The Scar and Node: Border Science Fiction and the *Mise-en-scène* of Globalized Labor," *The Global South* 8, no. 1 (2014): 83.

75. Ibid., 85.

76. For different considerations of the post-continental philosophies on speculative realism, see Ray Brassier, Iain Hamilton Grant, Graham Harman, and Quentin Meillassoux, "Speculative Realism," *Collapse: Philosophical Research and Development* 3 (2007): 307–449; Levi Bryant, Nick Srnicek, and Graham Harman, eds., *The Speculative Turn: Continental Materialism and Realism* (Melbourne: Re.press, 2010); and Steven Shaviro, The *Universe of Things: On Speculative Realism* (Minneapolis: University of Minnesota Press, 2018). The philosophy of speculative realism deemphasizes the human in measuring life and reality. While these philosophies are outside the purview of this book, they resonate in my considerations of how life is now measured by capital rather than the human. While these philosophies champion object-oriented ontology, new materialisms, and the posthuman, cultural production complicates this understanding of speculative realism. Chelsea Birks describes speculative realism through the medium of cinema, where films' mediated and unmediated relationship to reality "expose conflicting truths: on one level they draw attention to an objective world in excess of the human (thereby resisting the phenomenological basis of the apparatus), but on another they self-consciously indicate the ways that this world is necessarily framed in a subjective way." In some ways, Birks's understanding of film's contradictory relationship with the human asks us to think about what (human) worlds and truths are being constructed in film. Similarly, Critical Art Ensemble (CAE) describes a need for an "emergent necropolitics" that forces us to question how the speculative arts, especially those that are transhumanist and posthumanist, pretend that life can be without human death. Birks, "Objectivity, Speculative Realism, and the Cinematic Apparatus," *Cinema Journal* 57, no. 4 (2018): 11; Critical Art Ensemble, *Aesthetics, Necropolitics, and Environmental Struggle* (New York: Autonomedia, 2018), 27, 30, 32.

77. Ramón Saldívar, "Historical Fantasy, Speculative Realism, and Postrace Aesthetics in Contemporary American Fiction," *American Literary History* 23, no. 3 (2011): 585, 577.

78. Baudrillard, *Symbolic Exchange and Death*, 39–40.

79. Achille Mbembe, *Necropolitics* (Durham, NC: Duke University Press, 2019), 75.

80. Baudrillard, *Simulations*, 142. He also uses the verb "sealed off" in *Symbolic Exchange and Death*, 72.

81. Mbembe, *Necropolitics*, 75.

82. A. Gabriel Meléndez, *Hidden Chicano Cinema: Film Dramas in the Borderlands* (New Brunswick, NJ: Rutgers University Press, 2013), 103.

83. Ibid., 191–193.

84. Machado Sáez, *Market Aesthetics*, 81–83.

85. Mbembe, *Necropolitics*, 84, 80–83.

86. Ibid., 88.

87. Puar, *Terrorist Assemblages*, 72.

88. Mbembe, *Necropolitics*, 89.

89. Jasbir Puar, "Queer Times, Queer Assemblages," *Social Text* 23, nos. 3–4 (2005): 128.

90. Baudrillard, *Symbolic Exchange and Death*, 39–40. Baudrillard's idea of sacrifice aligns with Giorgio Agamben's idea of the *homo sacer*: a person of contradictory traits who is rendered sacred and whose killing is thus unpunishable. Agamben unpacks how a person deemed sacred (in the sense of god anointed) could be killed without

those doing the killing not being punished by the gods. On one level, the killing must either be seen as a sacrifice to the gods, or the *homo sacer* is already understood as possessed by god, so this person's killing is inconsequential to her/his/their sacred status. Agamben, *Homo Sacer: Sovereign Power and Bare Life* (Stanford, CA: Stanford University Press, 1998), 72–74.

91. Mbembe and Agamben locate much of necropolitics and biopolitics as growing out of a Fordist sensibility that desired mass production. Agamben explores how twentieth-century Nazism and racism fully realized and enacted thanatopolitics with technologies produced for efficient and mass genocide, eugenics, and ethnic cleansing. Mbembe locates this sensibility in the earlier spectacles of execution during the French Revolution: "In a context in which decapitation is viewed as less demeaning than hanging, innovations in the technologies of murder aimed not only at 'civilizing' the ways of killing. They also aimed at disposing of a large number victims in a relatively short span of time." Agamben, *Homo Sacer*, 122–123; Mbembe, *Necropolitics*, 73.

92. This sweatshop looks very different from the image of Mexican and Mexican American textile labor given in Josefina López's *Real Woman Have Curves*. Both exemplify the conditions of what we may call a "sweatshop": labor within hot and enclosed spaces, the lack of any running fans because these raise dust, being at the whim of ready-to-wear buyers (in both cases represented as white women). Nevertheless, *Real Woman Have Curves* is a familial business and has an incredibly large space with few workers, which starkly contrasts *La Ciudad*'s slave-like and cramped representation of the textile sweatshop. We may think of *La Ciudad* as demonstrating a more realistic version of this space; however, the difference between these two representations is not necessarily about which representation is more verisimilar but about whether they are capturing different forms of exploitation or not. One may appear less insidious that the other, but they both portray an economy that reduces Latinx subjects to laboring bodies. See also Harvey, *Spaces of Hope*, 110.

93. This is most commonly discussed under the topic of "model minority," where ethnic immigrants are ranked according to how well they assimilated or how economically successful they are in the United States. For a more nuanced reading of the model minority and its ramifications in Latina/o performance, specifically for the Cuban American experience, see José Esteban Muñoz, "No es fácil," *TDR: The Drama Review* 39, no. 3, (1995): 76–82.

94. Karl Marx, *Capital*, vol. 1 (London: Penguin, 1990), 279.

95. Aihwa Ong describes how transnational companies prefer "third world female workers" because of their perceived docility. For Ong, the third world female body becomes a selling point for buyers who want higher production on lower wages, so that her "nimble fingers," her "eyes and fingers adapted for assembly work," and her "natural attributes" are synonymous with wage work. Ong, "The Gender and Labor Politics of Postmodernity," 73. See also Marx, *Capital*, vol. 1, 481–482, 508; and Harvey, *Spaces of Hope*, 103–104.

96. Mel Y. Chen explores how the "animateness or inanimateness of entities" denote a living or dead binary. Chen argues against the parallel conception that collapses inanimateness into nonlife because certain situations and contexts—such as air pollution, queerness, or race—offer us a "different way to conceive of relationality and intersubjective exchange." Nevertheless, the idea that inanimateness is nonlife, according to Chen, extends from an ontological desire to make the human cohesive and centered

in discourse: "entities as variant as disability, womanhood, sexuality, emotion, vegetal, and the inanimate become more salient, more palpable as having been rendered proximate to the human, though they have always subtended the human by propping it up." I note Chen's ideas in my discussion of Ana's protest because her inanimate body also troubles the binary between life and death; her inanimateness is not synonymous with death or the nonhuman but instead produces what Chen calls an inanimate life or what Mbembe calls life-in-death: she is living dead. Chen, *Animacies* (Durham, NC: Duke University Press, 2012), 10–11, 98.

97. Arrizón, *Latina Performances*, 121, 124.

98. Dalleo and Machado Sáez, *The Latino/a Canon*, 41.

99. Baudrillard, *Symbolic Exchange and Death*, 39, 175.

100. Harvey, *Spaces of Hope*, 115.

101. Ibid., 101.

102. Ibid., 102.

103. Saldívar, *Chicano Narrative*, 108–109, 131.

104. Baudrillard, *Symbolic Exchange and Death*, 75.

Chapter 4: Markets of Resurrection

1. Judith Ortiz Cofer, *Silent Dancing: A Partial Remembrance of a Puerto Rican Childhood* (Houston: Arte Publico, 1990), 30.

2. Ibid., 30.

3. See John D. Márquez, "Latinos as the 'Living Dead': Raciality, Expendability, and Border Militarization," *Latino Studies* 10, no. 4 (2012): 475.

4. See Annie McClanahan, *Dead Pledges: Debt, Crisis, and Twenty-First-Century Culture* (Stanford, CA: Stanford University Press, 2017), 143, 176, 182.

5. Ibid., 31.

6. Ortiz Cofer, *Silent Dancing*, 31.

7. Ibid., 35.

8. Although Ortiz Cofer does not directly point to the real political counterpart for this labor-captivity narrative, she may be alluding to the Farm Placement Program (FPP, also known as the Farm Labor Program) between Puerto Rico and the United States. For a discussion on the FPP and the problem with labor contracts within this program, see Edgardo Meléndez, *Sponsored Migration* (Columbus: Ohio State University Press, 2017).

9. Ortiz Cofer, *Silent Dancing*, 35.

10. See Jessica Magnani, "Colonial Subjects, Imperial Discourses: Rosario Ferré's *The House on the Lagoon* and Judith Ortiz Cofer's *The Line of the Sun*," *Centro Journal* 21, no. 1 (2009): 156–179; Carmen Faymonville, "New Transnational Identities in Judith Ortiz Cofer's Autobiographical Fiction," *MELUS* 26, no. 2 (2001): 129–158.

11. Maya Socolovsky, "Telling Stories of Transgression: Judith Ortiz Cofer's *The Line of the Sun*," *MELUS* 34, no. 1 (Spring 2009): 96; David J. Vázquez, *Triangulations: Narrative Strategies for Navigating Latino Identity* (Minneapolis: University of Minnesota Press, 2011), 124.

12. Notably, representation from Belize is missing in the novel. Maritza E. Cárdenas maps the historical contours of this absence and its relation to blackness. Panama is also historically left out of the Confederación de Centro America (COFECA), although

Goldman includes Panamanian characters. Furthermore, US imperialism and intervention in Central America is not a recent phenomenon, and Cárdenas shows how this goes back to the nineteenth century. See Cárdenas, *Constituting Central American-Americans: Transnational Identities and the Politics of Dislocation* (New Brunswick, NJ: Rutgers University Press, 2019), 16, 32–34, 51.

13. See Ralph Armbruster-Sandoval, *Globalization and Cross-Border Labor Solidarity in the Americas: The Anti-Sweatshop Movement and the Struggle for Social Justice* (New York: Routledge, 2005).

14. Michael Templeton, "Becoming Transnational and Becoming Machinery in Francisco Goldman's *The Ordinary Seaman*," *Symploke* 14, nos. 1–2 (2006): 286.

15. Ibid., 287.

16. Francisco Goldman, *The Ordinary Seaman* (New York: Grove, 1997), 47.

17. Kristen Silva Gruesz, "Utopía Latina: *The Ordinary Seaman* in Extraordinary Times," *MFS: Modern Fiction Studies* 49, no. 1 (2003): 73.

18. Goldman, *The Ordinary Seaman*, 154.

19. María DeGuzmán, *Buenas Noches, American Culture: Latina/o Aesthetics of Night* (Bloomington: Indiana University Press, 2012), 173.

20. Lisa Marie Cacho, *Social Death: Racialized Rightlessness and the Criminalization of the Unprotected* (New York: New York University Press, 2012), 129–131.

21. Karina O. Alvarado, Alicia Ivonne Estrada, and Ester E. Hernández, "Introduction: U.S. Central American (Un)Belongings," in *U.S. Central Americans: Reconstructing Memories, Struggles, and Communities of Resistance*, ed. Alvarado, Estrada, and Hernández (Tuscon: University of Arizona Press, 2017), 21–22. See also Walter E. Little, "Maya Handicraft Vendors' CAFTA-DR Discourses," in *Central America in the New Millennium: Living Transition and Reimagining Democracy*, ed. Jennifer L. Burrell and Ellen Moodie (New York: Berghahn, 2012), 181–195.

22. Cacho, *Social Death*, 123–125.

23. See Kati L. Griffith, "U.S. Migrant Worker Law: The Interstices of Immigration Law and Labor and Employment Law," *Comparative Labor Law and Policy Journal* 31, no. 1 (2009): 125–162. See also Kitty Calavita, *Inside the State: The Bracero Program, Immigration, and the I.N.S.* (New York: Routledge, 2010), 182–183.

24. Ana Patricia Rodríguez, "Refugees of the South: Central Americans in the U.S. Latino Imaginary," *American Literature* 73, no. 2 (2001): 405.

25. Achille Mbembe, *Necropolitics* (Durham, NC: Duke University Press, 2019), 86–87; Jasbir Puar, *Terrorist Assemblage: Homonationalism in Queer Times* (Durham, NC: Duke University Press, 2007), 112.

26. Lee Edelman, *No Future*: Central Americans in the U.S. Latino Imaginary (Durham, NC: Duke University Press, 2004), 3, 10–14, 58, 64. Edelman draws heavily on Lacanian understandings of the death drive. For Lacan, the death drive is a psychic formation and social manifestation that has meaning only when caught between two contrary terms. On one level, the death drive describes (at its broadest and simplest) the contradiction between instinct, which denotes biological vitality, and death, which is the destruction of that vitality (or life). On another level, however, it describes how the discontents of civilization intersect with a subject's own anxieties, thereby splitting this subject and making him constitute the world, modernity, and life itself through his own end. In this sense, Lacan sees the death drive as both the beginning and the end of subjectivity—it is primordial and before speech—but it also becomes the very mecha-

nism that affirms the subject's life/being for others, giving him his essential image. Antonio Viejo takes up what Lacanian theory may offer to Latino studies. He contends that Latino studies currently employs an approach to subjectivity that cannot imagine a whole, complete, and transparent subject and ego, creating a notion of subjectivity that actually enables racist and white supremacist discourses. In his theorization of a Latino futurity, he argues that the Latinization of the United States "works to erase that specious border" in the face of significant demographic changes but also signals new forms of revitalization and "resuscitation"—thereby "breathing new life"—into the decaying neighborhoods and ghost towns and making the Latino future "what will have been." Jacques Lacan, *Écrits* (New York: Norton, 1977), 101–102, 28, 103–105; Antonio Viejo, *Dead Subjects: Toward a Politics of Loss in Latino Studies* (Durham, NC: Duke University Press, 2007), 4, 116–118, 122.

27. José Esteban Muñoz, *Cruising Utopia: The Then and There of Queer Futurity* (New York: New York University Press, 2009), 83.

28. Gruesz, "Utopía Latina," 80.

29. A. Rodríguez, "Refugees of the South," 402.

30. Goldman, *The Ordinary Seaman*, 116.

31. Ibid., 68.

32. Ibid., 116

33. Ibid., 124, 237.

34. Ibid., 318–322, 330.

35. Ibid., 371.

36. Ibid., 369.

37. Gruesz, "Utopía Latina," 78.

38. Mbembe, *Necropolitics*, 92

39. David McNally, *Monsters of the Market: Zombies, Vampires, and Global Capitalism* (Chicago: Haymarket Books, 2012), 4.

40. bell hooks, *Black Looks: Race and Representation* (Boston: South End, 1992), 168.

41. See David William Foster, "Latino Comics: Javier Hernandez's *El Muerto* as Allegory of Chicano Identity," in *Latinos and Narrative Media: Participation and Portrayal*, ed. Frederick Luis Aldama (New York: Palgrave Macmillan, 2013), 225.

42. I cannot talk about Hernandez's comic books or comic strips without talking about the film *The Dead One*. Partly the reason for this is that Hernandez's series is an unfinished and incomplete narrative, so the film helps to fill out the narrative. This interchangeability between the forms and the writers of this story is arguably problematic, but it fruitfully decenters the author as the central agent of the narrative. Accordingly, I read this story without the affective or authorial fallacy.

43. Javier Hernandez, "Weapon Tex-Mex vs. El Muerto," in *The Los Comex Codex* (Whittier, CA: Los Comex, 2013), 16.

44. Mauricio Espinoza, "The Alien Is Here to Stay: Otherness, Anti-Assimilation, and Empowerment in Latino/a Superhero Comics: *Latino Comic Books Past, Present, and Future*," in *Graphic Borders*, ed. Frederick Luis Aldama and Christopher González (Austin: University of Texas Press, 2016), 187.

45. Ibid., 187.

46. Sheila Maria Contreras, *Blood Lines: Myth, Indigenism, and Chicana/o Literature* (Austin: University of Texas Press, 2008), 54–56.

47. Claudio Lomnitz, *Death and the Idea of Mexico* (New York: Zone Books, 2005), 41–46.

48. Ibid., 28, 407–408.

49. Ibid., 450–451.

50. Ibid., 45. This is also clear in the Santa Muerte and San Malverde celebrations (unsanctioned by the Catholic Church), which sometimes are associated with the narco-economics of the borderlands. David Rochkind also produced a photography exhibit and book that capture the growing popularity of these celebrations amid the drug war in Mexico. See Rochkind, *Heavy Hand, Sunken Spirit* (Stockport, UK: Dewi Lewis Publishing, 2012).

51. See Michael Valdes Moses, "Magical Realism at World's End," *Margin: Exploring Magical Realism*, March 27, 2003, http://www.angelfire.com/wa2/margin/nonficMoses .html. He critiques how the presentation and promotion of magical realism gave the First World reader a Latin American reality that was essentially fantastic and fundamentally illogical. As such, the literary market tapped into a very colonial ideology that exoticizes, racializes, and inferiorizes the (Third World) Other. Emilio Sauri argues that First World readers notice the magic over the realism in boom literature because they need to depoliticize its radical and social content to maintain their worldview of social inequality. See Sauri, "'A la pinche modernidad': Literary Form and the End of History in Roberto Bolaño's *Los detectives salvajes*," *MLN* 125, no. 2 (March 2010): 419–420.

52. The Haitian zombie signifies both historical loss and colonial labor enslavement. The zombie is a product of African spiritual practices but also connotes a person who must labor indefinitely *after* death. Jerry Philogene argues that images of Haiti and Haitians—whether as zombies or as a powerless, poor, and abject people—construct a visual discourse that creates a country of "dead citizens" who are "perceived as ineligible for personhood." Philogene, "'Dead Citizen' and the Abject Nation," *Journal of Haitian Studies* 21, no. 1 (Spring 2015): 102.

53. For a look at the history of comic book advertisements, see Sara Century, "The Strange History of Comic Book Advertisements," *SYFY Wire*, May 31, 2018, https:// www.syfy.com/syfywire/the-strange-history-of-comic-book-advertisements.

54. Cacho, *Social Death*, 20, 63.

55. McNally, *Monsters of the Market*, 210.

56. Ibid., 210–213.

57. Ibid., 261.

58. Ibid. This also may be the structure of the economy itself. Chris Harman argues that our current boom/bust economy mimics the erratic actions of a zombie, dead when basic human goals are on the line but with "sudden spurts of activity that cause chaos," yet these economic patterns, which have been a strategic form of violent governmentalities since Bretton Woods (1944), enable the livelihood of some at the expense of others. Harman, *Zombie Capitalism: Global Crisis and the Relevance of Marx* (Chicago: Haymarket Books, 2009), 12.

59. Frederick Luis Aldama, *Your Brain on Latino Comics* (Austin: University of Texas Press, 2009), 14 (my emphasis).

60. McClanahan, *Dead Pledges*, 133.

61. Edelman, *No Future*, 3.

62. Muñoz, *Cruising Utopia*, 87.

63. Latinx literature and film has often produced these questions of gender, especially around abuelas, brujas, and curanderas: Ultima in Rudolfo Anaya's *Bless Me, Ultima* (1972), Mamá Cielo in Judith Ortiz Cofer's *Line of the Sun* (1989), Celia in Cristina Garcia's *Dreaming in Cuban* (1992), Doña Felicia in Ana Castillo's *So Far from God* (1993), and Lolita Lebrón in Irene Vilar's *The Ladies Gallery* (1996), to name only a few. Gisela Norat argues that some of these gendered and aged figures inspire returns to the ancestral homeland, thereby giving authority to these Latina daughters/writers. Irene Lara considers how being named a bruja mala/evil witch and producing her social death is a disciplining strategy to put all women back into their place, but these enactments make the bruja a transgressive figure of feminine power. Norat, "US Latinas Write through Carnal Mothers Back to Ancestral Homelands," *Letras Femeninas* 34, no. 1 (Summer 2008): 32; Lara, "Bruja Positionality: Toward a Chicana/Latina Spiritual Activism," *Chicana/Latina Studies* 4, no. 2 (2005): 11–12.

64. Melissa W. Wright, "Necropolitics, Narcopolitics, and Femicide: Gendered Violence on the Mexico-U.S. Border," *Signs* 36, no. 3 (2011): 709, 725, 726.

65. Russ Castronovo, *Necro Citizenship: Death, Eroticism, and the Public Sphere in the Nineteenth-Century United States* (Durham, NC: Duke University Press, 2001), 137.

66. McNally, *Monsters of the Market*, 44–45.

67. Ibid., 142–143. McNally also quotes here Peter Dendle, "The Zombie as Barometer of Cultural Anxiety," in *Monsters and the Monstrous: Myths and Metaphors of Enduring Evil*, ed. Niall Scott (Amsterdam: Rodopi, 2007), 48.

68. Castronovo, *Necro Citizenship*, 140. See also Gilles Deleuze and Félix Guattari, *A Thousand Plateaus: Capitalism and Schizophrenia* (Minneapolis: University of Minnesota Press, 1987); and Slavoj Žižek, *Organs without Bodies: On Deleuze and Consequences* (New York: Routledge, 2003).

69. See Fredric Jameson, *The Antinomies of Realism* (London: Verso, 2013), 28.

70. Avery Gordon, *Ghostly Matters: Hauntings and the Sociological Imagination* (Minneapolis: University of Minnesota Press, 1997), 24.

Chapter 5: Speculative Governances of the Dead

1. Stefano Harney and Fred Moten, *The Undercommons* (New York: Autonomedia, 2017), 55.

2. This violence of governance is also about the interplay between nation-state politics and the global economy. Drawing on David Marriot, Wilderson argues that blackness is a "locus of abjection," in which the libidinal economy "usurps me as an instrument *for*, though never a beneficiary *of*, every nation's woes." In this sense, economy situates bodies in violent ways as a way to maximize its capital. Saidiya Hartman also maps this contradictory corporealization, arguing that the black body and its givenness are constructed as a phobogenic object. Frank B. Wilderson III, *Afropessimism* (New York: Liveright, 2020), 12, 13; Hartman, *Scenes of Subjection: Terror, Slavery, and Self-Making in Nineteenth-Century America* (Oxford: Oxford University Press, 1997), 57.

3. Harney and Moten, *The Undercommons*, 17–18.

4. Ibid., 55.

5. Ibid., 57.

6. Ibid., 56–57.

7. Achille Mbembe, *Necropolitics* (Durham, NC: Duke University Press, 2019), 92.

8. Jack Halberstam, "The Wild Beyond: With and for the Undercommons," in Harney and Moten, *The Undercommons*, 11.

9. Daniel José Older, *Salsa Nocturna* (New York: JABberwocky Literary Agency, 2016), 171.

10. Marc C. Jerng, *Racial Worldmaking: The Power of Popular Fiction* (New York: Fordham University Press, 2018), 9–12.

11. Ibid., 155.

12. Ibid., 150, 156. Arturo Escobar's idea of the pluriverse also questions the possibilities of world-making under market imperatives, and he argues that the creation, design, and composition of worlds is always "collective, emergent, and relational" and must be understood as a social phenomenon. See Escobar, *Designs for the Pluriverse: Radical Interdependence, Autonomy, and the Making of Worlds* (Durham, NC: Duke University Press, 2018), xvi–xvii.

13. Older, *Salsa Nocturna*, 27, 240.

14. Ibid., 102–103.

15. Ibid., 236.

16. Harney and Moten, *The Undercommons*, 52–53.

17. Ibid., 53.

18. Ibid., 54.

19. Ibid., 55.

20. Ibid., 55–57. Wendy Brown argues that self-interest does not quite capture neoliberal transformations; instead, the market asks us to self-invest. Self-management, however, seems to cover both the proliferation of interest-making in the market and the market necessities for human capital. Brown, *Undoing the Demos: Neoliberalism's Stealth Revolution* (New York: Zone Books, 2015), 22, 33, 41–42, 70–71.

21. Lauren Berlant, "The Commons: Infrastructures for Troubling Times," *Environment and Planning D: Society and Space* 34, no. 3 (2015): 394.

22. Mbembe, *Necropolitics*, 86, 96–97. The term "multitude" may bring to mind Michael Hardt and Antonio Negri's call for the multitude: a network of plural singularities, internally different, whose actions, constitutions, and participatory democracy are based not on identity but on what they have in common. For Hardt and Negri, the multitude is a "living alternative" within the violences of globalization. But the potential for new networks and social mobilizations that globalization gives us is most reminiscent of Lisa Lowe's claim that the capital labor industry creates "necessary alliances between racialized and third world women within, outside, and across the borders of the United States" giving rise to "the emergence of politicized critiques." Aihwa Ong also sees potential in these globalized and transnational mobilizations and networks because the worldview allows for alliances and allegiances that are deterritorialized and, thus, always against the logic of sovereignty. But, again, this floating abstract called "sovereignty" disrupts the very material actions that social mobilization and politicizing bring out. I continue to be skeptical of their hope to outmaneuver and exceed the violences of late capitalism. Hardt and Negri, *Multitude: War and Democracy in the Age of Empire* (New York: Penguin, 2004)), xiii, 100; Lowe, "Work, Immigration, Gender," in *The Politics of Culture in the Shadow of Capital*, ed. Lisa Lowe and David Lloyd (Durham, NC: Duke University Press, 1997), 363; Ong, *Neoliberalism as Exception: Mutations in Citizenship and Sovereignty* (Durham, NC: Duke University Press, 2006), 122.

23. Mbembe, *Necropolitics*, 97.

24. Older, *Salsa Nocturna*, 12.

25. Ibid., 11.

26. Ibid., 27–28.

27. Ibid., 22.

28. Harney and Moten, *The Undercommons*, 80.

29. Older, *Salsa Nocturna*, 27.

30. Ibid., 171.

31. Harney and Moten, *The Undercommons*, 42–43.

32. Irene Mata, *Domestic Disturbances: Re-imagining Narratives of Gender, Labor, and Immigration* (Austin: University of Texas Press, 2014), 129.

33. Ibid., 134–135.

34. Dulce Pinzón, *The Real Story of the Superheroes* (Barcelona: RM, 2012).

35. Frances Negrón-Muntaner, *Boricua Pop: Puerto Ricans and the Latinization of American Culture* (New York: New York University Press, 2004), 8.

36. Mata, *Domestic Disturbances*, 141.

37. Media and scholars identify Batman and Robin's sexual relationship in multiple ways. The SNL cartoon short "The Ambiguously Gay Duo" satirizes the Batman-Robin relationship, regularly pointing to the homosexual undertones of their homoerotic partnership. See Glen Weldon, *The Caped Crusade: Batman and the Rise of Nerd Culture* (New York: Simon and Schuster, 2017). Mata also considers this history through their age difference. Mata, *Domestic Disturbances*, 139, 143.

38. Ibid., 139.

39. Older, *Salsa Nocturna*, 214.

40. Ibid., 207.

41. Ibid., 114. The trope of the parasite also imbues racial and colonial discourse, as noted in the introduction. Wilderson describes, "Though Blacks suffer the time and space subjugation of cartographic deracination and the hydraulics of the capitalist working day, we also suffer as the hosts of Human parasites, though they themselves might be the hosts of parasitic capital and colonialism." Wilderson, *Afropessimism*, 16. See also Orlando Patterson, *Slavery and Social Death: A Comparative Study* (Cambridge, MA: Harvard University Press, 1982), 334–342.

42. Older, *Salsa Nocturna*, 144.

43. Lee Edelman, *No Future: Queer Theory and the Death Drive* (Durham, NC: Duke University Press, 2004), 117.

44. Berlant, "The Commons," 403.

45. Harney and Moten, *The Undercommons*, 18.

46. Berlant, "The Commons," 408.

47. Harney and Moten, *The Undercommons*, 19, 20.

48. Mbembe, *Necropolitics*, 89.

49. Edelman, *No Future*, 13, 21.

50. José Esteban Muñoz, *Cruising Utopia: The Then and There of Queer Futurity* (New York: New York University Press, 2009), 49. I also touch on these issues in my article : Labour and Motherhood in *Lunar Braceros 2125-2148*," *Feminist Review* 116, no. 1 (2017): 85–100.

51. Older, *Salsa Nocturna*, 237.

52. Ibid., 106.

53. Harney and Moten, *The Undercommons*, 50–51.

54. Mbembe, *Necropolitics*, 84–85.

55. Ibid., 86.

56. Older, *Salsa Nocturna*, 239.

57. Ibid., 237, 244.

58. Ibid., 241.

59. Ibid., 242.

60. Norma Chinchilla, Nora Hamilton, and James Loucky, "Central Americans in Los Angeles: An Immigrant Community in Transition," in *In the Barrios: Latinos and the Underclass Debate*, ed. Joan Moore and Raquel Pinderhughes (New York: Sage, 1993), 66–67.

61. Mbembe, *Necropolitics*, 83. See also Zygmunt Bauman, "Wars of the Globalization Era," *European Journal of Social Theory* 4, no. 1 (2001): 11–28.

62. Harney and Moten, *The Undercommons*, 40.

63. Gilberto Rosas, "The Fragile Ends of War: Forging the United States—Mexico Border and Borderlands Consciousness," *Social Text* 25, no. 2 (2007): 81–102, 97. Rincón also argues that "neoliberal militarism fails to achieve the privatization of security because of its own role in fomenting social disorder." Rincón draws out a paradox within urban warfare, whose promises and practices of security actually produce the ungovernable, insecurable subjectivities it claims to be reining in, making "the idealized notion of home/land security unattainable." Rincón, "Home/Land Insecurity, or, *un Desmadre en Aztlán*," *MFS: Modern Fiction Studies* 63, no. 2 (2017): 262.

64. Ibid., 98.

65. Older, *Salsa Nocturna*, 253.

66. Ibid., 134.

67. Ibid., 146; Hartman, *Scenes of Subjection*, 57, 70–71, 76.

68. Older, *Salsa Nocturna*, 134.

69. Ibid., 132, 140.

70. Harvey, *Spaces of Capital*, 333, 343.

71. Coya Paz, "About," *The Lovely and Talented Coya Paz*, www.coyapaz.com/bio.

72. "All Events for *Still/Here: Manifestos for Joy and Survival*," *Free Street Theater*, https://freestreet.org/show/still-here/all/.

73. *Still/Here: Manifestos for Joy and Survival*, Free Street Theater, April 8, 2020. https://vimeo.com/405465504.

74. Ibid.

75. Harney and Moten, *The Undercommons*, 66.

76. Frances R. Aparicio, *Listening to Salsa: Gender, Latin Popular Music, and Puerto Rican Cultures* (Hanover, NH: Wesleyan University Press, 1998), 92, 95.

77. Older, *Salsa Nocturna*, 32–33.

78. Ibid., 33.

79. Ibid., 86.

80. Michelle Habell-Pallán, *Loca Motion: The Travels of Chicana and Latina Popular Culture* (New York: New York University Press, 2005), 48, 150.

81. Ibid., 38.

82. Daniel José Older, "Microfiction and a Short Speech for #BannedBooksWeek," Talk at Housing Works Bookstore, New York City, September 27, 2016, https://www.youtube.com/watch?v=L01qiU1jUKU.

83. Harney and Moten, *The Undercommons*, 26.

84. See Gloria Anzaldúa, *Borderlands/La Frontera: The New Mestiza* (San Francisco: Aunt Lute Books, 1999), 27, 100.

85. Jerng, *Racial Worldmaking*, 207.

86. Aimee Bahng, *Migrant Futures: Decolonizing Speculation in Financial Times* (Durham, NC: Duke University Press, 2018), 17.

87. Daniel José Older, "On *Shadowshaper* and Diverse Literature," lecture, Ruha Benjamin's course "Black to the Future," Princeton University, Princeton, NJ, April 22, 2015, https://www.youtube.com/watch?v=TC1eI3oEX7U.

88. Hartman, *Scenes of Subjection*, 57.

Coda: Dreaming of Deportation, or, When Everything "Goes South"

1. Javier Zamora, *Unaccompanied* (Port Townsend, WA: Copper Canyon Press, 2017), 3.

2. The webpages we explore most closely are https://www.uscis.gov/ and https://www.usa.gov/immigration-and-citizenship.

3. See https://www.uscis.gov/archive/consideration-of-deferred-action-for-childhood-arrivals-daca. In 2021, it has been unarchived and reinstated under the Biden administration, and information on DACA can be found across the various government pages (although information for DAPA is still relatively difficult to retrieve).

4. Sara Ahmed, *Queer Phenomenology: Orientations, Objects, Others* (Durham, NC: Duke University Press, 2006), 160.

5. Tanya Maria Golash-Boza, *Deported: Immigrant Policing, Disposable Labor, and Global Capitalism* (New York: New York University Press, 2015), 256–257.

6. Ibid., 4.

7. Ibid., 176–177.

8. Ibid., 259.

9. Wendy Brown, *Walled States, Waning Sovereignty* (New York: Zone Books, 2010), 114–123.

10. Ibid., 122.

11. Saskia Sassen, *Expulsions: Brutality and Complexity in the Global Economy* (Cambridge, MA: Belknap, 2014), 75.

12. Ibid., 88–89. See also David Harvey, A *Brief History of Neoliberalism* (Oxford: Oxford University Press, 2005).

13. Maceo Montoya, "The Anxiety of Influence," *Aztlán* 40, no. 2 (2015): 263.

14. In his *Los Angeles Review of Books* interview, Montoya explains that he wrote Wopper and Mija to be characters entirely constructed by perceptions, and as such, Wopper specifically becomes stunted in Woodland: "Everyone in Woodland views Wopper as your average loser, but when seen through the eyes of the characters in Mexico he becomes a mysterious figure who emerges out of nowhere. This change in perception allows Wopper to transform himself, to become someone new." These perceptions inhibit "his inability to imagine himself as being anything other than what he was," but leaving the US opens the possibility of subverting this social construction by imagining otherwise. Montoya, "Three Questions for Maceo Montoya," interview by Daniel Olivas, *Los Angeles Review of Books*, May 14, 2015, https://lareviewofbooks.org/article/three-questions-maceo-montoya/.

15. Maceo Montoya, *The Deportation of Wopper Barraza* (Albuquerque: University of New Mexico Press, 2014), 18.

16. Malín Alegría, *Sofi Mendoza's Guide to Getting Lost in Mexico* (New York: Simon and Shuster, 2008), 215.

17. Ibid., 250, 259, 265.

18. Montoya, *The Deportation of Wopper Barraza*, 75.

19. Montoya, "Three Questions for Maceo Montoya."

20. Ibid.

21. Kandace Chuh, *Imagine Otherwise: On Asian Americanist Critique* (Durham, NC: Duke University Press, 2003), 10.

22. Aimee Bahng, *Migrant Futures: Decolonizing Speculation in Financial Times* (Durham, NC: Duke University Press, 2018), 18–19.

23. Karla Cornejo Villavicencio, *The Undocumented Americans* (New York: One World, 2020), xv.

24. Ibid., 47.

25. Ibid., 156.

26. Ibid., 172.

27. Claudia Milian, "Central American-Americanness, Latino/a Studies, and the Global South," *The Global South* 5, no. 1 (2011): 150.

28. For more on development discourse within economic theory and practice, see Arturo Escobar, *Encountering Development: The Making and Unmaking of the Third World* (Princeton, NJ: Princeton University Press, 1995), 74–85; David Harvey, *Brief History of Neoliberalism* (Oxford: Oxford University Press, 2005), 90–93; David Harvey, *Spaces of Global Capitalism: Towards a Theory of Uneven Geographical Development* (New York: Verso, 2006), 71–75; Neil Smith, *Uneven Development: Nature, Capital, and the Production of Space* (Athens: University of Georgia Press, 2008), 187–188.

29. María Josefina Saldaña-Portillo, *The Revolutionary Imagination in the Americas and the Age of Development* (Durham, NC: Duke University Press, 2003), 5–7.

Bibliography

Adler, Rudy, Victoria Criado, and Brett Huneycutt. *Border Film Project: Photos by Migrants and Minutemen on the U.S.-Mexico Border*. New York: Abrams, 2007.

Agamben, Giorgio. *Homo Sacer: Sovereign Power and Bare Life*. Stanford, CA: Stanford University Press, 1998.

Ahmed, Sara. *Queer Phenomenology: Orientations, Objects, Others*. Durham, NC: Duke University Press, 2006.

Aldama, Frederick Luis. *A User's Guide to Postcolonial and Latino Borderlands Fiction*. Austin: University of Texas Press, 2009.

———. *Your Brain on Latino Comics: From Gus Arriola to Los Bros Hernandez*. Austin: University of Texas Press, 2009.

Alegría, Malín. *Sofi Mendoza's Guide to Getting Lost in Mexico*. New York: Simon and Shuster, 2008.

Alex, Stacey. "Undocumented Latinx Life-Writing: Refusing Worth and Meritocracy." *Prose Studies* 41.2 (2020): 108–128.

"All Events for *Still/Here: Manifestos for Joy and Survival*." *Free Street Theater*. https://freestreet.org/show/still-here/all/.

Alvarado, Karina O., Alicia Ivonne Estrada, and Ester E. Hernández. "Introduction: U.S. Central American (Un)Belongings." In *U.S. Central Americans: Reconstructing Memories, Struggles, and Communities of Resistance*, edited by Alvarado, Estrada, and Hernández, 3–35. Tucson: University of Arizona Press, 2017.

Alvarado, Leticia. *Abject Performance: Aesthetic Strategies in Latino Cultural Production*. Durham, NC: Duke University Press, 2019.

Amnesty International. *In Hostile Terrain: Human Rights Violations in Immigration Enforcement in the US Southwest*. New York: Amnesty International Publications, 2012. http://www.amnestyusa.org/files/ai_inhostileterrain_final031412.pdf.

Andreas, Peter. *Border Games: Policing the U.S.-Mexico Divide*, Ithaca, NY: Cornell University Press, 2000.

———. *Smuggler Nation: How Illicit Trade Made America*. Oxford, UK: Oxford University Press, 2013.

Anzaldúa, Gloria. *Borderlands/La Frontera: The New Mestiza*. San Francisco: Aunt Lute Books, 1999.

Aparicio, Frances R. "Jennifer as Selena: Rethinking Latinidad in Media and Popular Culture." *Latino Studies* 1, no. 1 (2003): 90–105.

———. *Listening to Salsa: Gender, Latin Popular Music, and Puerto Rican Cultures.* Hanover, NH: Wesleyan University Press, 1998.

Aradau, Claudia, and Rens van Munster. *Politics of Catastrophe: Genealogies of the Unknown.* London: Routledge, 2013.

Arias, Arturo. "Central American-Americans: Invisibility, Power and Representation in the U.S. Latino World." *Latino Studies* 1, no. 1 (2003): 168–187.

Armbruster-Sandoval, Ralph. *Globalization and Cross-Border Labor Solidarity in the Americas: The Anti-Sweatshop Movement and the Struggle for Social Justice.* New York: Routledge, 2005.

Arrizón, Alicia. *Latina Performances: Traversing the Stage.* Bloomington: Indiana University Press, 1999.

Azoulay, Ariella. *The Civil Contract of Photography.* New York: Zone Books, 2008.

Bahng, Aimee. *Migrant Futures: Decolonizing Speculation in Financial Times.* Durham, NC: Duke University Press, 2018.

Balibar, Étienne. *Citizenship.* Cambridge, UK: Polity, 2015.

———. "Is There a Neo-Racism?" In Balibar and Wallerstein, *Race, Nation, Class: Ambiguous Identities,* 17–28. London: Verso, 1991.

Barder, Alexander D. "Power, Violence, and Torture: Making Sense of Insurgency and Legitimacy Crises in Past and Present Wars of Attrition." In *The Geopolitics of American Insecurity,* edited by François Debrix and Mark J. Lacy, 54–70. London: Routledge, 2009.

Barthes, Roland. *Camera Lucida: Reflections on Photography.* New York: Hill and Wang, 1981.

Bartletti, Don. "Between Two Worlds." *Don Bartletti Photography.* https://donbartlettiphotography.com/between-two-worlds.

———. *Between Two Worlds: The People of the Border.* Oakland: Oakland Museum, 1992.

———. "Don Bartletti: Spotlight on Immigration." Interview by Dean Brierly. *Photographers Speak,* February 19, 2010. http://photographyinterviews.blogspot.com/2010/02/don-bartletti-spotlight-on-immigration.html.

———. "Enrique's Journey." *Don Bartletti Photography.* https://donbartlettiphotography.com/enriques-journey/.

———. "Framework: Enrique's Journey; #25." *Los Angeles Times,* June 29, 2010. https://web.archive.org/web/20161116210447/http://framework.latimes.com/2010/06/29/enrique%E2%80%99s-journey/#/24.

Baudrillard, Jean. *Simulations.* New York: Semiotext(e), 1983.

———. *Symbolic Exchange and Death.* London: Sage Publications, 1993.

Bauman, Zygmunt. "Wars of the Globalization Era." *European Journal of Social Theory* 4, no. 1 (2001): 11–28.

Becquer, Marcos, and Alisa Lebow. "Docudrag, or, 'Realness' as a Documentary Strategy." In *The Ethnic Eye,* edited by Chon Noriega and Ana M. López, 143–170. Minneapolis: University of Minnesota Press, 1996.

Bell, Daniel. *The Cultural Contradictions of Capitalism.* New York: Basic Books, 1976.

Beltrán, Cristina. *The Trouble with Unity: Latino Politics and the Creation of Identity.* Oxford: Oxford University Press, 2010.

Benjamin, Walter. *Illuminations*. New York: Schocken Books, 1968.

Berlant, Lauren. "The Commons: Infrastructures for Troubling Times." *Environment and Planning D: Society and Space* 34, no. 3 (2016): 393–419.

———. "Slow Death (Sovereignty, Obesity, Lateral Agency)." *Critical Inquiry* 33, no. 4 (2007): 754–780.

Birks, Chelsea. "Objectivity, Speculative Realism, and the Cinematic Apparatus." *Cinema Journal* 57, no. 4 (2018): 3–24.

Böger, Astrid. *People's Lives, Public Images: The New Deal Documentary Aesthetic*. Tübingen, Germany: Gunter Narr, 2001.

Bolton, Richard. "Introduction." In *The Contest of Meaning: Critical Histories of Photography*, edited by Richard Bolton, ix–xix. Cambridge, MA: MIT Press, 1992.

Bourdieu, Pierre. *Photography: A Middle-Brow Art*. Stanford, CA: Stanford University Press, 1990.

Brady, Mary Pat. "The Fungibility of Borders." *Nepantla: Views from the South* 1, no. 1 (2000): 171–190.

Brassier, Ray, Iain Hamilton Grant, Graham Harman, and Quentin Meillassoux. "Speculative Realism." *Collapse: Philosophical Research and Development* 3 (2007): 307–449.

Brown, Wendy. *Undoing the Demos: Neoliberalism's Stealth Revolution*. New York: Zone Books, 2015.

———. *Walled States, Waning Sovereignty*. New York: Zone Books, 2010.

Bryant, Levi, Nick Srnicek, and Graham Harman, eds. *The Speculative Turn: Continental Materialism and Realism*. Melbourne, Victoria: Re.press, 2010.

Burton, Julianne. "Don (Juanito) Duck and the Imperial-Patriarchal Unconscious: Disney Studios, the Good Neighbor Policy, and the Packaging of Latin America." In *Nationalisms and Sexualities*, edited by Andrew Parker, Mary J. Russo, Doris Sommer, and Patricia Yaeger, 21–41. New York: Routledge, 1992.

Butler, Judith. *Notes toward a Performative Theory of Assembly*. Cambridge, MA: Harvard University Press, 2015.

Cacho, Lisa Marie. *Social Death: Racialized Rightlessness and the Criminalization of the Unprotected*. New York: New York University Press, 2012.

Calavita, Kitty. *Inside the State: The Bracero Program, Immigration, and the I.N.S.* New York: Routledge, 2010.

Caminero-Santangelo, Marta. *Documenting the Undocumented: Latino/a Narratives and Social Justice in the Era of Operation Gatekeeper*. Gainesville: University Press of Florida, 2017.

Campt, Tina M. *Listening to Images*. Durham, NC: Duke University Press, 2017.

Cárdenas, Maritza E. *Constituting Central American–Americans: Transnational Identities and the Politics of Dislocation*. New Brunswick, NJ: Rutgers University Press, 2019.

Carroll, Amy Sara. "From *Papapapá* to *Sleep Dealer*: Alex Rivera's Undocumentary Poetics." *Social Identities* 19, nos. 3–4 (2013): 485–500.

Castronovo, Russ. *Necro Citizenship: Death, Eroticism, and the Public Sphere in the Nineteenth-Century United States*. Durham, NC: Duke University Press, 2001.

Century, Sara. "The Strange History of Comic Book Advertisements." *SYFY Wire*, May 31, 2018. https://www.syfy.com/syfywire/the-strange-history-of-comic-book-advertisements.

Chacón, Justin Akers, and Mike Davis. *No One Is Illegal: Fighting Violence and State Repression on the U.S.-Mexico Border*. Chicago: Haymarket Books, 2006.

Chatterjee, Partha. "Sovereign Violence and the Domain of the Political." In *Sovereign Bodies: Citizens, Migrants, and States in the Postcolonial World*, edited by Thomas Blom Hansen and Finn Sepputat, 82–100. Princeton, NJ: Princeton University Press, 2005.

Chavez, Leo. *Covering Immigration: Popular Images and the Politics of Nation*. Berkeley: University of California Press, 2001.

———. *Latino Threat: Constructing Immigrants, Citizens, and the Nation*. Stanford, CA: Stanford University Press, 2008.

Chen, Mel Y. *Animacies: Biopolitics, Racial Mattering, and Queer Affect*. Durham, NC: Duke University Press, 2012.

Chinchilla, Norma, Nora Hamilton, and James Loucky. "Central Americans in Los Angeles: An Immigrant Community in Transition." In *In the Barrios: Latinos and the Underclass Debate*, edited by Joan Moore and Raquel Pinderhughes, 51–78. New York: Sage Publications, 1993.

Christian, Karen. *Show and Tell: Identity as Performance in U.S. Latina/o Fiction*. Albuquerque: University of New Mexico Press, 1997.

Chuh, Kandace. *Imagine Otherwise: On Asian Americanist Critique*. Durham, NC: Duke University Press, 2003.

*La Ciudad/*The City. Directed by David Riker. New York: Zeitgeist Films, 1998. [DVD.]

Clune, Michael W. *American Literature and the Free Market, 1945–2000*. Cambridge: Cambridge University Press, 2010.

Cohen, Deborah. *Braceros: Migrant Citizens and Transnational Subjects in the Postwar United States and Mexico*. Chapel Hill: University of North Carolina Press, 2011.

Contreras, Sheila Maria. *Blood Lines: Myth, Indigenism, and Chicana/o Literature*. Austin: University of Texas Press, 2008.

Cornejo Villavicencio, Karla. *The Undocumented Americans*. New York: One World, 2020.

Critical Art Ensemble. *Aesthetics, Necropolitics, and Environmental Struggle*. New York: Autonomedia, 2018.

Cutler, John Alba. "The New Border." *College Literature* 44, no. 4 (2017): 498–503.

Dalleo, Raphael, and Elena Machado Sáez. *The Latino/a Canon and the Emergence of Post-Sixties Literature*. New York: Palgrave Macmillan, 2007.

Daou, Daniel. "The End of Civilization." *Thresholds* 40 (2012): 245–254.

"David Riker and the People of 'La Ciudad.'" *Revolutionary Worker*, March, 26, 2000. https://revcom.us/a/v21/1040-049/1048/riker.html.

Dávila, Arlene. *Latinos, Inc.: The Marketing and Making of a People*. Berkeley: University of California Press, 2001.

Davis, Mike. *Magical Urbanism: Latinos Reinvent the US City*. New York: Verso, 2001.

The Dead One/El Muerto. Directed by Brian Cox. La Crosse, WI: Echo Bridge Home Entertainment, 2007. [DVD.]

Dean, Jodi. *Democracy and Other Neoliberal Fantasies: Communicative Capitalism and Left Politics*. Durham, NC: Duke University Press, 2009.

de Duve, Thierry. "Time Exposure and Snapshot: The Photograph as Paradox." In *Photography Theory*, edited by James Elkins, 109–123. New York: Routledge, 2007.

De Genova, Nicholas. *Working the Boundaries: Race, Space, and "Illegality" in Mexican Chicago.* Durham, NC: Duke University Press, 2005.

DeGuzmán, María. *Buenas Noches, American Culture: Latina/o Aesthetics of Night.* Bloomington: Indiana University Press, 2012.

De León, Jason. *The Land of Open Graves: Living and Dying on the Migrant Trail.* Oakland: University of California Press, 2015.

Deleuze, Gilles, and Félix Guattari. *A Thousand Plateaus: Capitalism and Schizophrenia.* Minneapolis: University of Minnesota Press, 1987.

Detained in the Desert. Directed by Iliana Sosa. Los Angeles: Real Women Have Curves Studio, 2012. [DVD.]

Duran, Javier. "Virtual Borders, Data Aliens, and Bare Bodies: Culture, Securitization, and the Biometric State." *Journal of Borderlands Studies* 25, nos. 3–4 (2010): 219–230.

Edelman, Lee. *No Future: Queer Theory and the Death Drive.* Durham, NC: Duke University Press, 2004.

Entin, Joseph B. *Sensational Modernism: Experimental Fiction and Photography in Thirties America.* Chapel Hill: University of North Carolina Press, 2007.

Escobar, Arturo. *Designs for the Pluriverse: Radical Interdependence, Autonomy, and the Making of Worlds.* Durham, NC: Duke University Press, 2018.

———. *Encountering Development: The Making and Unmaking of the Third World.* Princeton, NJ: Princeton University Press, 1995.

Espinoza, Mauricio. "The Alien Is Here to Stay: Otherness, Anti-Assimilation, and Empowerment in Latino/a Superhero Comics." In *Graphic Borders: Latino Comic Books Past, Present, and Future,* edited by Frederick Luis Aldama and Christopher González, 181–202. Austin: University of Texas Press, 2016.

Esposito, Roberto. *Bios: Biopolitics and Philosophy.* Minneapolis: University of Minnesota Press, 2008.

Etzioni, Amitai. "The Liberal Narrative Is Broken, and Only Populism Can Fix It." *The Atlantic,* May 8, 2013. https://www.theatlantic.com/politics/archive/2013/05/the-liberal-narrative-is-broken-and-only-populism-can-fix-it/275600/.

Faymonville, Carmen. "New Transnational Identities in Judith Ortiz Cofer's Autobiographical Fiction." *MELUS* 26, no. 2 (2001): 129–158.

Ferraro, Thomas J. *Ethnic Passages: Literary Immigrants in Twentieth-Century America.* Chicago: University of Chicago Press, 1993.

Fisher, Mark. *Capitalist Realism: Is There No Alternative?* Winchester, UK: Zero Books, 2009.

Flores, Juan. "Nuevo York—Diaspora City: U.S. Latinos Between and Beyond." *NACLA Report on the Americas* 35, no. 6 (2002): 46–59.

Flynn, James R. *What Is Intelligence?* Cambridge: Cambridge University Press, 2007.

Foster, David William. "Latino Comics: Javier Hernandez's *El Muerto* as Allegory of Chicano Identity." In *Latinos and Narrative Media: Participation and Portrayal,* edited by Frederick Luis Aldama, 225–240. New York: Palgrave Macmillan, 2013.

Foucault, Michel. *The Birth of Biopolitics: Lectures at the Collège de France, 1978–1979.* New York: Palgrave Macmillan, 2008.

———. *History of Sexuality,* vol. 1: *An Introduction.* New York: Vintage, 1990.

Fox, Claire F. "Establishing Shots of the Border: The Fence and the River." In *Border Culture,* edited by Ilan Stavans, 30–49. Santa Barbara, CA: Greenwood, 2010.

———. "The Fence and the River: Representation of the U.S.-Mexico Border in Art and Video." *Discourse* 18, nos. 1–2 (1995–1996): 54–83.

———. *The Fence and the River: Culture and Politics at the U.S.-Mexico Border*. Minneapolis: University of Minnesota Press, 1999.

Fregoso, Rosa Linda. "We Want Them Alive!: The Politics and Culture of Human Rights." *Social Identities* 12, no. 2 (2006): 109–138.

Frieser, Hannah. "Surcando el margen/Navigating the Margin." In David Taylor, *Working the Line*, 19–27. Santa Fe, NM: Radius Books, 2010.

Galindo, René, and Jami Vigil. "Are Anti-immigrant Statements Racist or Nativist? What Difference Does It Make?" In *Immigration and the Border: Politics and Policy in the New Latino Century*, edited by David Leal and José Limón, 363–399. Notre Dame, IN: University of Notre Dame Press, 2013.

García Canclini, Nestor. *Consumers and Citizens: Globalization and Multicultural Conflicts*. Translated by George Yúdice, Minneapolis: University of Minnesota Press, 2001.

García-Peña, Lorgia. *The Borders of Dominicanidad: Race, Nation, and the Archives of Contradiction*. Durham, NC: Duke University Press, 2016.

Glazener, Nancy. *Reading for Realism: The History of a U.S. Literary Institution, 1850–1910*. Durham, NC: Duke University Press, 1997.

Golash-Boza, Tanya Maria. *Deported: Immigrant Policing, Disposable Labor, and Global Capitalism*. New York: New York University Press, 2015.

Goldman, Francisco. *The Ordinary Seaman*. New York: Grove, 1997.

Gómez-Peña, Guillermo, Felicia Rice, Jennifer A. González, Gustavo Vasquez, and Zachary James Watkins. *Doc/Undoc: Documentado/Undocumented; Ars Shamánica Performática*. San Francisco: City Lights Books, 2017.

González, Jennifer. "A Critical Commentary." In Guillermo Gómez-Peña et al., *Doc/Undoc: Documentado/Undocumented Ars Shamánica Performática*, 14–19. San Francisco: City Lights Books, 2017.

González, Marcial. *Chicano Novels and the Politics of Form: Race, Class, and Reification*. Ann Arbor: University of Michigan Press, 2009.

Gonzalez-Barrera, Ana. "More Mexicans Leaving than Coming into U.S." Pew Research Center, November 19, 2015. http://www.pewhispanic.org/2015/11/19/more-mexicans-leaving-than-coming-to-the-u-s/.

Gonzalez-Barrera, Ana, and Jens Manual Krogstad. "What We Know about Illegal Immigration from Mexico." Pew Research Center, December 3, 2018. http://www.pewresearch.org/fact-tank/2018/12/03/what-we-know-about-illegal-immigration-from-mexico/.

Gordon, Avery. *Ghostly Matters: Hauntings and the Sociological Imagination*. Minneapolis: University of Minnesota Press, 1997.

Grewal, Inderpal. *Saving the Security State: Exceptional Citizens in Twenty-First-Century America*. Durham, NC: Duke University Press, 2017.

Griffith, Kati L. "U.S. Migrant Worker Law: The Interstices of Immigration Law and Labor and Employment Law." *Comparative Labor Law and Policy Journal* 31, no. 1 (2009): 125–162.

Grise, Virginia. *Your Healing Is Killing Me*. Pittsburg, PA: Plays Inverse, 2017.

Gruesz, Kristen Silva. "Utopía Latina: *The Ordinary Seaman* in Extraordinary Times." *MFS: Modern Fiction Studies* 49, no. 1 (2003): 54–83.

Guidotti-Hernández, Nicole. *Unspeakable Violence: Remapping the U.S. and Mexican National Imaginaries.* Durham, NC: Duke University Press, 2011.

Guterman, Gad. *Performance, Identity, and Immigration Law: A Theater of Undocumentedness.* New York: Palgrave Macmillan, 2014.

Habell-Pallán, Michelle. *Loca Motion: The Travels of Chicana and Latina Popular Culture.* New York: New York University Press, 2005.

Halberstam, Jack. "The Wild Beyond: With and for the Undercommons." In Harney and Moten, *The Undercommons*, 5–12. New York: Autonomedia, 2017.

Hardt, Michael, and Antonio Negri. *Multitude: War and Democracy in the Age of Empire.* New York: Penguin, 2004.

Harman, Chris. *Zombie Capitalism: Global Crisis and the Relevance of Marx.* Chicago: Haymarket Books, 2009.

Harney, Stefano, and Fred Moten. *The Undercommons.* New York: Autonomedia, 2017.

Hartman, Saidiya. *Scenes of Subjection: Terror, Slavery, and Self-Making in Nineteenth-Century America.* Oxford: Oxford University Press, 1997.

Harvey, David. *A Brief History of Neoliberalism.* Oxford: Oxford University Press, 2005.

———. *Seventeen Contradictions and the End of Capitalism.* Oxford: Oxford University Press, 2014.

———. *Spaces of Capital: Towards a Critical Geography.* New York: Routledge, 2001.

———. *Spaces of Global Capitalism: Towards a Theory of Uneven Geographical Development.* New York: Verso, 2006.

———. *Spaces of Hope.* Berkeley: University of California Press, 2000.

Hayek, Friedrich A. *The Constitution of Liberty.* Chicago: University of Chicago Press, 2011.

———. *The Political Order of a Free People: Law, Legislation, and Liberty.* Vol. 3. Chicago: University of Chicago Press, 1979.

Hernandez, Javier. *El Muerto: The Aztec Zombie.* Whittier, CA: Los Comex, 2002.

———. "El Muerto vs. El Cucuy." In *Comics!*, n.p. Whittier, CA: Los Comex, 2013.

———. "Weapon Tex-Mex vs. El Muerto." In *The Los Comex Codex*, 15–35. Whittier, CA: Los Comex, 2013.

Hernandez, Javier, and Michael Aushenker. "El Muerto in Ghost Pirate." In *El Muerto*, n.p. Whittier, CA: Los Comex, 2002.

Hodge, Roger D. "Borderworld: How the U.S. Is Reengineering Homeland Security." *Popular Science,* January 17, 2012. http://www.popsci.com/technology/article/2011 -12/how-us-reengineering-homeland-security-borders.

Holland, Sharon P. *Raising the Dead: Readings of Death and (Black) Subjectivity.* Durham, NC: Duke University Press, 2000.

Holmes, Seth M. *Fresh Fruit, Broken Bodies: Migrant Farmworkers in the United States.* Berkeley: University of California Press, 2013.

hooks, bell. *Black Looks: Race and Representation.* Boston, MA: South End Press, 1992.

Inda, Jonathan Xavier. *Targeting Immigrants: Government, Technology, and Ethics.* Malden, MA: Blackwell, 2006.

"Interview with Director Alex Rivera." Latino Film Festival and Conference, Bloomington, IN, 2012. https://www.youtube.com/watch?v=dtbBG48m_Eo.

Irizarry, Ylce. *Chicana/o and Latina/o Fiction: The New Memory of Latinidad.* Urbana: University of Illinois Press, 2016.

Jacobs, Elizabeth. "Undocumented Acts: Migration, Community and Audience in

Two Chicana Plays." *Comparative American Studies: An International Journal* 14, nos. 3–4 (2016): 277–288.

Jameson, Fredric. *The Antinomies of Realism*. London: Verso, 2013.

Jerng, Marc C. *Racial Worldmaking: The Power of Popular Fiction*. New York: Fordham University Press, 2018.

Krauss, Rosalind. "Photography's Discursive Spaces." In *The Contest of Meaning*, edited by Richard Bolton, 287–301. Cambridge, MA: MIT Press, 1992.

Lacan, Jacques. *Écrits*. New York: Norton, 1977.

Lam, C. Christina. "Bearing Witness: Alternate Archives of Latinx Identity in Raquel Cepeda's *Bird of Paradise: How I Became a Latina*." *Studies in American Culture* 43, no. 1 (2020): 26–40.

Lara, Irene. "Bruja Positionality: Toward a Chicana/Latina Spiritual Activism." *Chicana/Latina Studies* 4, no. 2 (2005): 10–45.

Little, Walter E. "Maya Handicraft Vendors' CAFTA–DR Discourses." In *Central America in the New Millennium: Living Transition and Reimagining Democracy*, edited by Jennifer L. Burrell and Ellen Moodie, 181–195. New York: Berghahn, 2012.

Lomnitz, Claudio. *Death and the Idea of Mexico*. New York: Zone Books, 2005.

López, Josefina. *Detained in the Desert and Other Plays*. Carlsbad, CA: WPR, 2011.

López, Tiffany A. "Introduction." In Josefina López, *Detained in the Desert and Other Plays*, 17–18. Carlsbad, CA: WPR, 2011.

Louie, Miriam Ching Yoon. *Sweatshop Warriors: Immigrant Women Workers Take on the Global Factory*. Cambridge, MA: South End Press, 2001.

Lowe, Lisa. "Work, Immigration, Gender: New Subjects of Cultural Politics." In *The Politics of Culture in the Shadow of Capital*, edited by Lisa Lowe and David Lloyd, 354–374. Durham, NC: Duke University Press, 1997.

Luiselli, Valeria. *Tell Me How It Ends: An Essay in Forty Questions*. Minneapolis: Coffee House Press, 2017.

Machado Sáez, Elena. *Market Aesthetics: The Purchase of the Past in Caribbean Diasporic Fiction*. Charlottesville: University of Virginia Press, 2015.

Magnani, Jessica. "Colonial Subjects, Imperial Discourses: Rosario Ferré's *The House on the Lagoon* and Judith Ortiz Cofer's *The Line of the Sun*." *Centro Journal* 21, no. 1 (2009): 156–179.

Maguire, Mark. "The Birth of Biometric Security." *Anthropology Today* 25, no. 2 (2009): 9–14.

Malthus, Thomas Robert. *An Essay on the Principle of Population*. New York: Norton, 2018.

Marcks, Holger, and Janina Pawelz. "From Myths of Victimhood to Fantasies of Violence: How Far-Right Narratives of Imperilment Work." *Terrorism and Political Violence* (2020). https://doi-org.du.idm.oclc.org/10.1080/09546553.2020.1788544.

Márquez, John D. "Latinos as the 'Living Dead': Raciality, Expendability, and Border Militarization." *Latino Studies* 10, no. 4 (2012): 473–498.

Marx, Karl. *Capital*. Vol. 1. London: Penguin, 1990.

Mata, Irene. *Domestic Disturbances: Re-imagining Narratives of Gender, Labor, and Immigration*. Austin: University of Texas Press, 2014.

Mbembe, Achille. *Necropolitics*. Durham, NC: Duke University Press, 2019.

McClanahan, Annie. *Dead Pledges: Debt, Crisis, and Twenty-First-Century Culture*. Stanford, CA: Stanford University Press, 2017.

McCloskey, Deirdre. *The Rhetoric of Economics*. Madison: University of Wisconsin Press, 1998.

McCracken, Ellen. *New Latina Narrative: The Feminine Space of Postmodern Ethnicity*. Tucson: University of Arizona Press, 1999.

McNally, David. *Monsters of the Market: Zombies, Vampires, and Global Capitalism*. Chicago: Haymarket Books, 2012.

Meléndez, A. Gabriel. *Hidden Chicano Cinema: Film Dramas in the Borderlands*. New Brunswick, NJ: Rutgers University Press, 2013.

Meléndez, Edgardo. *Sponsored Migration: The State and Puerto Rican Postwar Migration to the United States*. Columbus: Ohio State University Press, 2017.

Mendieta, Eduardo. "The U.S. Border and the Political Ontology of 'Assassination Nation': Thanatological *Dispositifs*." *Journal of Speculative Philosophy* 31, no. 1 (2017): 82–100.

Michaels, Walter Benn. "Empires of the Senseless: (The Response to) Terror and (the End of) History." *Radical History Review* 85 (2003): 105–113.

Milian, Claudia. "Central American–Americanness, Latino/a Studies, and the Global South." *The Global South* 5, no. 1 (2011): 137–152.

Mills, Charles. *The Racial Contract*. Ithaca, NY: Cornell University Press, 1999.

Miyoshi, Masao. "A Borderless World? From Colonialism to Transnationalism and the Decline of the Nation-State." *Critical Inquiry* 19, no. 4 (1993): 726–751.

Molina, Natalia. *Fit to Be Citizens?: Public Health and Race in Los Angeles, 1879–1939*. Berkeley: University of California Press, 2006.

Montoya, Maceo. "The Anxiety of Influence." *Aztlán* 40, no. 2 (2015): 261–266.

———. *The Deportation of Wopper Barraza*. Albuquerque: University of New Mexico Press, 2014.

———. "Three Questions for Maceo Montoya." Interview by Daniel Olivas. *Los Angeles Review of Books,* May 14, 2015. https://lareviewofbooks.org/article/three-questions-maceo-montoya/.

"Monuments: 276 Views of the U.S.-Mexico Border by David Taylor." Exhibitions, Museum of Fine Arts, Houston. https://www.mfah.org/exhibitions/monuments-276-views-us-mexico-border-david-taylor.

Moses, Michael Valdez. "Magical Realism at World's End." *Margin: Exploring Magical Realism,* March 27, 2003. http://www.angelfire.com/wa2/margin/nonficMoses.html.

Muller, Benjamin J. *Security, Risk, and the Biometric State*. London: Routledge, 2010.

Muñoz, José Esteban. *Cruising Utopia: The Then and There of Queer Futurity*. New York: New York University Press, 2009.

———. *Disidentifications: Queers of Color and the Performance of Politics*. Minneapolis: University of Minnesota Press, 1999.

———. "No es fácil: Notes on the Negotiation of Cubanidad and Exilic Memory in Carmelita Tropicana's 'Milk of Amnesia.'" *TDR: The Drama Review* 39, no. 3 (1995): 76–82.

Nair, Parvati. "The Razor's Edge." In *Photography and Migration*, edited by Tanya Sheehan, 83–99. London: Routledge, 2018.

Nazario, Sonia. *Enrique's Journey*. New York: Random House, 2014.

Negrón-Muntaner, Frances. *Boricua Pop: Puerto Ricans and the Latinization of American Culture*. New York: New York University Press, 2004.

Nichols, Bill. *Representing Reality: Issues and Concepts in Documentary.* Bloomington: Indiana University Press, 1991.

Nixon, Rob. *Slow Violence and the Environmentalism of the Poor.* Cambridge, MA: Harvard University Press, 2013.

Norat, Gisela. "US Latinas Write through Carnal Mothers Back to Ancestral Homelands." *Letras Femeninas* 34, no. 1 (2008): 31–54.

Oboler, Suzanne. *Ethnic Labels, Latino Lives: Identity and the Politics of (Re)Presentation in the United States.* Minneapolis: University of Minnesota Press, 1995.

Older, Daniel José. "Microfiction and a Short Speech for #BannedBooksWeek." Talk at Housing Works Bookstore, New York City, September 27, 2016. https://www.youtube.com/watch?v=L01qiU1jUKU.

———. "On *Shadowshaper* and Diverse Literature." Lecture for Ruha Benjamin's course "Black to the Future," Princeton University, Princeton, NJ, April 22, 2015. https://www.youtube.com/watch?v=TC1eI3oEX7U.

———. *Salsa Nocturna.* New York: JABberwocky Literary Agency, 2016.

———. "*Salsa Nocturna* Promo #1: The Passing." May 20, 2012. https://www.youtube.com/watch?v=e5EaOcaOXPI.

———. *Salsa Nocturna* Promo #2: Midnight Mambo." June 15, 2012. https://www.youtube.com/watch?v=Cw8_nXVOR0o.

Ong, Aihwa. "The Gender and Labor Politics of Postmodernity." In *The Politics of Culture in the Shadow of Capital,* edited by Lisa Lowe and David Lloyd, 61–97. Durham, NC: Duke University Press, 1997.

———. *Neoliberalism as Exception: Mutations in Citizenship and Sovereignty.* Durham, NC: Duke University Press, 2006.

Ortiz, Ricardo. *Latinx Literature Now: Between Evanescence and Event.* Cham, Switzerland: Palgrave Macmillan, 2016.

Ortiz Cofer, Judith. *Silent Dancing: A Partial Remembrance of a Puerto Rican Childhood.* Houston: Arte Publico, 1990.

Passel, Jeffrey S., and D'vera Cohn. "U.S. Unauthorized Immigration Flows Are Down Sharply since Mid-Decade." Pew Research Center. September 1, 2010. http://www.pewhispanic.org/2010/09/01/us-unauthorized-immigration-flows-are-down-sharply-since-mid-decade/.

Pateman, Carole. *The Sexual Contract.* Stanford, CA: Stanford University Press, 1988.

Patterson, Orlando. *Slavery and Social Death: A Comparative Study.* Cambridge, MA: Harvard University Press, 1982.

Paz, Coya. "About." *The Lovely and Talented Coya Paz.* www.coyapaz.com/bio.

Paz, Octavio. *Poesia en movimiento: México, 1915–1966.* Mexico, D.F.: Siglo Veintiuno Editores, 1991.

Phelan, Peggy. *Unmarked: The Politics of Performance.* London: Routledge, 1993.

Philogene, Jerry. "'Dead Citizen' and the Abject Nation: Social Death, Haiti, and the Strategic Power of the Image." *Journal of Haitian Studies* 21, no. 1 (2015): 100–126.

Piketty, Thomas. *Capital and Ideology.* Cambridge, MA: Belknap Press, 2020.

Pinzón, Dulce. *The Real Story of the Superheroes.* Barcelona: RM, 2012.

Puar, Jasbir. "Queer Times, Queer Assemblages." *Social Text* 23, nos. 3–4 (2005): 121–139.

———. *Terrorist Assemblages: Homonationalism in Queer Times.* Durham, NC: Duke University Press, 2007.

Rabinowitz, Paula. *They Must Be Represented: The Politics of Documentary*. London: Verso, 1994.

Rao, Mohan. "An Entangled Skein: Neo-Malthusianism in Neo-liberal Times." In *Markets and Malthus: Population, Gender, and Health in Neo-liberal Times*, edited by Mohan Rao and Sarah Sexton, 103–126. Los Angeles: Sage Publications, 2010.

Rhodes, Gary D., and John Parrish Springer. "Introduction." In *Docufictions: Essays on the Intersection of Documentary and Fictional Filmmaking*, edited by Gary D. Rhodes and John Parrish Springer, 1–10. Jefferson, NC: McFarland, 2006.

Riker, David. "David Riker and the People of 'La Ciudad.'" *Revolutionary Worker*, March, 26, 2000. https://revcom.us/a/v21/1040-049/1048/riker.htm.

Rincón, Belinda Linn. "Home/Land Insecurity, or, *un Desmadre en Aztlán*: Virginia Grise's *blu*." *MFS: Modern Fiction Studies* 63, no. 2 (2017): 247–269.

Robertson, Thomas. *The Malthusian Moment: Global Population Growth and the Birth of American Environmentalism*. New Brunswick, NJ: Rutgers University Press, 2012.

Rochkind, David. *Heavy Hand, Sunken Spirit* (Stockport, UK: Dewi Lewis Publishing, 2012.

Rodríguez, Ana Patricia. "Refugees of the South: Central Americans in the U.S. Latino Imaginary." *American Literature* 73, no. 2 (2001): 387–412.

Rodríguez, Ralph. *Latinx Literature Unbound: Undoing Ethnic Expectation*. New York: Fordham University Press, 2018.

Rosas, Gilberto. "The Fragile Ends of War: Forging the United States—Mexico Border and Borderlands Consciousness." *Social Text* 25, no. 2 (2007): 81–102.

Saldaña-Portillo, María Josefina. *The Revolutionary Imagination in the Americas and the Age of Development*. Durham, NC: Duke University Press, 2003.

Saldívar, Ramón. *Chicano Narrative: The Dialectics of Difference*. Madison: University of Wisconsin Press, 1990.

———. "Historical Fantasy, Speculative Realism, and Postrace Aesthetics in Contemporary American Fiction." *American Literary History* 23, no. 3 (2011): 574–599.

Sassen, Saskia. "Black and White Photography as Theorizing: Seeing What the Eye Cannot See." *Sociological Forum* 26, no. 2 (2011): 438–443.

———. *Expulsions: Brutality and Complexity in the Global Economy*. Cambridge, MA: Belknap, 2014.

———. *The Global City: New York, London, Tokyo*. Princeton, NJ: Princeton University Press, 2001.

———. *Globalization and Its Discontents: Essays on the New Mobility of People and Money*, New York: New Press, 1998.

———. *Losing Control? Sovereignty in an Age of Globalization*. New York: Columbia University Press, 1996.

Sauri, Emilio. "'A la pinche modernidad': Literary Form and the End of History in Roberto Bolaño's *Los detectives salvajes*." *MLN* 125, no. 2 (2010): 406–432.

Schreiber, Rebecca M. *The Undocumented Everyday: Migrant Lives and the Politics of Visibility*. Minneapolis: University of Minnesota Press, 2018.

Sekula, Allan. "The Body and the Archive." In *The Contest of Meaning*, edited by Richard Bolton, 343–388. Cambridge, MA: MIT Press, 1992.

———. *Photography against the Grain: Essays and Photo Works, 1973–1983*. Halifax: Press of the Nova Scotia College of Art and Design, 1984.

Seltzer, Mark. *The Official World*. Durham, NC: Duke University Press, 2016.

Sexton, Jared. "Unbearable Blackness." *Cultural Critique* 90 (2015): 159–178.

Schmidt Camacho, Alicia. *Migrant Imaginaries: Latino Cultural Politics in the U.S.-Mexico Borderlands*. New York: New York University Press, 2008.

Schmitt, Carl. *Political Theology: Four Chapters on the Concept of Sovereignty*. Chicago: University of Chicago Press, 1985.

Shaviro, Steven. *The Universe of Things: On Speculative Realism*. Minneapolis: University of Minnesota Press, 2018.

Sheehan, Tanya. "Introduction: Questions of Difference." In *Photography, History, Difference*, edited by Tanya Sheehan, 1–10. Lebanon, NH: Dartmouth College Press, 2015.

Sicker, Martin. *The Geopolitics of Security in the Americas*. Westport, CT: Praeger, 2002.

"Similarities." Photo Gallery, *Border Film Project*. https://web.archive.org/web/20190 322164854/http://www.borderfilmproject.com/en/photo-gallery/.

Sleep Dealer. Directed by Alex Rivera. New York: Likely Story, 2008.

Smith, Neil. *Uneven Development: Nature, Capital, and the Production of Space*. Athens: University of Georgia Press, 2008.

Snyder, Rachel Louise. *Fugitive Denim: A Moving Story of People and Pants in the Borderless World of Global Trade*. New York: Norton, 2009.

Socolovsky, Maya. "Telling Stories of Transgression: Judith Ortiz Cofer's *The Line of the Sun*." *MELUS* 34, no. 1 (2009): 95–116.

Sontag, Susan. *On Photography*. New York: Farrar, Straus and Giroux, 1977.

Sontag, Susan, and Jonathan Cott. *Susan Sontag: The Complete Rolling Stone Interview*. New Haven, CT: Yale University Press, 2013.

Sorkin, Amy Davidson. "Countering Trump at the Border." *The New Yorker*, December 10, 2018. https://www.newyorker.com/magazine/2018/12/10/countering-trump-at-the-border.

Stewart, Garrett. *Transmedium: Conceptualism 2.0 and the New Object Art*. Chicago: University of Chicago Press, 2018.

Still/Here: Manifestos for Survival and Joy. Free Street Theater, April 8, 2020. https://vimeo.com/405465504.

Tancredo, Thomas G. *In Mortal Danger: The Battle for America's Border and Security*. Nashville, TN: Cumberland House, 2006.

Taylor, Charles. "The Politics of Recognition." In *Multiculturalism: Examining the Politics of Recognition*, edited by Amy Gutmann, 25–74. Princeton, NJ: Princeton University Press, 1994.

Taylor, David. "David J. Taylor 1994." In *100 Stories Archives, 1990s*, May 16, 2012. https://design.uoregon.edu/david-j-taylor-1994.

———. *Working the Line*. Santa Fe, NM: Radius Books, 2010.

Templeton, Michael. "Becoming Transnational and Becoming Machinery in Francisco Goldman's *The Ordinary Seaman*." *Symploke* 14, nos. 1–2 (2006): 271–288.

Ulibarri, Kristy L. "Agua, Inc.: Water Wars, Aqua-Terrorism, and Speculative Economy in Latinx and Transborder Cinema." *ASAP/Journal* 6, no. 2 (2021): 431–458.

———. "Speculating Latina Radicalism: Labour and Motherhood in *Lunar Braceros 2125–2148*." *Feminist Review* 116, no. 1 (2017): 85–100.

Urrea, Luis Alberto. *The Devil's Highway*. New York: Back Bay Books, 2004.

———. "Saluda a los malos/Say Hello to the Bad Guy." In David Taylor, *Working the Line*, 83–95. Santa Fe, NM: Radius Books, 2010.

US DHS and DOJ Form I-598. Rev. 5/16/17.

Vázquez, David J. *Triangulations: Narrative Strategies for Navigating Latino Identity.* Minneapolis: University of Minnesota Press, 2011.

Viejo, Antonio. *Dead Subjects: Toward a Politics of Loss in Latino Studies.* Durham, NC: Duke University Press, 2007.

Weheliye, Alexander G. *Habeas Viscus: Racializing Assemblages, Biopolitics, and Black Feminist Theories of the Human.* Durham, NC: Duke University Press, 2014.

Weldon, Glen. *The Caped Crusade: Batman and the Rise of Nerd Culture.* New York: Simon and Schuster, 2017.

Wells, Sarah Ann. "The Scar and Node: Border Science Fiction and the *Mise-en-Scène* of Globalized Labor." *The Global South* 8, no. 1 (2014): 69–90.

Who Is Dayani Cristal? Directed by Marc Silver. London: Pulse Films, 2014. [DVD.]

Wilderson III, Frank B. *Afropessimism.* New York: Liveright, 2020.

Wilkinson, Jayne. "Art Documents: The Politics of Visibility in Contemporary Photography." *InVisible Culture* 22 (2015): https://du.idm.oclc.org/login?url=https://www-proquest-com.du.idm.oclc.org/scholarly-journals/art-documents-politics-visibility-contemporary/docview/1771029175/se-2?accountid=14608.

Winston, Brian. *Claiming the Real: Documentary; Grierson and Beyond.* Hampshire, UK: Palgrave Macmillan, 2008.

Wright, Melissa W. "Necropolitics, Narcopolitics, and Femicide: Gendered Violence on the Mexico-U.S. Border." *Signs* 36, no. 3 (2011): 707–731.

Zamora, Javier. *Unaccompanied.* Port Townsend, WA: Copper Canyon Press, 2017.

Zaya, Luis H. *Forgotten Citizens: Deportation, Children, and the Making of American Exiles.* Oxford: Oxford University Press, 2015.

Zengerle, Patricia, and David Adams. "U.S. Turns Back Central Americans, Welcomes 'Dusty Foot' Cubans." *Reuters*, July 23, 2016. https://www.reuters.com/article/us-usa-immigration-cuba/u-s-turns-back-central-americans-welcomes-dusty-foot-cubans-idUSKBN0FZ2E420140730.

Žižek, Slavoj. *Organs without Bodies: On Deleuze and Consequences.* New York: Routledge, 2003.

Index

Note: Page numbers in *italics* indicate figures.